The Seventh-day Adventist
THEOLOGY CRISIS

**TWENTY ONE BURNING ISSUES CONCERNING
JUSTIFICATION BY FAITH (RIGHTEOUSNESS BY FAITH)
IN THE SEVENTH-DAY ADVENTIST CHURCH TODAY-2010**

21 FALSE PRESUPPOSITIONS CONCERNING THE GOSPEL

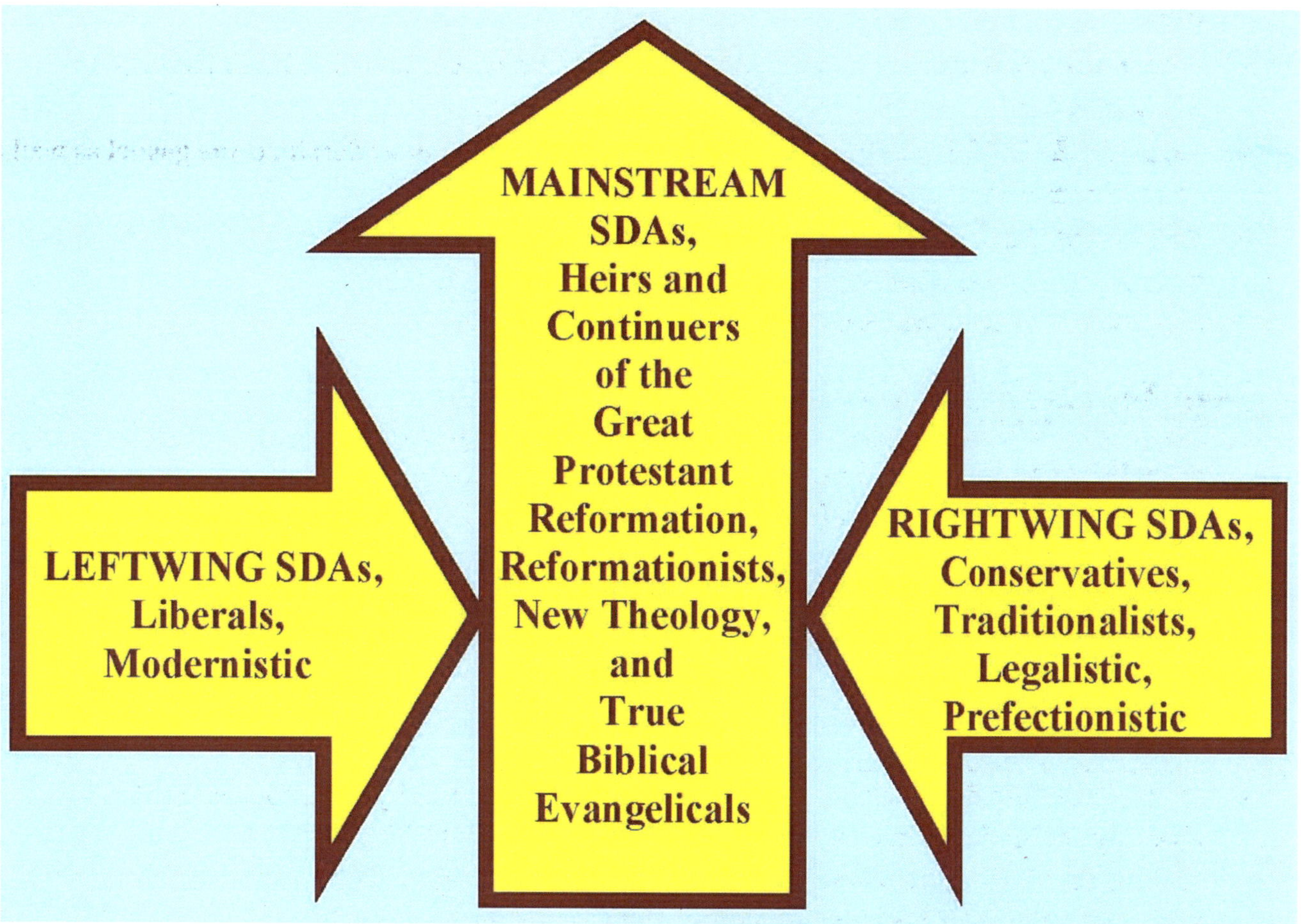

MAINSTREAM SDAs, Heirs and Continuers of the Great Protestant Reformation, Reformationists, New Theology, and True Biblical Evangelicals

LEFTWING SDAs, Liberals, Modernistic

RIGHTWING SDAs, Conservatives, Traditionalists, Legalistic, Prefectionistic

Seventh-day Adventism's
RENDEZVOUS
With Destiny!

Gordon Wm. Collier, Sr.

THE SEVENTH-DAY ADVENTIST THEOLOGY CRISIS

Christian Classics - Volume Two
Gordon Wm. Collier, Sr.

ISBN 978-1-4276-4599-9

1. Seventh-day Adventists—Righteousness by Faith
2. Seventh-day Adventists—Justification by Faith
3. Seventh-day Adventists and the Gospel

ISBN 978-1-4276-4599-9 (paperback)

Additional Copies of this book are available by order at:

gcollierjr@aol.com
Subject Line: Christian Classics - Volume Two

Printed in the United States of America

Volume TWO
THE SEVENTH-DAY ADVENTIST THEOLOGY CRISIS

Table of Contents

Table of Contents 3
Acknowledgements and Dedication 4
Foreword 5
Loma Linda Campus Hill Church Gospel Statement 6
For Entrance Into Heaven, What Does God Require of us? 12
A Key Prophetic Statement by Mrs. E. G. White 13
Romans, Chapter 4 and 5:1 14

Twenty-One Issues

ISSUE ONE: The Christian's HIGHEST AUTHORITY 16
ISSUE TWO: The Legal, Judicial, Forensic NATURE of Justification 21
ISSUE THREE: The DEFINITION of Justification 36
ISSUE FOUR: DISTINCTIONS Between imputed and imparted righteousness 52
ISSUE FIVE: WHOSE Righteousness it is that Justifies? 60
ISSUE SIX: WHERE is Justifying Righteousness? 62
ISSUE SEVEN: The BASIS of Justification 70
ISSUE EIGHT: The MEANS of Justification 75
ISSUE NINE: The ROOOT AND the FRUIT of Justification 88
ISSUE TEN: The ONLY CONDITION of Justification 93
ISSUE ELEVEN: STANDING and STATE 99
ISSUE TWELVE: SANCTIFICATION 112
ISSUE THIRTEEN: BIBLICAL (CHRISTIAN) PERFECTION—WHAT IS IT? 119
ISSUE FOURTEEN: THE ATONEMENT 128
ISSUE FIFTEEN: THE JUDGEMENT is Good News! 131
ISSUE SIXTEEN: PAUL AND JAMES 133
ISSUE SEVENTEEN: ASSURANCE of Salvation 135
ISSUE EIGHTEEN: Often MISUNDERSTOOD BIBLE STATEMENTS 138
ISSUE NINETEEN: Often MISUNDERSTOOD E. G. W. STATEMENTS 141
ISSUE TWENTY: The WEDDING GARMENT 143
ISSUE TWENTY ONE: RIGHTEOUSNESS BY FAITH—what is it? 146
RECAPITULATION 150
AN OPEN LETTER to our Leaders 153
MY CLOSING APPEAL to our Pastors and Laymembers 154
ABREVIATIONS TO E. G. W. Sources 155
Table of Contents For Volume One 156
Table of Contents For Volume Three 158
Table of Contents For Volume Four 159
Index of Important Gospel Subjects 161
Look and Live 162
The Two Different Aspects of Righteousness 163
20 E. G. W. DEFINITIONS OF JUSTIFICATION 164

Acknowledgements & Dedication

All that I have said in "Acknowledgements" in Volume One also applies to this volume.

But for Volume Two, I wish to express my heartfelt appreciation to two very special people who have contributed greatly to the creation of this volume.

The first is to **Elder Alton Johnson**, retired SDA pastor, evangelist and publisher, who prepared many pages of Volumes One and Two and also published *Christian Classics* ● *Volume One—Blessed Assurance*.

Gordon Wm. (Bill) Collier, Jr.

The second is to my son, **Gordon Wm. Collier, Jr.**, for contributing so much of his time and for his computer expertise in preparing this manuscript for publication.

Bill has spent hundreds of hours in travel in the air and on land, and hundreds of hours working with his laptop on these books. He has greatly improved the formatting of this book and has brought it to the point of publication.

Words are inadequate in expressing my profound appreciation for his wonderful contribution to the production of these books.

Ever since Bill was born, I have dreamed of the two of us partnering together in God's cause of spreading the gospel to the world.

My thanks also to Brother Lee Greer, Sr., and Sister Indra Greer of Loma Linda and to Estella Gaytan of Calistoga, California, for editing this book manuscript.

And so, I gratefully dedicate this book *Christian Classics* ● *Volume Two*—THE SEVENTH-DAY ADVENTIST THEOLOGY CRISIS—to my dear son, Gordon Wm. Collier, Jr., thanking and praising God for making my dream come true!

Thanks Be To God!

Gordon Wm. Collier, Sr.

Foreword

The Gospel which proclaims the Good News that believers are Justified by the Grace of God through faith in Jesus, apart from their obedience and good works, is not well understood in the right wing of the Seventh-day Adventist church.

To meet this challenge, in March 2001, the members of the Loma Linda, California Campus Hill Church have drawn up a definitive truly biblical and Christ centered statement explaining the gospel.

As was expected, this statement has been challenged by some sincere Seventh-day Adventists. One such challenge is a 48 page critique by an earnest SDA laymember. This book, which you hold in your hands, is my respectful REPLY to this challenge.

Having, for 26 years, as an SDA pastor-evangelist, believed like the challenger believes about Justification by Faith (Righteousness by Faith), this writer wishes to share with the challenger and others THE BIBLICAL AND ELLEN G. WHITE EVIDENCE that "turned him around"–that led him out of a legalistic, perfectionistic concept of the Gospel to the truly Scriptural teaching.

I am writing this defense of the gospel as much for the members of my beloved church as I am for the benefit of the critic who raises 21 EXTREMELY IMPORTANT ISSUES in the Seventh-day Adventist Church concerning the gospel. This is AN ASTOUNDING REVELATION! This is not an overstatement.

So, This book is **MY CRITIQUE OF A CRITIQUE** of the Loma Linda Campus Hill Church's statement of the gospel.

Beginning on page 16, I will present the "critiquer's" 21 Erroneous Presuppositions followed by my Comments and what The Bible Teaches.

Whenever I speak of the Roman Catholic doctrine of justification, it is always with respect to the Roman Catholic Church.

Also, when I speak of Jones' and Waggoner's 1888 message of Righteousness by Faith — Justification by Faith, like—Mrs. White, I am **not** endorsing all that they taught about Righteousness by Faith.

They correctly taught that we are justified solely by Faith, but they erroneously taught that God's act of justifying us included His act of **MAKING** us actually, personally, inwardly, morally righteous. This was a grave error and is similar to the Roman Catholic doctrine of justification by faith.

May we all see light in God's light is my earnest prayer for every reader.

This is the Loma Linda Campus Hill Church Statement of The Gospel

2001
My personal Union with Christ and His Church

I accept the Gospel of Jesus Christ: God the Father so loved the world that He gave Christ who offered Himself through the eternal Spirit, died on behalf of all our sins, was buried, and was raised again the third day according to the Scriptures[1] to intercede on our behalf at the right hand of God.[2] *Justification by faith alone*: *So*, I am persuaded that God *justifies* me, even me, by faith alone without works of any kind for the sake of His own Son.[3] That is, *God pardons* and *accepts me*, the *believing sinner, counting Christ's perfect life of obedience and death as though they were my own.*[4] This is my only claim to eternal life both now and forever![5] Indeed as a believer I know that God has chosen me in Christ from the foundation of the world, and blessed me with all spiritual blessings in Christ in heavenly places.[6]

- *God and Scripture.* Jesus the living Word is the ultimate revelation of God[7] and the Scriptures are *the testimony of Jesus,*[8] inspired by the Holy Spirit[9] who convicts of sin, righteousness, and judgment.[10] The Scriptures are the only rule of faith and practice[11] and the gifts of the Spirit continue to be manifested in the church, which is to be an ever reforming community of faith.[12,47] So the Father, Son, and Holy Spirit work together for our salvation.[13]

I. **The doctrine of sin**: "*Because they do not believe in Me*"

- Seeing Calvary, I am more than ever convicted of the awfulness of sin, which is

  - Rejecting Christ,[14]
  - 'Whatsoever is not of faith,'[15]
  - The transgression of God's Law – lawlessness,[16]
  - Knowing to do good and doing it not,[17]
  - Continuing to fall short of the glory of God,[18]

- 'Even as a believer indwelt by the Holy Spirit, nothing good is in my flesh, but only sin[19] – All I do and all I am continue to fall short of God's glory[20] so my only claim is Jesus' continuous unmerited justification.[21] Like every human I was a sinner from the moment of conception,[22] by nature a child of wrath,[23] a transgressor, estranged from the womb,[24] and constituted a sinner because of the fall of Adam,[25] thereby losing immortality.[26] Until Jesus comes again whether we are alive or dead, just as our righteousness is in Him, so our life is in Him and not in ourselves.[27]

- The holy Law of God brings a full knowledge of sin[28] and drives us to Christ in order that we might be justified by faith.[29]

II. **The doctrine of righteousness**: "*Because I am going to the Father and you no longer see Me*"

- *Justification by faith alone*: Because only a perfect doer of the Law can ever be justified,[30] the Law can never justify *me* in the sight of God.[31] I am justified by faith only in a Righteousness outside of myself or any of my works, even the righteousness of Christ my Substitute, which I can *neither see nor grasp* except by faith alone.[32,3] His perfect Righteousness reckoned mine[33,3,4,21] is what Scripture calls 'the righteousness of faith.'[34] The one who is just by faith shall live.[35]

- *Fruit in sanctification*: Being justified by faith alone for the sake of Jesus my Substitute in heaven[36] is the sole reason, the only lawful and ethical foundation upon which He sends the Holy Spirit to *sanctify* me down here on earth, yielding the fruit of the Spirit[37] as exemplified in Jesus my Example.[38] In Christ, He has given me assurance,[39] a new birth and freedom to be an overcomer,[40] to choose obedience in thought, word, and deed to all God's commandments,[41] including the seventh-day Sabbath, the emblem of creation, Gospel rest,[42] and sanctification.[43] Thus in sanctification:

    - God's laws are being written in my heart[44] as promises for happiness.[45]

    - Faith operating by love purifies the soul temple, spiritually, mentally, physically, and socially[46] including pure love for family and defense of the poor and defenseless.[47,12]

    - Because God for Jesus' sake has accepted me, a sinner, as righteous,[48] I accept others also. Therefore, where I have hurt them or they have hurt me, I am willing to confess my own faults and forgive theirs so we can pray together for healing.[49]

    - Because Jesus paid it all for me, I am happy to consecrate my all to Him, including life, time, talents, personal efforts, health, influence, a tithe of all my increase and my free will offerings,[50] in order to spread the Gospel.

    - Not that I have attained but I press forward forgetting what is behind;[51] He has begun a good work in me and He will perform it until the day of Jesus Christ.[52]

- Church. Jesus has called me into His Church Universal founded on the Rock, against which hell can never prevail, because in the 'keys of the kingdom' He has given her one authority: **To proclaim on earth below God's merciful verdict in Christ above on behalf of believing sinners– Justification by faith.**[53] In the last days, His calling includes fellowship with those who keep God's commandments and 'the faith of Jesus,' which is justification by faith alone.[54] His calling is signified by

    - Being baptized into His life, death, and resurrection to begin my new life in Him[55]
    - Partaking in corporate worship in the church[56]
    - Coming gratefully to the Lord's table 'in remembrance' of Jesus[57] to show His death till He comes again in glory[58]
    - Entering heaven itself in the priesthood of all believers in Christ[59]
    - Growing in discipleship, developing my own unique spiritual gifts and talents in His church[60] which will again become a common community in defense of the poor and defenseless.[47, 12]
    - Becoming a minister of reconciliation to carry the Gospel to a lost and dying world.[61]

III. The doctrine of judgment: "*Because the ruler of this world has been judged*"

- The slain Lamb of God, our Advocate and Surety, has already prevailed in court against our adversary;[62] our accuser has been cast down![63] It is God who justifies![3,21] Who can bring any charge against believers in Him?[64,3,4,21]

- By His Holy Law, God brings every work, thought, deed, and motive into judgment, whether good or evil, and the whole world is summoned.[65] However, as a repentant believer I appear only in the person of my Redeemer and Surety who has borne my sin[66] and appears in my stead.[67,3,4,21] Therefore with the Psalmist I can anticipate that day with solemn joy, "Judge me O Lord my God according to Your righteousness"[68,3,4,21] and exclaim with Martin Luther, "O happy judgment day!" Only the persistently impenitent must stand alone – alone in their sin, shame, and despair.[6]

- *Second Advent.* Soon Jesus is coming again in person in the clouds of heaven before every eye,[70] bringing judgment on all that obey not the Gospel.[71] He will raise the dead in Christ and translate the living believers into glory incorruptible, bringing all His redeemed home,[72] and receiving His bride, as the new earth becomes the saints' possession forever![73] Even so, come, Lord Jesus! Amen![74]

The Campus Hill Church of Seventh-day Adventists, Loma Linda, California 2354, USA

---

[1] *John* 3: 16; 1: 29; *Heb.* 9: 14; *Rom.* 4: 21-5: 21; I *Cor.* 15: 1-4; II *Cor.* 5: 19, 21a–>b; *Col.* 3: 1-4; I *John* 2: 2

[2] *Rom.* 8: 34; *Ps.* 110 – the Old Testament passage most cited in the New Testament; *Ps.* 84: 9

[3] *Rom.* 3-4: 21-5: 11: Faith in itself has no merit but because it lays hold of the Object, Christ and His spotless righteousness which is accounted mine in God's merciful reckoning for Jesus' sake, it is said to be 'counted for righteousness' (*Heb.* 11: 1).

[4] *Rom.* 1: 16-17; 3: 20-31; 4-5; 8: 31-39; *Gal.* 2: 16-3: 29; I *Cor.* 15: 1-4; *Col.* 3: 1-4; *Eph.* 1:3; *Phil.* 3: 9; *Rom.* 1: 16-17; 3: 22; 4: 5, 9, 11, 13; 9: 30; 10: 6; *Gal.* 5: 5; *Heb.* 11: 7; II *Pet.* 1: 1; *Ps.* 32: 1-2; *Isa.* 53; *Lev.* 1-9; 16; 17: 11; *Hebrews*; *Luke* 20: 35; 21: 36; II *Thes.* 1: 5; The Gospels: *Mark* = *Matthew* = *Luke* = *John*; I *John* 2: 1-2; cf. *Jn.* 18: 7-8

[5] *John* 3: 12-18; *Rom.* 4-5; I *Cor.* 15: 1-4; *Luke* 20: 35; 21: 36; II *Thes.* 1: 5

[6] *Eph.* 1: 1-14; I *Cor.* 1: 2, 30; 6: 11; II *Thes.* 2: 13; I *Pet.* 1: 2; *John* 17: 19; *Heb.* 2: 11; 10: 10, 14, 29; 13: 12; *Job* 1: 5; *Jer.* 1: 5; *Jude* 1: 1

[7] *Heb.* 1: 1-2; *John* 1: 1

[8] *Luke* 24: 25-27, 44-46; *Acts* 10: 34-43; *John* 5: 38-39; *Rev.* 1: 2, 9; 12: 17; 19: 10

[9] II *Pet.* 1: 21

[10] *John* 16: 7-11

[11] II *Tim.* 3: 16; *Rev.* 22: 18-19; *Isa.* 8: 20

[12] I *Cor.* 12: 4-11; *Rev.* 19: 10; I *Pet.* 2:21; I *John* 2: 6; *Acts* 10: 38; 2: 2 (~*Phil.* 2: 2); 2: 41-47 = *Jas.* 2: 14-18; *Mic.* 6: 8

[13] *Matt.* 28: 19; *Heb.* 9: 14; *Deut.* 6: 4-5 = *Mark* 12: 29-31; *Gal.* 4: 6

[14] *John* 16: 9

[15] *Rom.* 14: 23

[16] I *John* 3: 4

[17] *James* 4: 17

[18] *Rom.* 3: 23

[19] *Rom.* 7: 17, 20; *Jer.* 17: 7-12; *Matt.* 12: 34; 11: 7 = *Luke* 11: 13

[20] *Rom.* 3: 23-24; 7-8; I *John* 1: 8; *Eccl.* 7: 20; *Luke* 17: 10

[21] cf. Greek continuous present (and future) tense(s) in many of the following: *Rom.* 3: 23-24, 28; 4: 1-24-25; 7-8(: *31-33-39*); 1: 16-17; *Heb.* 7: 25; 10: 14; *Gal.* 3: 11; 2: 16; I *Cor.* 4: 4; *Acts* 13: 39; *Luke* 18: 14; I *John* 2: 1; *Ps.* 32: 1-2, 5; 130: 3-4

[22] *Ps.* 51: 5, LB

[23] *Eph.* 2: 3; *Ps.* 58: 3

[24] *Isa.* 48: 8; *Ps.* 58: 3; *Rom.* 3: 1-19, 23

[25] *Rom.* 5: 19

[26] *Gen.* 3; *Rom.* 5; *Job* 3: 11-19; 7: 21; *Eccl.* 9: 5-10; *Ps.* 115: 17; *John* 11: 11-14; I *Thes.* 4: 13-19; *Dan.* 12: 2; *Isa.* 26: 19

[27] *Col.* 3: 3-4; I *John* 5: 11-13; *Eccl.* 9: 5-10; *Ps.* 115: 17; *John* 11: 11-14; I *Thes.* 4: 13-19; *Dan.* 12: 2; *Isa.* 26: 19

[28] *Rom.* 3: 20

[29] *Gal.* 3: 24

[30] *Rom.* 2: 13; 4: 2; *Gal.* 3: 12; *Eph.* 2: 8-10

[31] *Gal.* 2: 16; *Acts* 13: 39; *Rom.* 3: 20; *Gal.* 3: 11; 5: 4

[32] *Rom.* 3: 21-28; 4: 2-8, 22-5: 1; *Col.* 3: 1-4; *Gal.* 2: 16; 3: 11; 3: 24; II *Cor.* 5: 21b

[33] *Rom.* 4

[34] *Phil.* 3: 9; *Rom.* 1: 16-17; 3: 22; 4: 5, 9, 11, 13; 9: 30; 10: 6; *Gal.* 5: 5; *Heb.* 11: 7; II *Pet.* 1: 1

[35] *Rom.* 1: 16-17

[36] *Rom.* 3: 23-24; 8: 29-31; *Heb.* 7: 25; *Gal.* 2: 20a,d

[37] *John* 16: 7-8; 1: 12; 15: 1-10; *Tit.* 3: 4-8; *Rom.* 6: 19, 22; 8: 1-5; II *Cor.* 4: 14-16; *Col.* 3: 1-4 –> 5-25; *Eph.* 1: 1-12 –> 13; *Heb.* 11: 33; I *John* 2: 29; 3: 1-3, 6-7; *Gal.* 5: 6, 22-26; 2: 20b,c; *Romans* 3: 27-28; 4: 2-3, 4-5 - 25 hence –> *Jas.* 2: 20-26

[38] I *Pet.* 2:21; I *John* 2: 6; *Acts* 10: 38; 2: 2 (~*Phil.* 2: 2); 2: 41-47 = *Jas.* 2: 14-18; *Mic.* 6: 8

[39] I *John* 5: 12-13; *Isa.* 32: 17; *John* 3: 16; 5: 24; *Rom.* 8: 1, 31-39; *Col.* 2: 2-10; I *Thes.* 1: 5; *Heb.* 4: 16; 6: 11, 18-20; 10: 19-22, 35

[40] *John* 16: 33, *Rom.* 3: 4; *Rev.* 17: 4 therefore– *Rom.* 12: 21; *Num.* 13: 30; I *John* 2: 13-14; 4: 4; 5: 4-5; *Rev.* 2: 7, 11, 17, 26; 3: 5, 12, 21; 12: 11; 21: 7; II *Pet.* 2: 19

[41] *Rev.* 14: 12; cf. *Rom.* 6-8; *Gal.* 5-6; *Eph.* 5-6: 1-20; *Col.* 3: 5-25

[42] *Gen.* 2: 1-3; *Mark* 2: 27-28; *Ex.* 20: 8-11; *Deut.* 5: 15; II *Cor.* 10: 3-5; *Heb.* 4

[43] *Ex.* 31: 13; *Ez.* 20: 12, 20

[44] *Ez.* 36: 26; *Jer.* 31: 33; *Heb.* 8: 10; 10: 16; *Prov.* 3: 3; 7: 3; II *Cor.* 3: 3; cf. *Deut.* 5; 6: 4-5; *Ex.* 20; *Matt.* 5-7; *Mk.* 12: 28-34 = *Matt.* 22: 34-40 = *Luke* 10: 25-28

[45] *Heb.* 8: 10; 10:16; *Deut.* 4: 6

[46] *Rom.* 12: 1; I *Thess.* 5: 21; I *Cor.* 6: 18-20; III *John* 1: 2

[47] *Matt.* 25: 31-46; a community in common: *Acts* 10: 38; 2: 2 (~*Phil.* 2: 2); 2: 41-47 = *Jas.* 2: 14-18; *Mic.* 6: 8; I *John* 2: 6

[48] *Eph.* 4: 31-32

[49] *James* 5: 16; *Matt.* 6: 9-13 = *Luke* 11: 2-4

[50] *Mal.* 3: 8-12; I *Cor.* 16: 2

[51] *Phil.* 3: 9-14

[52] *Phil.* 1: 6

[53] *Matt.* 16: 15-19; 6: 9-13 = *Luke* 11: 2-4; *John* 20: 22-23; *Eph.* 2: 11-22

[54] *Rev.* 12: 17; 14: 12

[55] *Rom.* 6

[56] *Heb.* 10: 25; 12: 22-23; I *Cor.* 12; *Rom.* 12: 1

[57] *Mark* 14: 17, 22-25; *Matt.* 26: 20, 26-29; *Luke* 22: 14-20

[58] I *Cor.* 11: 23-29; I *Thess.* 4: 16-18

[59] *Lev.* 16; ch. 25-26; *Heb.* 4: 12-16; 6:19-20; 9: 7-15, 24-28; 10: 1-25 (~ *Mark* 15: 38 = *Matt.* 27: 51 = *Luke* 23: 45); 12: 22-29; 13: 10-14; *Rev.* 1: 6; 5: 10; I *Pet.* 2: 9; *Eph.* 1: 3; the Jubilee Day of Atonement: *Dan.* 8: 1-14 = 9: 24-27 (= *Lev.* 16; ch. 25-26; *Isa.* 61:1-2~*Luke* 4: 18-19; *Hebrews*)

[60] I *Cor.* 12; The ministry and writings of Ellen G. White are recognized as an example of the prophetic gift.

[61] II *Cor.* 5: 14-21

[62] The Jubilee Day of Atonement: *Dan.* 8: 1-14 = 9: 24-27 (= *Lev.* 16; ch. 25-26; *Isa.* 61:1-2~*Luke* 4: 18-19; *Hebrews*); note the 'scapegoat'/ *Azazel* type: *Lev.* 16 –> [*Job* 1: 6-12; 2: 1-7]; *John* 12: 31-33; 16: 11; *Rom.* 3; *Zech.* 3; *Dan.* 8: 1-14 = 9: 24-27; *Rev.* 4; 12; 20: 1-3, 10; cf. the temptation, *Mark* 1 = *Matt.* 4 = *Luke* 4

[63] *Rev.* 12; *John* 12: 31; 16: 11; the Jubilee Day of Atonement: *Dan.* 8: 1-14 = 9: 24-27 (= *Lev.* 16; ch. 25-26; *Isa.* 61:1-2~*Luke* 4: 18-19; *Hebrews* [64] *Rom.* 8: 31-39

[65] *Eccl.* 12; *Rev.* 4; 12; 11: 15-19; 14: 6-12; *Rom.* 3; 8; 14: 10; *Dan.* 7-9; *John* 5: 22, 27; 12: 31-33; *Acts* 17: 31; *Zech.* 3; *Ps.* 9: 7; *Rom.* 3: 4 '... when You are judged'; *Luke* 23: 40 'Do you not fear God... you are in the same judgment?'

[66] *Isa.* 53; I *Tim.* 5: 24a; *Rom.* 3

[67] *Lev.* 16; *Heb.* 4: 12-16; *Rom.* 3; *John* 3: 18; 5: 24; *Dan.* 7: 9-14, 22, 26-27 (= *Ps.* 22-24 = *Rev.* 12); 8: 1-14 = 9: 24-27 (= *Lev.* 16; ch. 25-26; *Isa.* 61:1-2~*Luke* 4: 18-19; *Isa.* 63: 1-7); *Dan.* 12: 1-3; *Luke* 20: 35; 21: 36; II *Thes.* 1: 5

[68] *Ps.* 35: 24; *Dan.* 9: 16, 19; *Ps.* 31: 1; 71:1-2; cf. *Ps.* 84: 9 & I *Sam.* 12: 7

[69] II *Tim.* 5: 24b; *Isa.* 2: 10-21; 47: 3; *Jer.* 8: 20; *Nah.* 3: 5; *Heb.* 10: 25-26; *Rev.* 3: 18; 6: 15-16; *Ez.* 33: 11

[70] *Acts* in 1: 9-11; *Rev.* 1: 7

[71] II *Thes.* 1: 8; *John* 12: 48; includes the final 'great white throne' judgment and destruction after the 1000 years of *Rev.* 20.

[72] I *Thes.* 4: 13-16, LB; *Mark* 13 = *Matt.* 24 = *Luke* 21; *Dan.* 12: 1-3; *Jude* 1: 14-15

[73] *Rev.* 19; 14: 14-16

[74] *Rev.* 22: 20b

My Personal Union with Christ and His Church

Summary

I believe –

1. Jesus Christ, fully God and fully man, was obedient unto death, even the death of the cross. Through faith in Him I am saved and enjoy eternal life now.
2. There is one God: Father, Son, and Holy Spirit, a unity of three co-eternal Persons, all working together for my salvation.
3. The Bible is the testimony of Jesus and is the only rule of faith and practice for the Christian.
4. Adam's fall brought sin, condemnation, and death upon humanity. The Ten Commandment Law declares God's will, reveals sin, and reminds all, including the saved, of their need of a Savior.
5. The Gospel proclaims that the one who is just by faith shall live. In justification, God declares believers righteous on the ground of Jesus Christ's substitutionary life and death apart from works.
6. The fruit of the Gospel includes the new birth and a life of progressive sanctification, which is a deepening repentance and a growing Christ-likeness until glorification at the Day of Jesus Christ.
7. Under the New Covenant, God writes His Law, including the Fourth Commandment, upon the hearts and minds of believers in Jesus. Loyalty to God's Law is a necessary fruit of the Gospel.
8. Joined by faith to Jesus Christ, I become a member of His body, the Church Universal.
9. Participation in His body includes baptism, corporate worship, the Lord's supper, exercising discipleship and spiritual gifts – fulfilling the great commission to take the Gospel to the world.
10. The Christian life is a personal relationship with Christ – a commitment to His steadfast love of ourselves, our time, talents, possessions (including tithes and offerings), health, and influence.
11. At the cross, Jesus stood in the Judgment for sinners and died in their place. Believers do not personally appear in Judgment because Jesus the Mediator presents them as righteous in Himself.
12. In the Final Judgment, the righteous receive immortality at Christ's return, and the wicked, eternal death at the Millennium's end as the new earth becomes the saints' possession forever.
13. Seventh-day Adventist Christians are called to announce Christ's return to the world by proclaiming the Gospel – preparing individuals to stand in the Judgment in the Person of their righteous Representative – Jesus Christ.

FOR ENTERANCE INTO HEAVEN WHAT DOES GOD REQUIRE OF US?

For Entrance into Heaven
God Requires of Us
"Perfect Obedience, Perfect Righteousness"
From the Cradle to the Grave!
See SC 62, 1 SM 367.

BUT, NOT ONE PERSON IN THE WORLD HAS THAT PERFECT RIGHTEOUSNESS TO PRESENT TO GOD! EVERYONE HAS A THREEFOLD PROBLEM!

1. We were all **BORN** with **a sinful nature**–the tendency to sin–which we retain until glorification,
2. We have all **SINNED** times without number, and
3. The best Christians in the world still come **SHORT** of perfectly satisfying, fulfilling and obeying God's infinitely righteous law!

●

What Then? Is There No Hope?
Ah, Yes! Thank God! There IS Hope!
And That Hope IS IN JESUS IN HEAVEN!

The perfect righteousness which God requires of us for entrance into heaven, He Himself has already provided for us in His Son, Jesus Christ, Which He CREDITS to us in His gift of Justification AS A FREE GIFT!

And that free gift is received and appropriated by us personally (individually) **solely through faith in Jesus, apart from anything else we may do** (Rom. 3: 28).

All that we do, by the grace of God through faith in Jesus, or that God does in us, is the **fruit (result)** of Jesus' atoning work for us and His justification of us.

We are **NOT** justified **BY** faith; we are justified **BY GOD THROUGH FAITH**. There is absolutely **NO** justifying merit whatsoever in faith. Faith is simply **the empty hand** that reaches up and accepts the **GIFT** of Christ's **IMPUTED** righteousness. **ALL** our hope of heaven is in the **IMPUTED** righteousness of Christ!

A KEY PROPHETIC STATEMENT
By Mrs. Ellen G. White

Mrs. White Predicted That
The Time Will Come
BEFORE THE END WHEN:

"ONE INTEREST WILL PREVAIL,
ONE SUBJECT WILL SWALLOW UP
EVERY OTHER—

Christ Our Righteousness."
SD 259

The Day is Coming Soon When
The Subject of This Set of Books,
JUSTIFICATION BY FAITH,
Will be THE MAIN THEME OF DISCUSSION
by the Seventh-day Adventist Administrators,
Theologians, Pastors and Laymembers
All Over The World.

*Dear Fellow Seventh-day Adventist
Believer in Christ,*
LET THE DISCUSSION BEGIN TODAY!

ABRAHAM IS GOD'S CLASSIC EXAMPLE OF HOW HE JUSTIFIES ALL SINNERS

Justification by Faith, Righteousness by Faith, is Explained Beautifully by the *New King James Bible*

Romans 4:1-17, 22-25

1: *What then shall we say that Abraham our father has found according to the flesh?*

2: *For If Abraham was justified by works, he has something to boast about, but not before God.*

3: *For what does the Scripture say? "Abraham believed God, and it was ACCOUNTED to him for righteousness."*

4: *Now to him who works, the wages are not COUNTED as grace but as debt.*

5-8: *But to him who does not work but believes on Him who justifies the ungodly, his faith is ACCOUNTED for righteousness, just as David also describes the blessedness of the man to whom God IMPUTES righteousness apart from works: "Blessed are those whose lawless deeds are forgiven, and whose sins are covered: Blessed is the man to whom the LORD shall not IMPUTE sin."*

9: *Does this blessedness then come upon the circumcised only, or upon the uncircumcised also? For we say that faith was ACCOUNTED to Abraham for righteousness.*

10: *How then was it ACCOUNTED? While he was circumcised, or uncircumcised? Not while circumcised, but while uncircumcised.*

11-12: *And he received the sign of circumcision, a seal of the righteousness of the faith which he had while still uncircumcised, that he might be the father of all those who believe, though they are uncircumcised, that righteousness might be IMPUTED to them also, and the father of circumcision to those who not only are of the circumcision, but who also walk in the steps of the faith which our father Abraham had while still uncircumcised.*

13: *For the promise that he would be the heir of the world was not to Abraham or to his seed through the law, but through the righteousness of faith.*

14-15: *For if those who are of the law are heirs, faith is made void and the promise made of no effect, because the law brings about wrath; for where there is no law there is no transgression.*

16-17: *Therefore it is of faith that it might be according to grace, so that the promise might be sure to all the seed, not only to those who are of the law, but also to those who are of the faith of Abraham, who is the father of us all (as it is written, "I have made you a father of many nations") in the presence of Him whom he believed—God, who gives life to the dead and calls those things which do not exist as though they did;*

22: And therefore "It was ACCOUNTED to him for righteousness."

23-25: Now it was not written for his sake alone that it was IMPUTED to him, but also for us. It shall be IMPUTED to us who believe in Him who raised up Jesus our Lord from the dead, who was delivered up because of our offenses, and was raised because of our justification.

Romans 5:1

1: Therefore, having been justified by faith, we have peace with God through our Lord Jesus Christ.

ISSUE ONE:

THE CHRISTIAN'S ULTIMATE AUTHORITY

What is the Seventh Day Adventist Christian's Highest Authority?

Is it the *Bible? Or is it Mrs. White? Or is it both equally?*

Are Mrs. White's writings an *inspired commentary, or interpreter* of the Bible?

ERRONEOUS PRESUPPOSITIONS

The Bible is *not our ultimate authority; Mrs. White is.*

Mrs. White is *an inspired interpreter of the Bible.*

Page 2.8*: *"We would be so much farther ahead [in our understanding of the Scriptures] if we had always valued and used her writings in conjunction with scriptures in developing and understanding these truths."*

Mrs. White's writings *are more clear, accurate, and reliable* than the Bible!

---

* Page 2.8 means page 2 of the 48 page Critique, 8/10 of the way down the page.

Comments by The Author

"Lay Sister White right to one side; lay her to one side. Don't you ever quote my words again as long as you live, until you can obey the BIBLE. When you take *THE BIBLE* and make that your food, and your meat, and your drink, and make that the elements of your character, when you can do that you will know better how to receive some counsel from God."3 SM 33.

"But here is *THE WORD*, the precious *WORD*, exalted before you today. *And don't you give a rap any more what 'Sister White said—Sister White said this, and Sister White said that, and Sister White said the other thing.' But say, 'Thus says the Lord God of Israel' [the Bible]* and then you do just what the Lord God of Israel does, and what He says… I don't want you ever to quote Sister White until you get your vantage ground where you know where you are. *QUOTE THE BIBLE.'"**   Spalding-Magan Collection, page 167 and 174.

The Bible Teaches That:

The Bible is the Christian's ultimate authority. We must not give Mrs. White veto-power over the Bible.

Dozens of times, Mrs. White herself taught that:
- *The Bible is the Christian's ultimate authority,*
- *All teachings must be tested by the Bible and*
- *SDAs Subscribe to the Protestant Reformer's slogan: Sola Scriptura.*

---

*Mrs. White's writings are not to be used to define doctrine.

Isa. 8:20: "To the law and to the testimony, if they speak not according to this word, there is no light in them."

Rev. 22:18, 19: "If any man shall *add unto these things, God shall add unto him the plagues that are written in this book: and if any man shall take away from the words of the book of this prophecy, God shall take away his part out of the book of life, and out of the holy city, and from the things which are written in this book.*"

Historic (traditional, conservative) Seventh-day Adventists may deny that they put her above the Bible, but this is the way they come across.

Anyone who says that "Mrs. White is an inspired interpreter or commentary on the Bible," automatically puts **her** *authority* **above** the Bible.

(We must interpret Mrs. White by the Bible, not the Bible by her!)

Mrs. White Strongly Endorsed The Great Protestant Slogan:

- **Sola Scriptura (Scripture alone),**
- **Sola Gratia (Grace alone),**
- **Solo Christo (Christ alone),**
- **Sola Fide (Faith alone).**

Biblical Evidence
The Bible Teaches that:

- **The Bible and the Bible alone**, without and apart from the traditions of men, should be our rule of faith.
- **The grace of God and the grace of God alone**, not any grace of priests, sacraments, and saints, is the procuring cause of our salvation.
- **Christ and Christ alone**, without and apart from the church, the sacraments, and our own obedience, good works, and self-sacrifice, is the only atonement for sin and basis of forgiveness, acceptance, and salvation.
- **Faith and Faith alone**, without and apart from our own repentance, conversion, obedience, good works, sanctification, self-sacrifice, growth in grace, perfecting of Christian character, and godly living, is the MEANS by which we appropriate God's gift of justification to ourselves personally.

E. G. White Evidence

For the sake of brevity we will refrain from commenting on Mrs. White's beliefs and teachings concerning the **WORD** of God, the **GRACE** of God, the one and only **BASIS** of salvation, and the one and only **MEANS** by which we accept God's great gift of salvation. We will let Mrs. White speak for herself.

Sola Scriptura – The Bible and the Bible Only

"In our time there is a wide departure from their [the Scriptures] doctrines and precepts, and there is a need of a return to the great Protestant principle–**THE BIBLE, AND THE BIBLE ONLY**, as a rule of faith and duty." GC 204, 205.

We Seventh-day Adventists Should Accept THE BIBLE AND THE BIBLE ONLY:

- "as [the] authoritative and infallible revelation of God's will. GC 7"
- "as the basis of SDA faith. PP 143"
- "as counselor. CH 369 - 72"
- "as educator. 7BC 989; FE 414; MYP 189"
- "as friend and guide. CT138-9; MYP 274"
- "as God's Inspired Word. 1SM 17"
- "as God's Word. MH 122"

Sola Scritura:

- "as infallible guide FE 394"
- "as instructor. Ev 629"
- "as light of God's people. FE 414"
- "as only food for soul. FE 379"
- "as only foundation of faith. COL 39-40; 8T 193"
- "as rule of daily life. 5T 264"
- "as study book. CT 455; GW 309"
- "as they are. 7BC 944-5; 1SM 17; 5T 388"
- "as they read. GC 599; 1SM 170; 5T 171"
- "The words of the Bible, and the Bible alone, should be heard from the pulpit." Prophets and Kings, pp. 624-626

The Scriptures:

- "alone are foundation of SDA faith. 2SM 85
- "alone are rule of faith and duty. CH 371"
- "alone can satisfy questionings of mind. CT 53-4
- "alone contain authentic account of creation. 5T 25"
- "alone enable men to distinguish path of life from path of death. FE 200"
- "alone give correct view of events now happening. PK 537"
- "alone give correct view of world conditions. Ed 180"
- "alone present authentic account of origin of nations. CT 52; MYP 263; Ed 173"
- "alone: religion of Protestants is based on.   GC 448"
- "alone reveal power that created heaven and earth. CT 52; MYP 263"
- "alone should be basis of all reforms. GC 595"
- "alone should be SDA creed. 1SM 416"
- "alone should be standard of all doctrines. GC 595"
- "alone should be teacher's counselor. CT 352-3"
- "alone should be your guide. CW 145"

"God help us to be *Bible* students. Until you can see the reason for it yourself and a '*thus saith the Lord*' in the Scriptures, don't trust any living man to interpret the Bible for you." (Emphasis added).

"And when you can see this, you know it for yourself, and know it to be the truth of God. You will say, 'I have read it [in the Bible], I have seen it [in the Bible], and my own heart takes hold upon it, and it is the truth God has spoken to me from His Word.'"

"Now this is what we are to be—individual Christians. We need to have an individual, personal experience. We need to be converted, as did the Jews. If you see a little light, you are not to stand back and say, 'I will wait until my brethren have seen it.' If you do, you will go on in darkness." FW 77, 78.

"The question is, 'What is truth?' It is not how many years have I believed that makes it the truth. You must bring your creed to the Bible and let the light of the Bible define your creed and show where it comes short and where the difficulty is." FW 77.

The Preamble to The Statement of FUNDAMENTAL BELIEFS OF THE SEVENTH-DAY ADVENTIST CHURCH states: "Seventh-day Adventists accept the Bible as their only creed..."

THE CHRISTIAN'S HIGHEST AUTHORITY
16 STATEMENTS BY MRS. WHITE

When Sister White's grandson, Elder Arthur White, was the secretary for the E. G. White Estate, he wrote and published a 37-page paper entitled: **"The position of the Bible and the Bible Only"** and **"The Relationship of This to The Writings of Ellen G. White."**

The following are 16 statements by Mrs. White quoted by Elder White in this paper on the subject.

1. **CSSW 84**– "The Bible and the Bible **ALONE**, is our rule of faith."
2. **PK 626**–"The words of the Bible, and the Bible **ALONE**, should be heard from the pulpit."
3. **Word to the Little Flock, p.13, by James White**–"The Bible is a perfect, and complete revelation. It is our **ONLY** rule of faith and practice."
4. **CWE 145**–"We then took the position that the Bible, and the Bible **ONLY**, was to be our **guide**; and we are **never** to **depart** from this position."
5. **1SM 416**–"The Bible, and the Bible **ALONE**, is to be our creed, the **SOLE** bond of union; all who bow to this Holy Word **will be in harmony.**
6. **GC 448**–"The Bible, and the Bible **ONLY**, is the religion of Protestants."
7. **GC 595**–"But God will have a people upon the earth to maintain the Bible and the Bible **ONLY** as the **STANDARD** of **ALL** doctrines and the **BASIS** of **all reforms**."
8. **FCE 126**–"The Bible is the **ONLY** rule of faith and doctrine."
9. **CSSW 84**–"Leave the impression upon the mind that the Bible, and the Bible **ALONE**, is our rule of faith, and that the sayings and doings of men [or modern-day prophets] are not to be a criterion for our doctrines."
10. **FCE 200**–"The Bible **ALONE** affords the means of distinguishing the path of life from the broad road that leads to perdition and death."
11. **2SM 85**–"I am fully in harmony with you [A. T. Jones] in your work when you present the Bible, and the Bible **ALONE**, as the **foundation** of our faith."

12. **Ed 179,180; PK 537**–"The Bible, and the Bible **ONLY**, gives a correct view of these things [last-day events]. Here are revealed the great final scenes in the history of our world."

13. **5T 25**–"In God's word **ALONE** we find an authentic account of creation....Here **ONLY** can we find a [an inspired] history of our race."

14. **CT 352, 353**–"Teachers need an intimate acquaintance with the Word of God. The Bible, and the Bible **ALONE**, should be their counselor."

15. **EW 78**–"I recommend to you, dear reader, the Word of God as **the rule** of your faith and practice. **BY THE WORD** we are to be judged."

16. **1 SM 416**–"Our own views and ideas must not control our efforts. Man is fallible, but **God's Word is infallible**. Let us meet all opposition as did our Master, saying, **'It is written.'** Let us life up the banner on which is inscribed, The Bible our rule of faith and discipline."

Elder White concludes with these words: "THERE ARE MANY [MORE] LIKE STATEMENTS, but to multiply their duplication would add little to the discussion." (Signed, A. L. White)

**Jesus Said,
"And I, if I be lifted up . . .
Will draw all men unto Me."
John 12:32**

ISSUE TWO:
THE NATURE OF JUSTIFICATION

What is the *NATURE* of Justification?
Is Justification *a legal, judicial, forensic act* by God in behalf of believers?

    Or, is it God's gracious *creative* act of converting, sanctifying, transforming and dwelling in Christians by the Holy Spirit?

Is God's *act* of justifying us strictly a *judicial* act by which He sets us free from condemnation?

    Or is God's *act* of justifying us His *creative, converting, sanctifying, transforming act* of imparting to us Christ's redeeming love that transforms the heart?

Does God's *act* of *justifying* believers include His work of *making* them inwardly righteous in nature, character or life?

    Or, does God's *act* of justifying believers include His gracious gifts of (1) *forgiveness* (2) Christ's perfect righteousness *credited* to them, (3) God's *acceptance* of them unto eternal life, and (4) God's *treatment* of believers during this life on earth *as if* they had not sinned?

ERRONEOUS PRESUPPOSITIONS

God's **ACT** of justifying (forgiving) sinners **is not restricted** to a **legal, judicial, forensic** act in behalf of sinners, outside of sinners.

That is to say: God's **act** of **justifying** sinners is **not** restricted to His **forgiveness** of sinners, His **crediting** Christ's righteousness to sinners, His act of **accepting** sinners unto adoption and eternal life, and His act of **treating** them during this life on earth, **AS IF** they had never sinned.

God's act of **justifying** sinners **IS** a **creative, converting, sanctifying and transforming** act of **imparting** the Holy Spirit to them and **making** them inwardly righteous, pleasing and acceptable to Himself in nature, character, and life.
Justification is a creative, converting, sanctifying, transforming act by God in believers.

Page 28.10: "'Fruit in *sanctification*' are components of 'Justification by faith alone!' So when someone says, '*Justification* by faith alone' they are *including* 'Fruit in *sanctification*.'"

Page 43.5: "To be pardoned [justified] in the way that Christ pardons, is not only to be forgiven, but to be renewed [converted] in the spirit of our mind." RH, Aug. 19, 1890 par. 7.

Page 43.6: "God's forgiveness is *not* merely a *judicial* act by which He sets us free from condemnation. It [God's forgiveness] is not only forgiveness for sin, but *reclaiming* from sin. It [God's forgiveness] is the outflow of redeeming love that *transforms* the heart. David had the true conception of forgiveness when he prayed, '*Create* in me a clean heart...' " MB 114

The Bible Teaches That:

Justification is *not* a creative, converting, sanctifying, transforming act of God in *believers* by which He *makes* them actually, inwardly righteous, pleasing and acceptable to Himself

Biblical Justification *is* a *legal, judicial, forensic law-court word* which means: To *reckon, declare, and treat as if* we were *innocent* of any wrongdoing—*as if* we were *perfectly righteous.*

The EGW Statements above, separated from her *balancing, complementary* definitions of justification are misleading.

The *few, isolated problem* statements by Mrs. White must be interpreted in harmony with her great *many balancing, complementary* statements like the following statement.

The following EGW quotations in this book clearly state that God's act of justifying believers is *not* a *creative, converting* act in *making* them righteous, but is instead a *judicial* act of *crediting* Christ's righteousness to them, *forgiving* their sins and *accepting and treating* them *as if* they had never sinned!

Our brother's paper, page 42.9 correctly says, "Sinners can be *justified* by God only when He *pardons* their sins, *remits* the punishment they deserve, and *treats* them *as though* they were really just [righteous] and had not sinned, receiving them into divine favor and *treating* them *as if* they were righteous. They are *justified alone* through the **IMPUTED** righteousness of Christ. The Father accepts the Son, and through the atoning sacrifice of His Son, accepts the sinner." (8MR 355.3)

I marvel that our brother quotes this clear EGW statement on page 42.9 of his critique of the Campus Hill Church Statement of the gospel since it *contradicts* his major premise that justification is *not only a forensic act* by God *outside* of believers, but a *creative, converting, sanctifying, transforming* act *inside* of *believers* in which He *makes* them righteous, pleasing, and acceptable to Himself!

Let's face it; Mrs. White sometimes uses interchangeably the words, *impute* and *impart.* Sometimes she uses the word *impute* to mean *impart,* and sometimes she uses the word *impart* to mean *impute.*

See Issue 19 entitled "Often Misunderstood EGW Statements" for additional material concerning Mrs. White's problem statements.

Both the Bible and Mrs. White, hundreds of times, teach clearly and decisively that *our hope of justification and acceptance by God* is *not* in a righteousness *inside* of us, but in Christ's righteousness *outside* of us—an infinite righteousness *that is always, in Him in heaven!*

This reply to our SDA brother's critique will prove conclusively that God's act of *justifying* believers is *NOT a morally transforming act* in them, but is, instead, *a legal, judicial, forensic verdict outside* of believers in which He *forgives* their sins, *credits* Christ's righteousness to them and *accepts and treats* them *as if* they were righteous.

Our brother may not be aware of it, but his view of Justification *coincides* with much of the Roman Catholic Church's doctrine of this subject.

The Roman Catholic Church teaches that God's justification of believers is based on His *sanctification* of them. When I speak of the Roman Catholic Church, it is always with respect. The Roman Catholic Church should thank me for explaining what it teaches about justification.

The church of Rome teaches that, We are **JUSTIFIED** by being *converted, sanctified and made* inwardly righteous, pleasing, and acceptable to God.

The teaching of every false religion in the world puts the righteousness that secures the Higher Power's acceptance of sinners *inside* of them—in *their* obedience, good works and self-sacrifice.

The **CHRISTIAN** religion is the only religion in the world that teaches that the righteousness that secures the favor of God is **OUTSIDE** of them—**ALWAYS ONLY IN JESUS IN HEAVEN.** This is the beauty of the Christian religion.

Holy, Holy, Is What the Angels Sing

There is singing up in heaven such as we have never known,
Where the angels sing the praises of the Lamb upon the throne;
Their sweet harps are ever tuneful and their voices always clear,
O that we might be more like them while we serve the Master here!

So, although I'm not an angel, yet I know that over there
I will join a blessed chorus that the angels cannot share;
I will sing about my Savior, *who upon dark CALVARY*
Freely PARDONED my transgressions, died to set a sinner FREE.

Johnson Oatman Jr., Church Hymnal, page 125.

The following is adapted, expanded and paraphrased from *Go Free* by Robert M. Horn, Appendix 1, Justification: A Ten-point summary, page 123, Inter Varsity Press, Powers Grove, Ill. 60515

THE BIBLE AND THE ORIGINAL PROTESTANT REFORMERS TEACH THAT:

1. *Justification* has to do with **the changed relationship** between a holy God and otherwise guilty, condemned unworthy sinners. God's sacrifice of His Son and His justification of sinners is His **revelation** to the world and to the universe of **His thinking** about Himself, His Son, righteousness, sin, and sinners.

2. Justification is **a legal, judicial, forensic verdict** by God, the Creator and Judge of the Supreme Court of the universe, in which He declares that, because of Jesus atoning work for sinners, (believers in Jesus) are no longer condemned, but are forgiven, adopted and accepted by Him unto eternal life.

3. Justification is God **not holding or counting** our sins against us, but is instead, **crediting** Christ's perfectly righteous character and sacrifice to our account in heaven and **treating** us during this life, **AS IF** we had never sinned.

4. God's free gift of justification gives believing sinners **a righteous legal STANDING** before Him and His law in the judgment in our **sinful moral STATE**.

5. The believing justified sinner's new righteous **standing** before God is **based** exclusively upon and is the direct **result** of Christ's **atoning** work for sinners outside of sinners 2000 years ago.

6. Christ's atoning work for guilty condemned sinners which secures their justification is not because of any supposed good **in us**, or because of anything **we have done or can do** by the grace of God through faith in Jesus or because of anything God may do in us, but solely because of **God's free grace.**

7. God took Jesus who was perfectly righteous and laid all our sins upon Him and reckoned and treated Him *AS IF* He were sinful, in order that He could justly take us who are exceedingly sinful and credit His perfect righteousness to us and reckon and treat us *AS IF* we were as righteous as He. (Isa. 53:6, 8, 10, 11, 12 and 2 Cor. 5:21.

8. God's transcendent gift of *justification* consists of four wonderful gifts of: (1) the *forgiveness* of all our sins, (2) Christ's perfectly obedient life, death, and resurrection *credited* to us, (3) *God's adoption and acceptance* of us unto eternal life, and (4) His *treatment* of us, during this life, *AS IF* we were as righteous as Christ.

9. It is God's gift of *faith* in Jesus and in His promises that *enables* us sinful sinners *to accept, receive and appropriate to ourselves personally* His fourfold gift of justification. *Faith* is *belief* plus *trust* plus *resting* in Christ's completed work for our justification 2000 years ago.

10. Since God's undeserved gift of justification does *not* depend upon something *IN US*, but wholly upon something *in Him and in Jesus*, we can have the *full assurance* that we are truly forgiven and fully accepted by God unto eternal life, and adopted into His heavenly family as His dear blood-bought children.

11. Our *reception* of God's unspeakable gift of justification solely through faith apart from anything else we may do, brings perfect *peace* with God, *joy* unspeakable and full of glory even in times of severe loss, suffering, trials, and spiritual depression.

12. Justification and Sanctification are always *distinct, but never separate.* The same faith that justifies, also, always, at the same time, sanctifies and brings forth in us the fruit of obedience, good works, and a godly life. We grow *in* sanctification, *not into* sanctification.

13. During this life on earth, *Christian perfect*ion is always *relative, never absolute*. Although we cannot *equal* the Pattern, we are to *copy* it, and, to the best of our ability, resemble it, by the grace of God through faith in Jesus. *True faith* always leads to a love for righteousness and a hatred of sin—to repentance, conversion, sanctification, obedience, to a godly life, and to the perfecting of Christian character. It is comforting to know that, while we are growing up into Christ, *forgiveness (justification) is always available.*

    Born again Christians are not in and out of grace, or justification many times every day or week or month every time we sin or come short of perfectly obeying God. As long as we continue to truly believe in Jesus and are sincerely striving by the grace of God, to overcome our besetting sins, we remain justified. God does not "divorce" us until we "divorce" Him. He is "married" to the backslider. Jer. 3:14.

    Of course, continual, habitual willful sin cancels our justification. It is the habitual trend of life that reveals our relationship to God and His relationship to us. We have to turn our backs upon

God, and deliberately quit being Christians in order to be lost. So long as we persevere in our personal faith-love relationship with God, we are in a saved condition. SC 57, 58.

Although we are not *perfect* children of God, we are *perfectly* His children the moment we truly believe in God and in Jesus whom He has sent. Justification is *eschatological*. We do not have to wait until the close of probation to be justified: We retain God's gift of justification solely through faith. In justification, we have God's verdict of the final judgment brought forward to *the present*.

14. For a correct understanding of the gospel and of justification, it is absolutely imperative that we clearly distinguish between *three aspects of justification*:
    1. *The objective meritorious BASIS* on which God justifies us,
    2. *The subjective instrumental MEANS* by which we accept (appropriate) His gift of justification, to ourselves personally.
    3. *The inevitable FRUIT (RESULT, EVIDENCE)* of justification.
       - The *BASIS* on which God justifies sinners is *Christ's atoning work.*
       - The *MEANS* by which we accept, receive, and appropriate God's gift of justification to ourselves personally is *faith.*
       - The *FRUIT* of justification is *the indwelling Holy Spirit, conversion, sanctification, obedience, good works, a godly life, and perfecting Christian character.*

    Again:
       - *Christ's atoning work for sinners* is the *BASIS* on which God justifies sinners.
       - *Faith* in Jesus is the *MEANS* by which we *appropriate* God's gift of justification to ourselves personally.
       - God's *gifts* of *the Holy Spirit, repentance, conversion, sanctification, and grace* to live a victorious Christian life are *the FRUIT (RESULT)* of justification and *the evidence* that our faith is *genuine.*

The essence of the ROMAN CATHOLIC doctrine of justification is that God justifies people by **making** them righteous, pleasing and acceptable to Himself. Having **made** them righteous, He then justifies them. The essence of the BIBLICAL-PROTESTANT doctrine is that God justifies people by Christ's life, death and resurrection and by **forgiving** their sins and **crediting** Christ's righteousness to them; God's gift of justification is believed, trusted and rested in **solely by faith, apart from works!**

DIFFERENT EXPRESSIONS THE BIBLE USES TO SAY THE SAME THING

1. We are **FORGIVEN** = pardoned, not on the **BASIS of our** faith, repentance, conversion, sanctification, obedience, good works, and godly lives, but on the **BASIS of Christ's** perfectly sinless life and His death on the cross, **THROUGH our faith in Jesus.**
2. We are **JUSTIFIED** = just as if I'd never sinned.
3. Justification by Faith = **RIGHTEOUSNESS BY FAITH.**
4. We are given **RIGHT STANDING** with God by faith.
5. We are **SET RIGHT = PUT RIGHT** with God by faith.

6. Christ's righteousness is **IMPUTED** to our account in heaven.
7. Christ's righteousness is **CREDITED** to our account in heaven.
8. We are **COUNTED** — accounted — righteous by God.
9. We are **RECKONED** — considered — righteous by God.
10. We are **DECLARED** — pronounced — righteous by God.
11. We are **ACCEPTED AND TREATED** by God, during this life, as if we were righteous.
12. We are **NOT NOW CONDEMNED.** John 3: 17,18; John 5: 24; 2 Cor. 5:19, 21.
13. "There is **NOW NO CONDEMNATION**" to those who believe in Jesus. Rom. 8: 1.
14. We shall **NOT PERISH.** John 3:16.
15. We "**HAVE ETERNAL LIFE**" — "have everlasting life." John 5:24; 3:18.
16. "We were [**LEGALLY**] **RECONCILED** to God by the death of His Son."
17. "We have **PEACE WITH GOD**." Rom. 5:1
18. We shall "**NOT BE ASHAMED.** "
19. JUSTIFICATION IS THREE THINGS:
    - The non-charging of our sins to us,
    - The charging of our sins to Christ,
    - The crediting of Christ's righteousness to us.
20. We are given a righteous legal **STANDING** by God in our sinful moral **STATE**.
21. We are not made inwardly righteous, but put into a right **RELATIONSHIP** with God.
22. **The Wedding Garment** of Matt. 22 symbolizes Christ's perfect obedience and His death which are **CREDITED** to our account in heaven in God's **GIFT** of "Justification by Faith"—"Righteousness by Faith." The wedding garment represents Christ's **IMPUTED** righteousness. (See Issue 20).
23. The parable of **The Pharisee and the Publican** of Luke 18:9—14 teaches that we are justified, forgiven, and accepted by God **solely through faith apart** from obedience and good works.
24. **Abraham is God's classic example** of how all sinners are saved. Abraham **believed** God; and God **counted** (reckoned, credited) it to him for righteousness. Gen. 15:16; Rom. 4:3; Gal. 3:6; Jas. 2:23.
    - The righteousness of **JUSTIFICATION IS NOT IN US.** It is **IN CHRIST** in heaven.
    - The **righteousness** of **RIGHTEOUSNESS BY FAITH IS NOT IN US.** It is **IN CHRIST** in heaven.
    - **PARDON, FORGIVENESS IS NOT IN US.** It is always **IN CHRIST** in heaven.

Volume Four soon to be published: "*The Third Angel's Message In Verity*", *20 EGW DEFINITIONS OF JUSTIFICATION* every one of which teaches that justification is *NOT* a *CREATIVE* act of God *IN US*, but that it is *a LEGAL, JUDICIAL, FORENSIC VERDICT* of acquittal by God *OUTSIDE* of us.

Table of Contents for *Christian Classics - Volume Four*

1. Justification is entirely **the GIFT of God** to unworthy sinners. Romans 5:15-18 -- six times.
2. Justification is by the **GRACE (goodness, mercy, kindness)** of God.
3. Justification is **SOLELY THROUGH FAITH in Jesus, apart from obedience and good works.**
4. Justification is **a LEGAL, judicial, forensic law-court verdict of pardon (forgiveness, innocence, not guilty), of being in harmony with God.**
5. Justification is **OBJECTIVE – outside of us – in the Godhead alone. The fruit and results** of justification are inside of us.
6. Justification is **ESCHATOLOGICAL.** We have the final verdict of the final judgment **now**--the verdict of **not guilty, of pardon.**

7. Justification does **not change** our characters or natures. **Justification** changes **God's RELATIONSHIP to us**; and Justification **by faith** changes **our** *relationship* **to God.** (During this life on earth, God does not judge or condemn or forsake us!)

8. Because of and on the **BASIS** of (1) Christ's incarnation, (2) sinless life, (3) death on the cross, and (4) resurrection from the dead, in justification, God **CREDITS** Christ's righteousness (perfect obedience) and His death to us and He **reckons, accepts, and treats us as if we were righteous**.

9. Justification is **"the OPPOSITE of condemnation."**

10. Justification is **"a full, complete PARDON** of sin" by God.

11. Justification is our being **CREDITED** with Christ's righteousness by God.

12. Justification is our being **ACCOUNTED** righteous by God.

13. Justification is our being **DECLARED legally** righteous by God.

14. Justification is **NOT** God's creative act of **MAKING** us inwardly righteous in the flesh.

15. Justification enables us to **STAND** before God in our sinful **STATE AS IF we were as righteous as Christ**.

16. Justification is the **SUBSTITUTION** of Christ's righteousness for our **unrighteousness**.

17. Justification is our being **RESTORED TO FAVOR** with God in a legal sense.

18. Justification gives us a righteous legal **STANDING (relationship)** before God and His infinitely righteous law in our sinful moral **STATE (inner moral condition)**.

19. Justification is the **IMPUTATION (RECKONING, CREDITING, COUNTING, AND ACCOUNTING)** of Christ's righteousness to us by God.
    This all amounts to one thing. During this life on earth **God does not hold our sins against us. He FORGIVES** all our sins and **CREDITS, IMPUTES** Christ's righteousness to us and treats us, during this life on earth, **as if** we were as righteous as Christ.

20. These are all truths taught by Mrs. White concerning Justification. Thank God for His wonderful **GIFT of Justification** which we receive **SOLELY BY FAITH, apart from our obedience and good works!**

Conclusion:

NOWHERE does the Bible say that justification is *a creative, converting, sanctifying, transforming* act of God *inside of* Christians in *making* them righteous, pleasing and acceptable to God in nature, character or life! **To the contrary, it teaches that in justifying us, God forgives our sins and IMPUTES, RECKONS, CREDITS Christ's righteousness to us–PERIOD!**

The BIBLE'S Threefold Definition of Justification:

1. Justification is God's Gracious Act of *NOT CHARGING* our sins against us! (5 Bible Texts - see pages 28 and 29).

2. Justification is God's Gracious Act of *CHARGING* our sins *TO CHRIST*! (7 Bible Texts - see pages 29 and 30).

3. Justification is God's Gracious Act of *CREDITING* Christ's righteousness (perfectly obedient life, substitutionary death, and resurrection from the dead) to us, to our account in heaven. (9 Bible Texts - see pages 30 and 31).

Justification has to do, *not* with **the Holy Spirit's** righteousness, but with **Christ's**! Justification *takes place, not IN US, but in Christ* and in God, the Father *who are in heaven.*

The Bible's Threefold DEFINITION of Justification

In order for us to really understand JUSTIFICATION, we must understand that there are three parts to justification. These three parts are: 1. the **non-charging** of our sins to us; 2. the **charging** of our sins to Christ; and 3. the **crediting** of Christ's righteousness to us. Let us look briefly at these three aspects of Justification, with the biblical evidence.

1. Justification is the NON-CHARGING of our Sins to Us

FIVE BIBLE TEXTS

God does not impute or charge our sins to us. This amounts to the forgiveness of all the sins of all believing sinners in the world during this life on earth. (At death all unconfessed sins are rolled back on sinners and they are then, rejected and condemned by God and eternally lost)!

1. **Psalm 32:1,2:** "Blessed is he whose transgression is **forgiven**, whose sin **is covered**. Blessed is the man unto whom the Lord **imputeth not iniquity**."

    Here the Bible says that God **does not impute our sins to us — does not charge our sins against us**—does not hold our sin against us—He lets us live—He postpones the death penalty!

2. **Isa 44:22:** God Says, "I have **blotted out**, as a thick cloud, thy transgressions, and as a cloud, thy sins: [therefore God pleads] return unto me; for I have redeemed thee." Here God plaintively appeals to Israel to **repent** of their sins **because** of His previous **forgiveness** of their sins!

    This text teaches that, during this life on earth, God does not hold or charge our sins against us. This is forgiveness! This is justification. God does not impute — charge — our sins against us. Justification is the **non-charging** of our sins to us and treating us, during this life on earth, **AS IF** we were perfectly righteous.

3. **Zech. 3:1-5:** "And he shewed me Joshua the high priest standing before the angel of the Lord, and Satan standing at his right hand to resist him. And the Lord said unto Satan, The Lord rebuke thee, O Satan; even the Lord that hath chosen Jerusalem rebuke thee: is not this a brand plucked out of the fire? Now Joshua was clothed with **filthy garments**, and stood before the angel. And he answered and spake unto those that stood before him, saying, Take away the filthy garments from him. And unto him he said, Behold, **I have caused thine iniquity to pass from thee [I have forgiven thee],** and I will clothe thee with a change of raiment. And I said, Let them set a fair mitre upon his head.

    So they set a fair mitre upon his head, and clothed him with **garments**. And the angel of the Lord stood by." Mrs. White explains that this **"change of raiment"** is the **IMPUTED** righteousness of

JUSTIFICATION, NOT the **imparted** righteous of **sanctification**. This is **the wedding garment** which Mrs. White says is the **imputed** righteousness of **justification**. (See Chapter 20).

4. **Rom. 4:7,8:** "Blessed are they whose iniquities are **forgiven** and whose sins are **covered** . . . Blessed is the man to whom the Lord **will not impute [charge] sin**." (Here Paul quotes David in Ps.32:1 and 2.)

5. **2 Cor. 5:19:** ". . . God was in Christ, reconciling the world unto Himself, **not imputing [not holding, charging or counting]** their trespasses unto them."

These five texts reveal the incredible truth that justification is **the non-imputation** of our sins to us. If God does not charge or hold our sins against us, what does He do with them? He can't just "sweep them under the rug" and forget about them. Satan would not be satisfied with that. This brings us to our **second definition** of justification.

---

2. Justification is THE CHARGING of our Sins to CHRIST

SEVEN BIBLE TEXTS
God imputed (charged) all our sins to Christ and dealt with them all in Him 2000 years ago.

1. **Isa.53:4,5,6,8,10,11,12:** "Surely he hath borne our griefs, and carried our sorrows: yet we did esteem him stricken, smitten of God, and afflicted. But he was **wounded for our transgressions, he was bruised for our iniquities:** the chastisement of our peace was upon him; and with his stripes we are healed. All we like sheep have gone astray; we have turned every one to his own way; and **THE LORD HATH LAID ON HIM THE INIQUITY OF US ALL.**

   " . . . For the transgression of my people was he stricken. . .
   "Yet it pleased the Lord to bruise him; he hath put him to grief: when thou shalt make his soul an offering for sin. . .
   "My righteous servant [shall] **JUSTIFY** many; for **HE SHALL BEAR THEIR INIQUITIES. . .**
   "He hath poured out his soul into death: and he was numbered with the transgressors; and he **bare the sin of many,** and made intercession for the transgressors."

2. **Matt. 8:17:** "That it might be fulfilled which was spoken by Esaias the prophet, saying, Himself **took our infirmities, and bare our sicknesses [sins]."**

3. **John 1:29:** "Behold the Lamb of God, which **taketh away [Greek–beareth away] the sin of the world."**

4. **2 Cor. 5:21:** "For he hath **made him to be sin for us,** who knew no sin; that we might be made the righteousness of God in him." (God **reckoned** Christ sinful and **treated** Him **AS IF** He were **sinful** in order that He might **reckon** us righteous and **treat** us **AS IF** we were righteous.) Incredible!

5. **Gal. 3:13:** "Christ hath **redeemed us from the curse of the law, being made a curse for us:** for it is written, Cursed is every one that hangeth on a tree."

6. **Heb. 9:28:** "So Christ was once offered **to BEAR the sins of many."**

7. **1 Peter 2:24:** "Who his own self **BARE our sins** in his own body on the tree."

God's **forgiveness** of all our sins and His **charging them to Christ**, and dealing with them **in Christ** leaves us **forgiven, but without the righteousness which we need** for entrance into God's presence in heaven. How does God meet this need? We discover the answer in our **third definition** of justification.

3. Justification is THE CREDITING of Christ's Righteousness to Us

NINE BIBLE TEXTS
God imputes (counts, reckons, credits) Christ's righteousness to us.

1. **Gen. 15:6:** "And he [Abraham] **believed** in the Lord; and he **COUNTED** it to him **for righteousness.**" This statement appears 4 times in the Bible. See also Rom. 4:3; Gal. 3:6, and James 2:23.

2. **Rom. 4:1-13:** "What shall we say then that **Abraham** our father, as pertaining to the flesh, hath found? For if Abraham were justified by works, he hath whereof to glory; but not before God. For what saith the Scripture? Abraham **BELIEVED** God, and it was **COUNTED** unto him for **righteousness**. Now to him that worketh is the reward not **RECKONED** of grace, but of debt. But to him that worketh not, but **believeth** on him that **justifieth the ungodly**, his **faith** is **COUNTED** for righteousness.

"Even as David also describeth the blessedness of the man, unto whom God **IMPUTETH** righteousness **without works**, Saying, Blessed are they whose iniquities are forgiven and whose sins are covered. Blessed is the man to whom the Lord will **not IMPUTE sin**.

"Cometh this blessedness then upon the circumcision only, or upon the uncircumcision also? For we say that **faith** was **RECKONED** to Abraham for righteousness. How was it then **RECKONED**? When he was in circumcision or in uncircumcision? Not in circumcision, but in uncircumcision.

"And he received the sign of circumcision, a seal of **the righteousness of the faith** which he had yet being uncircumcised: that he might be the father of all them that **believe,** though they be not circumcised; that righteousness might be **IMPUTED** unto them also.

"And the father of circumcision to them who are not of the circumcision only, but who also walk in the steps of that faith of our father Abraham, which he had being yet uncircumcised. For the promise, that he should be the heir of the world, was not to Abraham, or to his seed, through the law, but through **the righteousness of faith.**"

3. **Rom. 4:22-25:** "And therefore it was **IMPUTED** to him for righteousness. Now it was not written for his sake alone, that it was **IMPUTED** to him; But for us also, to whom it shall be **IMPUTED**, if we **believe** on him that raised up Jesus our Lord from the dead. Who was delivered for our offences, and was raised again for our justification."

4. **Rom. 5:15-19:** "But not as the offence, so also is **the free gift**. For if through the offence of one many be dead, much more the grace of God, and the gift by grace, which is by one man, Jesus Christ, hath

abounded unto many. And not as it was by one that sinned, so is **the gift**; for the judgment was by one to condemnation, but **the free gift** is of many offences unto **justification**.

"For if by one man's offence death reigned by one; much more they which receive abundance of grace and of **the gift of righteousness** shall reign in life by one, Jesus Christ.

"Therefore as by the offence of one judgment **CAME upon ALL men to condemnation**; even so by the righteousness of one **the free gift came upon ALL men unto JUSTIFICATION** of life. For as by one man's disobedience many were made [in God's eyes] sinners, so by the obedience of one shall many ["**ALL**"—verse 18] be made righteous [in God's reckoning]."

5. **Gal 3:6:** "Abraham believed God, and it was *ACCOUNTED, [CREDITED]* to him for righteousness."

6. **Phil. 3:9:** "And be found in him, not having mine own righteousness, which is of the law, but that which is **through the faith** of Christ, **the righteousness** which is of God **by faith.**"

7. **Col. 1:20-22, 28:** "And having made peace through the blood of his cross, by him to **reconcile** all things unto himself; by him, I say, whether they be things in earth, or things in heaven. And you, that were sometime alienated and enemies in your mind by wicked works, **yet now hath he reconciled in the body of his flesh through death, to present you holy and unblamable and unreproveable IN HIS SIGHT:** . . . Whom we preach, warning every man, and teaching every man in all wisdom; that we may present every man perfect [not inside of ourselves, but] **IN CHRIST JESUS.**"

8. **James 2:23:** "And the scripture was fulfilled which saith, Abraham **believed** God and it was **IMPUTED** unto him for **righteousness**: and he was called the Friend of God."

9. **2 Cor. 5:19, 21:** " God was in Christ, reconciling the world unto Himself, **NOT IMPUTING [not charging]** their trespasses unto them."

"For He hath made Him to be sin for us, who knew no sin; that we might be made the righteousness of God in Him." Verse 21 says that **Christ who was righteous, was reckoned sinful and treated as if He were sinful in order that we who are sinful, might be reckoned righteous and treated as if we were righteous.**

These nine texts support our third definition of justification: that justification is God's gracious act of crediting Christ's righteousness to us, and treating us, during this life on earth AS IF we were righteous.

"ALL that man can possibly DO toward his salvation
is to ACCEPT the invitation." 6BC 1071

THE JESUIT ERROR

THE Jesuits do not distinguish between the atoning work which God did **for us, outside** of us, **in Jesus, 2000 years ago,** and the converting work He does **inside** of us **now by the Holy Spirit.**

They do not distinguish between the righteousness of **Christ** which is the **BASIS** of our justification on the one hand, and the righteousness of the **Christian** which is the **FRUIT** of our justification on the other.

They do not distinguish between the righteousness of **CHRIST which reckons us infinitely sinless** and the righteousness of the **HOLY SPIRIT** which **never makes us perfect** during this life on earth.

They do not distinguish between the righteousness which **justifies and saves** them and the righteousness that does **NOT** justify and save them but that regenerates and sanctifies them.

They **believe** that God **infuses** His righteousness into them and, by that **infused** righteousness, actually **makes** them perfectly righteous within. Having **made** them perfectly righteous **within** by the **imparted** righteousness of **sanctification**, God simply justifies, forgives, and accepts them unto eternal life. **This is the great error of the Roman Catholic Jesuits.** They believe that they are saved by a righteousness that is **inside** of them.

At the peril of their lives, all the Protestant reformers **PROTESTED** against this extremely serious heresy. Many of them were burned at the stake while their wives and children looked on! The great truth of the gospel and this great demonstration of courage on the part of the martyrs is what aroused the nations of Europe in the 16th century and gave birth to the great Protestant–Reformation. Oh, what will it take to **arouse** Seventh-day Adventists in this matter? Let us no longer acquiesce and do nothing to combat this serious **Jesuit heresy** with which "certain independent SDA ministries" are attempting to force upon our beloved church!

On page number 89 of Volume One you see the picture of **Ignatius Loyola, the founder of the Jesuit order** in the Roman Catholic Church. Loyola's Jesuit priests **dominated** the Roman Catholic **Council of Trent** (1545-1563), which was convened to **COUNTER** the Protestant Reformation truth of Justification by Faith (Righteousness by Faith).

These Jesuit priests were ordered to make sure that in the Council of Trent, the Roman Catholic Church did not **compromise** its doctrine of Justification. These priests correctly taught that believers are justified and saved by **the GRACE AND RIGHTEOUSNESS of God through FAITH in Jesus!**

But they erroneously taught that **the GRACE AND RIGHTEOUSNESS** by which believers are justified and saved **is INSIDE** of them. Accordingly, it was the Jesuit-dominated Council of Trent **which perverted more fully and "set in concrete"** the false doctrine which declared that **the righteousness that justifies and saves** is the righteousness that God **INFUSES into believers!**

Accordingly, **the Jesuits** wrongly insisted that God's act of **justifying** people **actually MADE them inwardly righteous! They taught that God cannot justify, forgive, accept, and treat as righteous anyone who was NOT actually righteous!** "That would be **a lie,**" they claimed! In short, the Jesuits taught then, and they continue to teach now, that **Justification MAKES them inwardly righteous!** This is the **basis** of every false religious system in the world.

This is the major point of disagreement between the **true Biblical** Protestant doctrine of justification and **the false Jesuit** Roman Catholic doctrine. Now, do we begin to understand **the importance** of Seventh-day Adventist Christians understanding the **difference** between the true and the false doctrines of Justification by Faith?

As loyal, Biblical, Mainstream Seventh-day Adventist Christians let us rise up and teach **the truth** in this matter! Let us become **crusaders** for the true Biblical doctrine of **Righteousness by Faith—Justification by Faith. Jesus was an activist—a revolutionary—a crusader—for the truth about God. Let US become activists, revolutionaries, crusaders, for truth!** Fifty million Christians sacrificed their lives during **the Dark Ages** defending and promulgating this great truth. Can we do less?

> **T R A G I C A L L Y**
> **THE JESUIT DOCTRINE OF JUSTIFICATION BY FAITH**
> **IS IN THE SEVENTH-DAY ADVENTIST CHURCH TODAY (2010)**
> ★★★
> **HOW CAN WE COMBAT THIS PERNICIOUS SOUL-DESTROYING DOCTRINE**
> **WHICH TEACHES THAT THE RIGHTEOUSNESS OF**
> **"RIGHTEOUSNESS BY FAITH" IS INSIDE OF US?**

How can we **combat** this diabolical heresy in the rightwing of the Seventh-day Adventist Church which is teaching that the doctrine of Righteousness by Faith (Justification by Faith) **includes** sanctification, is **inside** of us and that it **makes** us inwardly righteous?

How can we **expose** this soul–destroying Jesuit error which does **NOT distinguish between** the **perfect,** finished, completed atoning work of Christ **outside** of Christians which justifies Christians, and the ongoing, regenerating work the Holy Spirit does **inside** of Christians which sanctifies them, but which never makes them absolutely sinless or perfectly righteous in nature, character, or outward life?

We are fighting the battle of the Reformation all over again in the Seventh-day Adventist Church!

Understanding the Gospel

Most Seventh-day Adventist Christians have fallen right into **the Jesuit trap** of **not** distinguishing between the two different aspects of righteousness.

Most Seventh-day Adventists are following the Jesuit heresy of **FUSING and thus CONFUSING** the two different aspects of righteousness into one and the same righteousness. As the result, they are looking **WITHIN** for the righteousness which both justifies and saves them. **This is disastrous!** Oh, how the Jesuits must be laughing at Seventh-day Adventists! This is Phariseeism Legalism, Perfectionism, Galatianism, **JESUIT Roman Catholicism,** and Heathenism!

> ## In order for us to really understand the GOSPEL, we must distinguish between the two different aspects of righteousness.

The two different aspects of righteousness are **DISTINCT (DIFFERENT), BUT NEVER SEPARATE.** What are these two different aspects of Righteousness, and **HOW** do they differ? How does the Bible distinguish between them?

WE SEVENTH-DAY ADVENTIST CHRISTIANS MUST DISTINGUISH BETWEEN:

1. THE RIGHTEOUSNESS that **justifies and saves** us;
   and the righteousness that does **NOT** justify and save us, but which, instead, **sanctifies and perfects us.**

2. THE RIGHTEOUSNESS that is the **ROOT** of our justification;
   and the righteousness that is the **FRUIT** of our justification.

3. THE RIGHTEOUSNESS that is **the MERITORIOUS BASIS** on which God **justifies and save us** on the one hand;
   and the righteousness that is **the non–meritorious, validating EVIDENCE** that our faith is genuine on the other.

4. THE RIGHTEOUSNESS that is **legally** (judicially, forensically) **IMPUTED (accounted, credited)** to us in God's gift of **JUSTIFICATION**;
   and the righteousness that is actually, experientially **IMPARTED TO—produced** and **developed** in us in **SANCTIFICATION.**

5. THE RIGHTEOUSNESS that is **NEVER INSIDE** of us, but that is always **outside** of us on the one hand;
   and the righteousness that **IS inside** of us on the other hand.

6. THE RIGHTEOUSNESS that is **solely through faith;**
   and the righteousness that is **NOT** solely by faith, but that **is by faith and works.**

7. THE RIGHTEOUSNESS of **Justification by Faith;**
   and the righteousness of **Sanctification by Faith and Works.**

8. THE RIGHTEOUSNESS of **Righteousness by Faith;**
   and the righteousness of **Sanctification by Faith and Works.**

9. THE RIGHTEOUSNESS that is our **key, ticket, title, and passport** to heaven on the one hand;
   and the righteousness that is **the validating evidence** that God's universal justification of the entire world of believers **collectively** has become ours personally, individually, on the other hand.

10. THE RIGHTEOUSNESS that is our **ASSURANCE** that our sins are all **forgiven** and that we are **accepted** by God unto eternal life on the one hand;
    and the righteousness that is our **ASSURANCE** that our faith, repentance, conversion, and sanctification are **GENUINE** on the other.

11. THE RIGHTEOUSNESS that is **absolutely** righteous;
    and the righteousness that is **never**, during this life on earth, absolutely righteous, but that is always only RELATIVELY righteous. (The **best** righteousness of the **best** Christians on earth always comes **short** of perfectly fulfilling God's infinitely righteous law for us.)

12. THE RIGHTEOUSNESS in which **all our HOPE** of heaven **resides,** and the righteousness in which **none** of our hope of heaven resides. (We are saved by the **first**. We are **never** saved by the second, **but** neither are we saved at last **without** the second.)

13. THE RIGHTEOUSNESS of Justification by Faith (Righteousness by Faith) which is **infinitely meritorious;** and the righteousness of sanctification by faith and works which is in us, but that has in it **absolutely no justifying merit whatsoever!**

14. THE RIGHTEOUSNESS that is the **BASIS** of our justification, and the **FAITH** that is the **MEANS** of our justification. (God's gift of justification is appropriated by us **solely by FAITH.**)

> ## THESE TWO DIFFERENT ASPECTS OF RIGHTEOUSNESS ARE DISTINCT, BUT NEVER SEPARATE

How can we claim to be loyal Seventh-day Adventist Christians—loyal to God, loyal to the Bible, loyal to TRUTH — and remain **INDIFFERENT** to the battle against truth and error that is raging in the Seventh-day Adventist Church today (2010)?

> **We must distinguish between the finished, completed atoning work of the SECOND member of the Godhead for us, outside of us, 2000 years ago, and the unfinished, incomplete regenerating work of the THIRD member of the Godhead in us now — during this life on earth!**

The Jesuit-controlled Council of Trent did not do this, but instead made the **regenerating** work of the **third** member of the Godhead **inside** of us **now the BASIS** on which God justifies, forgives, and accepts us unto eternal life.

The Jesuit doctrine of Justification by Faith — Righteousness by Faith—leads all who are deceived by it to look **WITHIN** for the righteousness that justifies and saves them. Mrs. White declares that all who do this, are **children of the devil and are lost!** 1SM 343. (See Volume ONE, Chapter 36).

We must **not** do this! We must **look AWAY from our sinful selves TO JESUS ALONE** for that righteousness that is good enough:

- **to atone for** our sins,
- **to perfectly satisfy** God's infinitely righteous law for us,
- **to get us through** the Investigative Judgment,
- **to bring to us** God's gifts of justification, forgiveness, adoption, eternal life, and heaven!

Only **Christ's** righteousness which is **IMPUTED (credited)** to us in God's gift of **Justification by Faith—Righteousness by Faith—is good enough to accomplish all the above for us.** (Vol. 1, pages xiii, 30, 47-53, 58, 65-68, 106-108, 110-112, 136-139).

ISSUE THREE:

DEFINITION OF JUSTIFICATION

WHAT IS JUSTIFICATION?

When God justifies a believer, *what* does He *DO*?

When God justifies believers, does He *FORGIVE AND TREAT* them *AS IF* they were righteous?

Or, does He also *MAKE* them inwardly righteous, pleasing, and acceptable to Himself?

ERRONEOUS PRESUPPOSITIONS

Justification is God's gracious *act* by which He *infuses* Christ's grace and righteousness into believers by which He converts, sanctifies, transforms and *makes* them inwardly righteous, pleasing and acceptable to Himself.

Having *made* believers righteous, pleasing and acceptable to Himself by *infusing* His grace and righteousness into them, God forgives them and ultimately takes them to heaven.

1. Page 12.10 and 13.2: "Having *made* us inwardly righteous…God pronounces us just [justifies us], and treats us as just."
2. Page 32.10: "He prepares us to stand [in the judgment] in the imputed *and imparted* righteousness of Christ."
3. Page 19.9: "Our *only ground* of hope is in the righteousness of Christ imputed [credited] to us *and in that wrought* by the Holy Spirit working *in* and through *us*."
4. Page 24.2: "To be *pardoned [justified]* in the way that Christ pardons [justifies] is *not* only to be forgiven, but to be *renewed* in the Spirit of our mind. The Lord says, '*a new heart* will I give thee.'"
5. Page 24.6: God's forgiveness *[justification] is not merely a judicial act* by which He sets us free from condemnation…it is *the outflow of redeeming love that transforms the heart."*

The Bible Teaches That:

Justification is the *OPPOSITE OF CONDEMNATION*.

Justification consists of *four* marvelous *gifts* of God to unworthy believing sinners who are not yet perfect (sinless).

Justification is: **(1)** *Forgiveness*, **(2)** Christ's perfectly righteous life, death, and resurrection *credited* to believers in Jesus, **(3)** God's *acceptance* of believers unto adoption and eternal life, and **(4)** God's *treatment* of believers, during this life on earth *as if* they had never sinned—*as if* they were now and always have been as righteous as Jesus!

We are never, during this life on earth, *inwardly* righteous, pleasing, and acceptable to God in nature, character or life.

God justifies us, not because we are righteous, but because **Jesus** was, and because He died on the cross to save us.

"Without the shedding of blood of Jesus, there is no forgiveness of sin." Heb. 9:22.
Justification is **a legal verdict.** God accepts believers on the basis of the righteousness and death of a **substitute**.

There is a God in the universe who **loves** you, and who **declares** all believers in Jesus righteous, pleasing and acceptable to Himself!

When God justifies believers in Jesus, He puts them in **a right relationship with Himself**.

Hebrews 9:24 says that Jesus is entered "into heaven itself now to appear in the presence of God for us." Rev. 5:6 says that the Father looks at our SUBSTITUTE, SURETY, AND REPRESENTATIVE WHO APPEARS BEFORE HIM "AS A LAMB AS IT HAD BEEN SLAIN."

Jesus forever bears the marks of His cruel sufferings. The Father ACCEPTS OUR SUBSITTUTE; WE ARE ACCEPTED BECAUSE HE IS ACCEPTED. O, "BEHOLD THE LAMB OF GOD WHICH TAKETH AWAY THE SIN OF THE WORLD." John 1:29

The DEFINITION of Justification

The Righteousness of "RIGHTEOUSNESS BY FAITH" and The Righteousness of "THE LAW" C—O—N—T—R—A—S—T—E—D

Millions of Christians do not understand the Gospel because they do not understand that:

- There are **TWO different ASPECTS** of Righteousness,
- In **TWO different PLACES**,
- Which **accomplish TWO** entirely different **things** for us, and
- **WHAT** these **TWO** different accomplishments are.

THE TWO DIFFERENT ASPECTS OF RIGHTEOUSNESS, WHAT EACH IS, WHERE EACH IS, AND WHAT EACH ACCOMPLISHES FOR US

- **Eight Bible texts which speak of the righteousness of "RIGHTEOUSNESS BY FAITH":** Gal. **5:5**—"For we through the Spirit wait for the hope of **righteousness by faith**." See also Rom. 3:22; 4:11; 4:13; 9:30; 10:6; Phil. 3:9; Heb. 11:7. Every one of these eight texts is speaking about

JUSTIFICATION BY FAITH. Therefore, **"Righteousness by Faith"** is exactly the same thing as **"Justification by Faith."**

- **Bible texts which speak of "The Righteousness of THE LAW" Rom. 8:4**—"That **the righteousness of THE LAW** might be fulfilled **IN US,** who walk not after the flesh, but after the Spirit." See also Rom. 2:26. The Righteousness of **The Law** is our **sanctification , obedience, and growing in grace** by faith and works.

- **Bible texts which speak of BOTH the righteousness of "Righteousness by Faith" and "the righteousness of THE LAW." Phil. 3:9**—"And be found in Him, not having mine own righteousness which is of **THE LAW,** but that which is through the faith of Christ, the righteousness which is of God **BY FAITH.**" See also Rom. 9:30; 10:6.

In the above texts we see that there are **TWO** different aspects of righteousness. There is the imputed righteousness of **"Righteousness by Faith"** and of **"Justification by Faith"** which is in Christ in heaven; and there is **"the imparted righteousness of THE LAW"** which is fulfilled **IN US**—in a relative sense—the righteousness of sanctification and of obedience and good works.

"And as Moses lifted up the serpent in the wilderness, even so must the Son of Man be lifted up: That whosoever believeth in Him

should not perish, but have eternal life."

John 3: 14, 15

Jesus' sinless life and His atoning sacrifice are the BASIES on which God justifies believers in Jesus.

And now, let us CONTRAST on a chart these TWO different aspects of RIGHTEOUSNESS

	The Righteousness of "RIGHTEOUSNESS BY FAITH"	"The Righteousness of THE LAW"
The Righteousness of "RIGHTEOUSNESS BY FAITH" And "The Righteousness of THE LAW" CONTRASTED		
1	IS NEVER IN US	IS ALWAYS
2	IS ALWAYS OUTSIDE OF US	IN BELIEVERS
3	IS ALWAYS IN CHRIST IN HEAVEN	ON EARTH
4	IS CHRIST'S perfect infinitely righteous nature, character, obedience, good works, and godly life on earth, His atoning death on the cross, and His resurrection from the dead 2000 years ago which are **credited** to believers in Christ.	Is the CHRISTIAN'S best **relatively** righteous character, obedience, good works, and godly life which is **NEVER perfectly righteous** during this life on earth, but which is always only **relatively** righteous.
5	IS CHRIST'S DOING AND DYING which **perfectly fulfills and satisfies** God's infinitely righteous law for us, atones for our sins, gets us through the Investigative Judgment, and secures for us God's gifts of forgiveness, Christ's righteousness, adoption, eternal life, and heaven. The righteousness which God **requires** of us, He Himself **provides** for us in His Son as a free gift.	Is THE CHRISTIAN'S best "righteousness" (obedience, good works, and godly life) which is never good enough to do any of these things for us. The Christian's **best** obedience always comes **short** of perfectly fulfilling God's infinitely righteous law for us. The Christian's righteousness is always only **relatively** righteous.
6	IS CHRIST'S righteousness which is reckoned **(credited, imputed)** to Christians in God's gift of **JUSTIFICATION**, which Christians believe, trust, appropriate to themselves, and **REST** in personally, **solely by faith, apart from works.** Christians contribute **absolutely nothing** toward their justification and forgiveness.	IS THE CHRISTIAN'S "righteousness" (obedience, good works, godly life, and perfecting Christian character), which is **IMPARTED TO AND DEVELOPED IN** Christians in **Sanctification** by the Holy Spirit and Christians working together by faith and love.
7	IS CHRIST'S perfect righteousness which gives **sinners** a righteous legal **STANDING** with God in their sinful moral **STATE**. Although Christians are still **sinful,** God accounts them **righteous!**	IS THE CHRISTIAN'S relative "righteousness" which, although pleasing to God and which helps Christians to perfect their character, has in it absolutely **no justifying merit** whatsoever.
8	IS CHRIST'S perfect righteousness which is every sinner's **KEY, TICKET, TITLE, PASSPORT TO, AND ASSURANCE** of heaven. This wonderful **TRUTH** concerning God's love, mercy, **righteousness**, and salvation is something we sinners can really get excited about! Although sin **remains** in Christians, it does not **reign** in them!	We are **NOT** justified and saved **BY this**. But **neither** are we justified and saved **WITHOUT this**. True faith will always inspire the sinner to repent, to be converted, to be sanctified, to be obedient, to perform good works, to live a godly life, and to perfect Christian character.

GOD'S TOTAL PLAN OF SALVATION
(Part One of Two Parts)

There are several ways in which we may study the biblical doctrine of salvation.

1. THE THREE TENSES OF SALVATION

One, is to think of salvation in three tenses, *past, present, and future.*

Thank God, because of Jesus redeeming work I can say, I *WAS* saved, I *am NOW BEING* saved, and I *WILL BE* saved.

- *In the past*, when Jesus died, *I was* saved from the *guilt and condemnation* of sin.
- *In the present*, day by day, I *am now being* saved from the *power and dominion* of sin.
- *In the future*, when Jesus returns, I *will be* saved from the *presence and effects* of sin.

The first is *JUSTIFICATION;* the second is *SANCTIFICATION;* the third is *GLORIFICATION.*

These are three chronological aspects of salvation, and they must not be confused or fused into one event, but be kept distinct, but never separate in the total history of the Christian.

2. THE BASIS, THE MEANS, AND THE RESULT OF JUSTIFICATION

It is of utmost importance that we clearly and decisively distinguish between:

- The objective, *meritorious BASIS* of justification.
- The subjective, non-meritorious *instrumental MEANS* of justification.
- And the subjective and objective *inevitable FRUIT* of justification.

Let us look at these three aspects of justification:

- *Christ's atoning work* for sinners outside of sinners, 2000 years ago is the *basis* on which God justifies believers.
- *Faith* in Christ's atoning work for sinners is the *means* by which we believe, trust, receive and rest in Christ's completed work 2000 years ago for our justification.
- *Obedience, good works, and a godly life* are the *result, fruit, evidence, and assurance* that our faith, repentance, and Christian experience are genuine. No fruit, no root!

Again

- The *BASIS* on which God justifies sinners is *Christ's atoning work for sinners.*
- The *MEANS* by which God's gift of justification is believed, trusted, accepted, received, and appropriated by us personally is *faith.*
- The *FRUIT* (result, evidence, assurance, and proof) that our faith, repentance, conversion, sanctification, and Christian experience is genuine, is *obedience, good works, a godly life, growing in grace, perfecting Christian character, and more and more victory over our besetting sins.* (Sanctification is the work of a lifetime.)

3. THE TOTAL PLAN OF SALVATION

God's *total* plan of salvation consists of at least *28 aspects* (Two aspects in each of the following 14 items). Let us now consider these 28 aspects of God's total plan of salvation.

1. We are *condemned* by our *sins*, Rom. 6:23,

2. We are *saved* by the *grace* of God, Eph. 2:8,9,

3. We are *redeemed* by the *blood* of Christ,

4. We are *justified (forgiven) meritoriously* on the *basis* of *Christ's atoning work* for sinners,

5. We are *enlightened* by the *Gospel*,

6. We are *brought* to *faith* by the *Word* of God,

7. We are *brought* to *repentance* by the *goodness (love)* of God,

8. We are *converted* by *the Holy Spirit*,

9. We are *sanctified* by the *truth* about God, John 17:17,

10. We are *perfected* by the *obedience* of faith,

11. We are *judged* by the *law*, James 2:10-12,

12. We are *justified evidentially* by our *obedience* and godly lives, James 2:24,

13. We are *rewarded* at last according to our *works*,

14. We are *perfectly restored* to our original physical, mental and spiritual perfection in which *we were created* in Adam and Eve before they sinned, by *Glorification!*

"In ourselves, we are sinners, but IN CHRIST we are RIGHTEOUS." 1SM 394

The DEFINITION of Justification
GUARDING AGAINST EXTREMES

It is very important for biblical students to seek to understand *THE CORRECT BALANCE* between the various aspects of the total plan of salvation such as:
Law and grace,
Faith and works,
The basis and the result
of Justification by Faith (Righteousness by Faith).

Some Christians make the serious mistake of *understanding and emphasizing* certain aspects of the total plan of salvation and, by lesser praise, *neglecting and downgrading* other aspects.

Some well meaning Christians will emphasize *justification* and neglect *sanctification*, and vice versa.

Some will emphasize *faith* to the exclusion of *obedience and good works*, and become careless and permissive about sin.

Some emphasize the importance of *imputed* righteousness and minimize the importance of *imparted* righteousness, and vice versa.

Likewise, some professing Christians will *emphasize* the importance of the **ROOT (BASIS)** of justification ("only believe, Jesus has done it all") and *minimize* the importance of the **FRUIT (RESULT)**.

Some Christians will emphasize obedience and good works and minimize faith, thus becoming legalistic in their Christian experience.

These emphasize the *fruit or result* of justification and *become perfectionistic Christians* and minimize the importance of the *basis* and become careless and permissive about sin. Often heated arguments and alienation result from the above.

Those well-meaning Christians who are guilty of one or the other of the above extremes tend to be *unbalanced* Christians, either *careless* (**antinomian**) Christians, or *overly strict* (*legalistic*) Christians!

We must strive for a *balanced* understanding and presentation of the *various aspects* of the gospel and the *total* plan of salvation.

Let us strive to be *balanced* Christians who do not go to one extreme either way, thus *correctly representing* what it means to be a Christian.

Truth honors Christ and Christianity, and *error dishonors* Christ and *helps Satan's cause* by spreading confusion, discouraging Christians, and alienating people. A winsome, Christlike Christian is *the strongest argument* in favor of Christianity.

Although We are not perfect Children of God, We are perfectly God's Children the moment we truly believe in Jesus.

Important Distinctions Between
Justifying Righteousness and
Sanctifying Righteousness

First: We need to distinguish between what God does outside of us and what He does inside of us.

Second: We need to distinguish between the imputed righteousness of justification and the imparted righteousness of sanctification.

Third: We need to distinguish between the BASIS, MEANS, and the FRUIT of Justification.

Fourth: We need to distinguish between Justification by Faith and Sanctification by Faith.

God's Total Plan of Salvation
(Part Two of Two Parts)

GOD'S TOTAL PLAN OF SALVATION CONSISTS OF MANY PARTS

1. Atonement

It begins with God *atoning* for our sins in Jesus, which consists of four unspeakable acts: Christ's (1) incarnation, (2) sinless life, (3) substitutionary, reconciling death, and (4) resurrection from the dead.

2. Justification (See pages 21 - 35).

It continues with God *justifying* sinners which consists of six marvelous acts:
    (1) His forgiveness of all our sins. His non-charging of our sins to us;
    (2) His charging our sins to Christ;
    (3) His crediting Christ's perfectly obedient life to us,
    (4) His adoption of us into His heavenly family,
    (5) His acceptance of believers unto eternal life, and
    (6) His treatment of us, during this life on earth *AS IF* we had never sinned.

3. Sanctification

It continues with God *sanctifying* believers which, in turn, consists of four wonderful acts of the Holy Spirit in believers:

    (1) Their conversion,
    (2) Their being indwelt by the Holy Spirit,
    (3) Their increasing victory over their besetting sins,
    (4) Their perfecting Christian character which isn't complete until glorification.

4. Glorification

It culminates with *our complete physical, mental, and spiritual restoration* to the perfection of Adam and Eve when they were first created.

●

A Threefold Deliverance

This threefold truth and deliverance *from Satan and sin and death* (sinfulness, guilt and condemnation) needs repeating over and over again.

1. Justification

In His gracious act of *justifying* us, God delivers us from the *guilt, condemnation, and wages* of sin.

2. Sanctification

In his gracious act of *sanctifying us*, God delivers us from the *power and dominion* of sin.

3. Glorification

In His gracious act of *glorifying* us, God delivers us from the *presence and effects* of sin!

A Divine Prohibition

Since God has ***distinguished betwe***en these three aspects of salvation, we must never ***FUSE*** and therefore ***CONFUSE*** these mighty acts of God for believing sinners into one and the same ***BASIS*** of justification, for they are not.

●

Standing, State, Nature

1. ***In justification***, God changes our ***standing*** (legal status) before Him and His law in the judgment from one of ***guilt and condemnation*** to one of ***pardon and acceptance***.
    Justification is relational. Justification changes God's ***relationship*** to sinners and sinners ***relationship*** to God from one of ***hostility*** to one of ***oneness and harmony***.

2. ***In Sanctification***, God changes our sinful ***state*** from one of habitual sin to one of ***more and more victory over sin***—Right-doing becomes the NORM, and wrong doing becomes the EXCEPTION.

3. ***In Glorification***, God changes our sinful, mortal ***nature*** to one of righteousness and immortality.

●

NOT Synonymous or Interchangeable Terms

These are ***not synonymous terms***; they cannot be ***equated*** with each other or ***fused*** into one and the same ***BASIS, GROUND, CAUSE, OR REASON*** for God's justification of believers.

To do so is to turn ***Roman Catholic*** and to teach that God's ***ACT*** of justifying believers ***MAKES*** them inwardly righteous, pleasing and acceptable to Himself. This spreads ***confusion***, legalism, and perfectionism, and despair among believers.

God's gracious act of justifying believers does not ***make*** them actually personally, inwardly, morally, sinless in nature, character or life. It ***credits*** Christ's righteousness to them and ***accounts*** and ***treats*** them ***AS IF*** they were actually inwardly righteous in nature, character, and life.

God's act of ***justifying*** believers gives them **A RIGHTEOUS LEGAL STANDING** before Him and His infinitely righteous law in the judgment in their **SINFUL MORAL STATE**.

●

Total Restoration

God justifies believers ***IN ORDER THAT*** He might gradually convert, sanctify, perfect and ultimately restore them completely to their original physical, mental and spiritual perfection at His Second Coming to this earth.

For born-again Christians these terms: justification, sanctification, imputed righteousness and imparted righteousness, have definite, distinct meanings.

"WE CANNOT SAY, 'I AM SINLESS,'"
till this vile body is CHANGED and fashioned like unto His
glorious [glorified] body." TIMK 361

Distinct, but Never Separate

Justification and sanctification are distinct, but never separate.

For believing Christians, **imputed** *righteousness and* **imparted** *righteousness are* **distinct, but never separate.**

To *justify* is *not* to *sanctify*; and to *sanctify* is *not* to *justify*! To *impute* righteousness is not to *impart* righteousness; and to *impart* righteousness is not to *impute* righteousness!

The same faith that *justifies* also always at the same time, *sanctifies*. Like the two natures in Christ, like heat and light in the sun, like the two rails of a railroad track, *justification and sanctification are always together.*

But they are *not the same thing*. Each is distinct, but never separate. To separate them leads to disaster. And to fuse them unto the one and same thing leads to **Roman Catholic confusion**.

●

NOT EQUATABLE

The Bible never equates justification with sanctification or sanctification with justification. It never equates *imputed* righteousness with *imparted* righteousness, or *imparted* righteousness with *imputed* righteousness.

It never equates what God does *outside* of us with what He does *inside* of us, or what He does *inside* of us with what He does *outside* of us.

It never equates the *basis* of justification with the *fruit* of justification, or the *fruit* of justification with the *basis* of justification.

●

Romans, Chapter four

Abraham is *God's classic example* of what happens when God *justifies* a believer.

When God *justified* Abraham, He did *three* things:
1. He did *not hold* Abraham's sins against him. See pages 28 - 31 for texts.
2. He *charged* Abraham's sins to Christ. See pages 28 - 31 for texts.
3. He *credited* Christ's righteousness to Abraham's account. See pages 28 - 31 for texts.
That's justification!

Accordingly, *justification is based on* something God *did for* us, *outside* of us, *in Jesus, 2000 years ago*!

The provision is there! All that *remains* is for us to *learn* of it, to *believe* it by faith, to *trust* it, to embrace it, and to *rest* in Christ's completed work for our justification for as long as we live! "Faith includes not only belief but trust." 1SM 389

•

Faith is not Static

Faith is dynamic. The faith that appropriates God's gift of justification to ourselves personally always leads to repentance, conversion, the indwelling Holy Spirit, sanctification, obedience, good works, a godly life, and to perfecting Christian character.

•

Synonyms For Justification

Justification is the same as:
- God *forgiving*, pardoning, covering our sins.
- God **not charging**, reckoning, counting or holding our sins against us.
- God *crediting*, reckoning, counting, imputing, Christ's righteousness to us.

•

Justification is the ***opposite*** of ***condemnation***.

1. Rom. 8:34: "It is God who ***justifies***. Who is he that ***condemns***?"
2. Deut. 25:1 "…the judges [will] decide between them, ***acquitting*** [*clearing, justifying*] the innocent and ***condemning*** the guilty."
3. 1 Kings 8:32: "…judge Thy servants, ***condemning*** the guilty…and ***vindicating***, [*clearing, justifying*] the righteous."
4. Rom. 8:33, 34: "Who shall lay anything to the charge of God's elect? It is God that ***justifieth***. Who is he that ***condemneth*** …"

•

Justification is Forgiveness

1. Acts 13:38,39 "Be it known unto you therefore, men and brethren, that through this man is preached unto you the **FORGIVENESS** of sins: And by him all that believe are **JUSTIFIED** from all things, from which ye could not be *justified* by the law of Moses."

2. Rom. 3:24-26,28 "Being **JUSTIFIED** freely by His grace through the redemption that is in Christ Jesus: Whom God hath set forth to be a propitiation through faith in His blood, to declare His righteousness for the **REMISSION** of sins that are past, through the forbearance of God; To declare, I say, at this time His righteousness: that He might be just, and *the justifier* of him which *believeth* in Jesus. Therefore we conclude that a man is **JUSTIFIED BY FAITH WITHOUT THE DEEDS OF THE LAW.**"

3. Rom. 4:5-6 "But to him that worketh not, but *believeth* on Him that ***JUSTIFIETH*** the ungodly, his faith is **COUNTED** for righteousness. Even as David also describeth the blessedness of the man, unto whom God **IMPUTETH** righteousness without works, saying, 'Blessed are they whose iniquities are ***FORGIVEN***, and whose sins are ***COVERED***. Blessed is the man to whom the Lord ***will not impute sin*** [to whom the Lord ***will not hold*** his sins against him]."

   This is ***FORGIVENESS!*** Justification is the same thing as ***pardon, forgiveness—a legal, judicial, law-court VERDICT of pardon, of forgiveness, of no condemnation outside of us.***

•

See Volume Four for 20 EGW definitions of Justification

1. Is God's *forgiveness* of our sins *inside* of us or *outside* of us?
2. Does God's act of *forgiving* our sins *MAKE* us inwardly righteous?
3. The correct answer to both of these questions is clear.
4. God's *forgiveness* of our sins is *in Himself in heaven—outside* of us.
5. God's act of *forgiving* our sins does not *make* us inwardly righteous; it *credits* Christ's righteousness to us and *treats* us *AS IF* we were actually righteous in nature, character and life.
6. So it is with *justification*! Justification is *outside* of us and it treats us *AS IF* we were righteous.
7. God accepts our substitute and He accepts us only because He is accepted. Heb. 9:24; Rev 5:6.

There Are TWO BASIC VIEWS of Justification in the Christian World and in the Seventh-day Adventist Church

The **FIRST** view is *BASED* on the *Bible*.

The **SECOND** view is *BASED* on *Tradition*.

The FIRST view is taught by:
- **The Bible,**
- **ALL of the great Protestant Reformers,**
- **Mrs. Ellen G. White**
- **MOST SDA Andrews University Ph.D. Theologians**
- **Evangelical Seventh-day Adventists in the U.S.A.**

The SECOND view is taught by
the **Roman Catholic Church,** and "Certain Independent Ministries" in the "historic," "traditional," "conservative" ("rightwing") segment of the Seventh-day Adventist Church! (I use these terms respectfully).

The FIRST View
The FIRST view, which is based on *THE BIBLE*, teaches that the righteousness of *justification* is *CHRIST'S atoning work* for sinners, outside of sinners, 2000 years ago.

The SECOND View
The SECOND view, which is based solely upon **ROMAN CATHOLIC or SDA TRADITION**, teaches that the righteousness of *justification* includes the converting, sanctifying transforming work of the Holy Spirit and Christ living His perfectly righteous life *INSIDE* of sinners now, during this life on earth!

The SECOND view is EXTREMELY DANGEROUS because those who are teaching it:

1. *Appear* to be teaching it from the Bible
2. Are teaching much **beautiful** truth.
3. Are *correctly* teaching that there is **NO** justifying (saving) merit whatsoever in **OUR** obedience and good works of faith and love.
4. Are *correctly* emphasizing **the importance and necessity** of conversion, sanctification, living a godly life, Christ living His perfectly righteous life inside of believers, and perfecting Christian character.
5. Are *correctly* teaching that we are justified by the grace of God through faith in Jesus, and
6. Are *correctly* teaching that the righteousness that *justifies* us **IS NOT OURS, BUT CHRIST'S.**

An Important Question!

What then is the problem with the teaching of the **Roman Catholic Church** and "Certain Independent SDA Ministries" concerning justification?

The six points **ABOVE** sound wonderfully true, and they are! But, let us *beware* because, after presenting many wonderful truths, Satan slips in some *error* in order to deceive sincere, unsuspecting seekers for truth. Satan *sugar-coats* his bitter pill of error with some sweet truth in order to deceive unwary seekers for truth.

In addition to teaching the above six wonderful truths, some very popular and influential SDA ministers are teaching to the SDA world *the VERY SERIOUS ERROR* that it is **OUR:** (1) conversion, (2) sanctification, and (3) Christ living His perfectly sinless (righteous) life *INSIDE* of us that justifies us!

Instead of teaching that the *BASIS* on which God justifies us is solely *GOD'S ATONING WORK* FOR US, OUTSIDE OF US, IN JESUS, *2000 YEARS AGO*, they are teaching that the *BASIS* on which God justifies us *INCLUDES* the Holy Spirit's converting, sanctifying, transforming work *IN US AND* Christ living His perfectly righteous life *INSIDE* of us now, during this life on earth!

> ## Let us look more closely at these *TWO VIEWS* of Justification by Faith–Righteousness by Faith– in the Christian world and in the SDA church.

There is the true, Biblical, Protestant View, and there is the false Roman Catholic View.

> ## *SINCE* some aspects of the false, **Roman Catholic view of Justification by Faith (Righteousness by Faith)** is being taught to the SDA world church by some very popular, influential SDA ministers, we would do well to make very plain *WHAT* each of these two views teaches lest we be deceived by the false view.
> Tragically, many well-meaning SDAs are being deceived by some extremely popular, highly educated, charismatic SDA ministers!

See Volume Four for 20 EGW DEFINITIONS of Justification.

These *two BASIC VIEWS in the Christian world are as follows:*

1. The FIRST (TRUE, Biblical, Protestant) view teaches that Justification by Faith (Righteousness by Faith) IS BASED ON:

1. *CHRIST'S atoning work* in behalf of sinners 2000 years ago,
2. *a legal, judicial, forensic act* by God in behalf of sinners,
3. *God's act outside* of sinners,
4. God's act of *forgiving* all our sins,
5. God's act of *crediting* Christ's righteousness to us,
6. God's act of *adopting us and accepting* us unto eternal life—postponing the eternal death sentence—giving the human race a second probation (opportunity) to be eternally saved, and
7. God's act of *treating* us, during this life on earth, *AS IF* we had never sinned!

ALL SEVEN of the above gracious acts of God are performed by Him for converted Christian believers *although they are not yet perfectly sinless (righteous)!*

EIGHT Results of Justification

The same faith that leads sinners to: (1) repentance, (2) conversion, (3) sanctification, and (4) the indwelling of the Holy Spirit, *also always leads them* (5) to obedience, (6) to performing good works, (7) to living a godly life, and (8) to the perfecting of Christian character!

All eight of the above *RESULTS* of justification *are the FRUIT and EVIDENCE, (not the ROOT) of justification.*

2. The SECOND, (FALSE) ROMAN CATHOLIC AND "CERTAIN SDA INDEPENDENT MINISTRIES" view teaches that Justification by Faith IS BASED ON:

1. *THE HOLY SPIRIT'S converting, sanctifying, transforming work* in behalf of believers now, during this life on earth,
2. an act of God *INSIDE* of sinners,
3. God's act of *converting* sinners,
4. God's act of *sanctifying* sinners,
5. God's act of *"infusing"* Christ and His righteousness *INTO* believers,
6. God's act of *making* believers actually, inwardly righteous, pleasing, and acceptable to Himself.

Roman Catholics and many SDA's are taught to believe that *ALL SIX* of the above gracious *ACTS* of God are performed by Him *INSIDE* of believers in order to *MAKE* them actually, inwardly righteous, pleasing, and acceptable to Himself and to *JUSTIFY* them!

The Bible teaches that God justifies us in order to sanctify us. The Roman Catholic Church and rightwing SDAs teach that God sanctifies us in order to justify us!

The above false teaching *ROBS* the believer of the *ASSURANCE* of God's forgiveness and acceptance of him unto eternal life!

Why is this? The answer is: If God's ultimate forgiveness and acceptance of us unto eternal life *depends* upon the above sixfold work of the Holy Spirit *INSIDE OF US*, how can we ever be *SURE* that the converting, sanctifying, perfecting work of the Holy Spirit inside of us is *perfect, complete, and acceptable* to God?

How can we be *SURE* that we are converted, sanctified, and righteous *enough to be saved?*

Therefore, we are forever *doing* this and that and the other thing in order to become *good enough* to be saved! And we are forever looking *within* for that perfect righteousness inside of us which secures God's acceptance of us!

And, so, instead of looking *away from* our sinful selves, *to Jesus alone,* for that perfect righteousness which saves us, we keep on *doing* this and that and the other thing in order to become *good enough* to pass the Judgment and to secure God's approval of us.

This erroneous philosophy of salvation does not lead one to true repentance, conversion, and sanctification, or to a truly godly life, but to a legalistic, perfectionistic, ego-centric religious experience.

Conclusion

Thank God for the wonderfully liberating truth of the *pure apostolic gospel* of salvation solely through faith in Jesus' perfectly righteous life, death, and resurrection from the dead outside of us 2000 years ago, all of which God *credits* to us in His gift of *justification!*

This wonderful truth does not lead one to become *careless and permissive about sin.* Instead, it leads us to *love* God more, to want to be more *like* Jesus in character, and to *obey and please* Him in all things. Truly converted Christians do this, *not* in order to be saved, but because they *love* God and righteousness and hate error and unrighteousness.

Because we LOVE Him, we OBEY Him!

Thank God! The righteousness which *justifies and saves* us is *not inside us on earth, but in Jesus in heaven!* The *knowledge* of this wonderful truth gives us the *calm, steadfast assurance* of God's forgiveness and acceptance of us unto eternal life, even when things go wrong!

Isn't that wonderful, dear reader? The righteousness of Righteousness by Faith is *not inside* of us; it is always, only *in Jesus in heaven!* This is the thrilling world-shattering, transforming truth of the gospel!

We do not have to be perfectly sinless (righteous) within in order to be saved! *ALL we have to DO* in order to be saved is to exercise true *faith* in Jesus–to truly: *(1) believe, (2) trust, and (3) rest* in Jesus' completed, atoning work for us, outside of us, 2000 years ago!

The *righteousness* that secures for us God's forgiveness and acceptance of us unto eternal life is nothing that *WE* do or that God does *IN* us!
We contribute NOTHING toward our JUSTIFICATION!

Blessed Assurance

Blessed assurance, Jesus is mine
    O, what a foretaste of glory divine!
Heir of salvation, purchase of God,
    Born of His Spirit, washed in His blood."

"This is my story, this is my song,
    Praising my Saviour all the day long;
This is my story, this is my song,
    Praising my Saviour all the day long."

–Fanny J. Crosby

Blessed Assurance!

Your Salvation Is Guaranteed
by Jesus' Incarnation, Sinless Life,
Substitutionary Death, Resurrection and Intercession

Christian Classics ● *Volume One*

Gordon Wm. Collier, Sr.

ISSUE FOUR:
DISTINCTIONS BETWEEN THE IMPUTED AND IMPARTED RIGHTEOUSNESS OF CHRIST

THE TWO ASPECTS OF CHRIST'S RIGHTEOUSNESS:
IMPUTED RIGHTEOUSNESS AND IMPARTED RIGHTEOUSNESS

What is the *meaning* of the word *impute*?

What is the *meaning* of the word *impart* (*infuse*)?

What is *imputed* righteousness? What is *imparted* righteousness?

When God *imputes* Christ's righteousness to us, *what does He do?*

When God *imparts* Christ's righteousness to us, *what does He do?*

ERRONEOUS PRESUPPOSITIONS

The meaning of the word *impute, must not be restricted to:* to *reckon* and to *treat as if* one were righteous.

The word, *impute* also means to *impart* righteousness and to *make* actually righteous.
- Page 12.10: "Having **made** us righteous through the **imputed** righteousness of Christ…"
- Page 13.2: "Having **made** us righteous through the **imputed** righteousness of Christ.
- Page 13.2: "This is a very **subjective**-oriented paragraph."

Comments by The Author

Those Seventh-day Adventists who are translating the word **impute** to mean **impart** and the word **impart** to mean **impute** are giving to these words meanings which no dictionary in the world gives to them.

We must interpret these words according to the obvious dictionary meaning—according to the common usage of these words by society.

The Bible Teaches That:

In reference to justification in the New Testament, the word *impute never means to impart or to infuse!* The words *impart* or *infuse never mean to impute.*

We must distinguish between:
- The *imputed (reckoned, credited)* righteousness of Christ and His *imparted* righteousness:
- The *righteousness of justification* and the *righteousness of sanctification*,
- The *righteousness that justifies* and the *righteousness* that *sanctifies*,
- The *righteousness that is* the *root* of justification *and the righteousness that is the fruit* of justification,
- The *righteousness* that is the *basis* of justification and the righteousness that is the *result* of justification,
- The *righteousness* that is the atoning work of the *Second* member of the Godhead outside of us 2000 years ago, and the righteousness that is the converting, sanctifying work of the *third* member of the Godhead in us now, during this life,

- The *righteousness* that is our **title** to heaven, and the **righteousness** that is our *fitness* for heaven in a relative sense.

In the New Testament, the word *impute never* means to *impart*; and the word *impart never means to impute*!

Imputed righteousness *never makes* a person *inwardly* righteous.

In speaking of justification and righteousness by faith, the Bible *never* uses the word *impute* in the sense of *making* righteous.

The Bible *restricts* the meaning of the word *impute* to: to *reckon* righteous, to *credit* Christ's righteousness to believers, to accept and to *treat* the believer in Jesus *as if* he were actually already righteous within.

Imputed righteousness and *justification* always refer to a righteousness that is *outside* of us.
The Roman Catholic Church officially puts the *imputed* righteousness that *justifies* believers *inside* of them!

The *reckoned, credited, imputed* righteousness of Christ and of justification does *not make* us inwardly righteous in nature, character or life; it *accounts* us righteous, *credits* Christ's righteousness to us and *treats* us *AS IF* we were righteous.

Far from being "a very subjective thing, Justification is a *very objective* gift of God. Forgiveness is *outside* of us, always, only in God in heaven.

We must not give to a word a meaning that is not found in the dictionary, in the Bible, or in the writings of truly Evangelical Christians.

To do so is to create confusion and to teach error.

There is *an irreconcilable difference* between the meaning of the words *impute and impart,* between *imputed* righteousness and *imparted* righteousness, between *justification* and *sanctification*, between the *root* of justification and the *fruit* of justification, between the *atoning* work of Christ and the *converting* work of the Holy Spirit, and between that righteousness that is *meritorious* and that righteousness that is not *meritorious*.

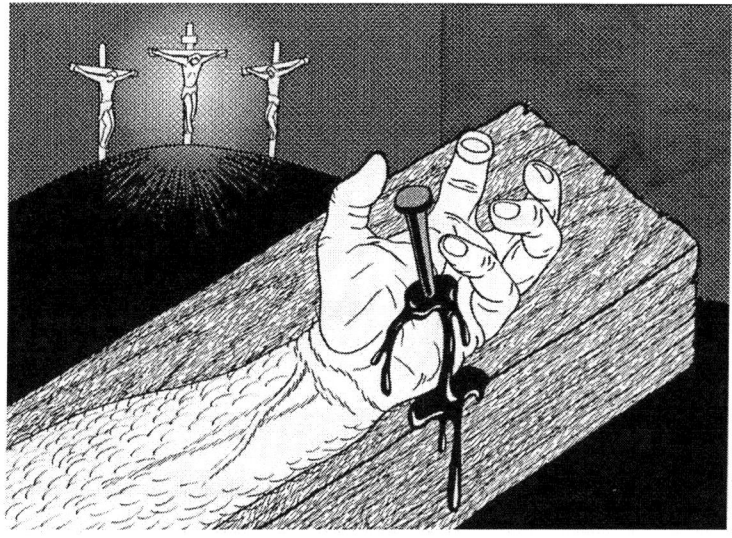

"The blood of Jesus Christ His Son cleanseth us from all unrighteousness."
1 John 1:7

The MEANING of the Greek Word,

LOGIZOMAI (IMPUTE),

"Reckon" [*logizomai*] in the NT and its Translations

Gordon W. Collier, Sr. (1994)

A careful study reveals that all the English translations of the New Testament (of which I am aware) recognized that the Greek word *logizomai* - impute - in its contextual usage with the NT doctrine of righteousness always means to reckon, count, or account righteous, never to make righteous. In any of its NT usages, *logizomai* never means "to make" but always to "consider" or to "reckon".

The Protestant Reformers and all these translations depicted in the chart below, rendered "justification by faith" is the same as "righteousness by faith." They believed that justification by faith—righteousness by faith—was not a **making** inwardly righteous, but a **"reckoning"** and **"declaring"** legally righteous.

In justification by faith, God does not impute (or charge) our sins against us, but rather He **credits** Christ's perfect righteousness (perfect obedience and death) to us, and therefore accepts us and treats us as though we were righteous. That is justification by faith or righteousness by faith. The inward renewal of the believing sinner is sanctification.

It bears repeating that *logizomai* in the context of the NT teaching of 'righteousness by faith' cannot be rendered to mean, making inwardly righteous. Accordingly, the righteousness of 'justification by faith' or 'righteousness by faith' is not in us! Our righteousness is only in Christ in heaven. The righteousness of sanctification by the indwelling Holy Spirit is in us on earth, but it is a lifelong process of growth and is always relative and never complete in this life.

Logizomai and its English translations

	Text	KJV	NIV	NEB	TEV	RSV	NASB	Others
1	Mark 15:28	numbered	counted	reckoned	-	reckoned	reckoned	counted - LB
2	Luke 22:37	reckoned	numbered	counted	shared	reckoned	classed	reckoned - Phillips
3	Rom. 3: 28	conclude	maintain	argument	conclude	hold	maintain	conclude - TCNT
4	Rom. 4: 3	counted	credited	counted	accepted	reckoned	reckoned	regarded - TCNT
5	Rom. 4: 4	reckoned	credited	counted	regarded	reckoned	reckoned	counted - Phillips
6	Rom. 4: 5	counted	credited	counted	account	reckoned	reckoned	regarded - TCNT
7	Rom. 4: 6	imputeth	credits	counts	accepts	reckons	reckons	charge - Williams
8	Rom. 4: 8	impute	count	count	account	reckon	account	regard - TCNT
9	Rom. 4: 9	reckoned	credited	counted	accepted	reckoned	reckoned	regarded – TCNT
10	Rom. 4:10	reckoned	credited	counted	accepted	reckoned	reckoned	credited - Weymouth

Logizomai and its English translations

	Text	KJV	NIV	NEB	TEV	RSV	NASB	Others
11	Rom. 4:11	imputed	credited	counted	accepted	reckoned	reckoned	credited - Weymouth
12	Rom. 4:22	imputed	credited	counted	accepted	reckoned	reckoned	regarded - TCNT
13	Rom. 4:23	imputed	credited	counted	accepted	reckoned	reckoned	counting - Phillips
14	Rom. 4:24	imputed	credit	counted	accepted	reckoned	reckoned	regarded - Phillips
15	Rom. 6:11	reckon	count	regard	think	consider	consider	look upon - Phillips
16	Rom. 8:18	reckon	consider	reckon	consider	consider	consider	accounted - ASV
17	Rom. 8: 36	accounted	considered	treated like	treated like	regarded	considered	reckoned - Knox
18	Rom. 9: 8	counted	regarded	reckoned	regarded	reckoned	regarded	considered - Phillips
19	Rom.14:14	esteemeth	regards	considers	believes	thinks	thinks	holds - TCNT
20	I Cor. 4:1	account	regard	regarded	look on	regard	regard	look upon - TCNT
21	II Cor. 5:19	imputing	counting	holding	account	counting	counting	reckoning - Conybeare
22	II Cor. 11: 5	suppose	think	think	think	think	consider	regard - TCNT
23	Gal. 3: 6	accounted	credited	counted	accepted	reckoned	reckoned	counted - Phillips
24	Phil. 3: 13	count	consider	reckon	think	consider	regard	consider - Phillips
25	Heb.11:19	accounting	reasoned	reckoned	reckoned	considered	considered	judging - Bas.
26	Jas. 2: 23	imputed	credited	counted	accepted	reckoned	reckoned	imputed - ASV
27	I Pet. 5: 2	suppose	regard	hold	regard	regard	regard	account - ASV

NIV = New International Version; NEB = New English Bible; TEV = Today's English Version; RSV = Revised Standard Version; NASB = New American Standard Bible; TCNT = The Twentieth Century New Testament; ASV = The American Standard Version; LB = Living Bible; Bas = New Testament in Basic English.

A Note To The Reader By The Author
These pages may be found on the Internet address: http://www.jesusinstituteforum.org/logizomai.html

"I was guilty with nothing to say;
    And they were coming to take me away;
But, then a voice from heaven was heard
    Which said,
'Let Him go; take me instead!'

I should have been crucified,
    I should have suffered and died,
I should have hung on the cross in disgrace,
    But, Jesus, God's Son
      Took my place."

THE WORDS OF THIS GOSPEL SONG express my sincere heartfelt testimony.

What Does THE BIBLE Teach About Justification?

Does **THE BIBLE teach that** Justification is a **LEGAL, JUDICIAL, FORENSIC, LAWCOURT VERDICT**, meaning **TO RELEASE from guilt, to RECKON, COUNT, ACCEPT and TREAT as righteous?** Or does **it** mean a **MAKING ACTUALLY, PERSONALLY, INWARDLY, MORALLY RIGHTEOUS in nature, character or life?**

ROMANS 4

We repeat: the Greek word, **LOGIZOMAI**, appears **ELEVEN** times in the fourth chapter of the book of Romans; and every time it is translated, **NOT TO MAKE INWARDLY RIGHTEOUS, BUT TO RECKON RIGHTEOUS.** When God **justifies** us, He **CREDITS** Christ's perfect obedience to us and **TREATS** us **AS IF** we were now and always have been perfectly righteous. Consequently, justification is **not** a **creating**, converting, sanctifying, transforming act of God in us. Justification is, instead, God's legal, judicial, forensic act in our behalf which graciously grants to us a righteous legal **STANDING** before Him in our sinful moral **STATE.** This will become **CLEAR** as we read Romans, Chapter **FOUR.**

1. What shall we say then that **ABRAHAM** our father, as pertaining to the flesh, hath found?
2. For if **ABRAHAM** were **JUSTIFIED** by works, he hath *whereof* to glory; but not before God.
3. For what saith the scripture? **ABRAHAM BELIEVED** God, and it was **COUNTED [1]** unto him **for righteousness.**
4. Now to him that worketh is the reward not **RECKONED [2]** of grace, but of debt.
5. But to him that worketh not, but **BELIEVETH** on Him that **JUSTIFIETH** the **ungodly**, his **FAITH** is **COUNTED [3]** for **RIGHTEOUSNESS.**
6. Even as David also describeth the blessedness of the man, unto whom God **IMPUTETH [4] RIGHTEOUSNESS without works,**
7. *Saying*, Blessed *are* they whose iniquities are **forgiven**, and whose sins are **covered.**
8. Blessed is the man to whom the Lord will **not IMPUTE [5]** sin.
9. *Cometh* this blessedness then upon the circumcision *only*, or upon the uncircumcision also? For we say that **FAITH** was **RECKONED [6]** to **ABRAHAM** for **RIGHTEOUSNESS.**
10. How was it then **RECKONED?** **[7]** when he was in circumcision, or in uncircumcision? Not in circumcision, but in uncircumcision.
11. And he received the sign of circumcision, a seal of **THE RIGHTEOUSNESS OF THE FAITH** which *he had yet* being uncircumcised: that he might be the father of all them that **BELIEVE**, though they be not circumcised; that **RIGHTEOUSNESS** might be **IMPUTED [8]** unto them also [that believe].
12. And the father of circumcision to them who are not of the circumcision only, but who also walk in the steps of that **FAITH** of our father **ABRAHAM**, which *he had* being *yet* uncircumcised.
13. For the promise, that he should be the heir of the world, *was* not to **ABRAHAM**, or to his seed, through the law, but through **THE RIGHTEOUSNESS OF FAITH.**
14. For if they which are of the law *be* heirs, **FAITH** is made void, and the promise made of none effect:
15. Because the law worketh wrath: for where no law is, *there is* no transgression.

16. Therefore *it is* of **FAITH**, that *it might be* **by grace**; to the end the promise might be sure to all the seed; not to that only which is of the law, but to that also which is of the **FAITH** of **ABRAHAM**; who is the father of us all,

17. (As it is written, I have made thee a father of many nations.) before him whom he **BELIEVED**, *even* God who quickeneth the dead, and calleth those things which be not as though they were.

18. Who against hope **BELIEVED** in hope, that he might become the father of many nations, according to that which was spoken, So shall thy seed be.

19. And being not weak in **FAITH**, he considered not his own body now dead, when he was about an hundred years old, neither yet the deadness of Sarah's womb:

20. He staggered not at the promise of God through unbelief; but was strong in **FAITH**, giving glory to God;

21. And being fully persuaded that, what he had promised, he was able also to perform.

22. And therefore it was **IMPUTED [9]** to him for **RIGHTEOUSNESS**.

23. Now it was not written for his sake alone, that it was **IMPUTED [10]** to him;

24. But for us also, to whom it shall be **IMPUTED [11]**, if we **BELIEVE** on Him that raised up Jesus our Lord from the dead;

25. Who was delivered for our offenses, and was raised again for our **JUSTIFICATION**.

ROMANS 5: 1

Therefore, being justified by faith, we have peace with God through our Lord Jesus Christ.

LINGUISTIC PROOF that JUSTIFICATION by Faith and Righteousness by Faith are exactly the same thing

The English Words, Just, Justify, Justification, Righteous and Righteousness are Translated from the SAME GREEK ROOT WORD

The best way to discover **the meaning** of a word in the English Bible is to find out the meaning of the Hebrew or Greek word in the original manuscripts. We must not give an English–1611–King James meaning to the original Hebrew or Greek word in the Bible. We **must** take the meaning the Hebrews and Greeks of Bible times gave to the word in question. **What did this word mean TO THEM THEN?**

The Hebrew and Greek words **righteous and righteousness are not primarily ethical words** having to do with **sinless moral nature, character or pure, honest, righteous ethical action**. They are, instead, primarily **RELATIONAL words** having to do with how God **relates** to sinners and how they **relate** to Him. **This is an extremely important truth which few rightwing Seventh-day Adventist's understand!**

Because of CHRIST'S righteousness (doing and dying), God justifies us–(1) forgives all our sins, (2) **credits** Christ's doing and dying to us, and (3) **treats** us, during this life on earth, **as if** we were now and always have been perfectly righteous–as righteous as Christ. **This is not a creative act of God in sinners. It IS a legal, judicial, forensic act of God in behalf of sinners, outside of sinners.** And **that** is "Righteousness by Faith," **not** Sanctification by Faith!

Let us now discover the Greek meaning of the English words **justification and righteousness**.

Depicting the Greek root word for **righteous** on a flow-chart will help us understand the meaning of the word.

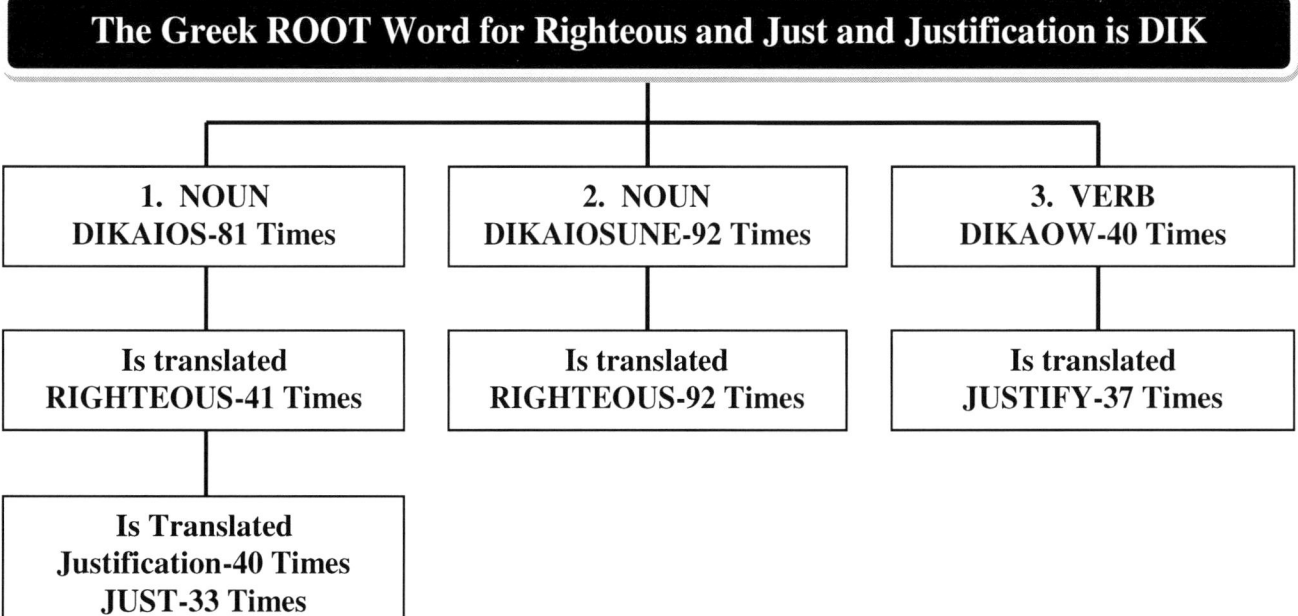

THE MEANING OF THE GREEK WORDS JUSTIFICATION AND RIGHTEOUSNESS IN THE GREEK NEW TESTAMENT

The Greek ROOT Word for Righteous and Just and Justification is DIK

1. NOUN DIKAIOS-81 Times	2. NOUN DIKAIOSUNE-92 Times	3. VERB DIKAOW-40 Times
Is translated RIGHTEOUS-41 Times	Is translated RIGHTEOUS-92 Times	Is translated JUSTIFY-37 Times
Is Translated Justification-40 Times JUST-33 Times		

The chart above makes it clear that the English words: **RIGHTEOUS** (righteousness) and **JUST** (justify, justification), **are the SAME words in Greek**. These English words are correctly translated from the same Greek **ROOT–DIK**.

Accordingly, the English expressions, "**Righteousness by Faith**" and "**Justification by Faith**" are exactly the same words in the original Greek manuscripts and are correctly translated either way: "**Righteousness by Faith**" or "**Justification by Faith**."

SUMMARY

The Greek noun **dikaios**, appears 81 times in the Greek New Testament. It is translated **RIGHTEOUS, 41 TIMES and JUST 33 times**. (See chart above).

The Greek noun **dikaiousune**, which is derived from **dikaios**, is translated **righteousness 92 times**.

The Greek verb **dikaiow**, which is also derived from **dikaios**, is translated **justify 37 times**.

The Greek noun **dikaiwma** (not shown above), which is derived from **dikaios** is translated: **justify 37 times, righteousness 4 times**, and justification one time.

The Greek noun **dikaiosis** (not shown) appears two times and is translated **justification both times**.

All of these Greek nouns, adjectives, verbs, and adverbs for **righteous, righteousness, justify, and justification**, are derived from the **same** Greek root or stem **DIK**.

The basic meaning of DIK is **not** a moral or an ethical purity, holiness, sinlessness, righteousness, or perfect **obedience** or behavior, but is **RELATIONAL—to be in a right RELATIONSHIP** with God or man—a relationship of faith and love and loyalty.

Thus in marriage, a husband or wife who is **faithful** to the other is not necessarily **sinless, but is basically LOYAL** to the other—in a right relationship to the other.

Likewise in Christianity, a Christian who intends to be faithful to God is not necessarily absolutely sinless, but is **basically loyal** to God and is in **a right relationship** with Him—a relationship of faith and love and loyalty.

From the above flowchart on the Greek word, **righteous (righteousness)**, we learn that **NOT ONCE** do these Greek words mean **SINLESS!**

We must repeat this important truth. The same is true of the Old Testament Hebrew words **righteous and righteousness**. The original Hebrew word that is translated righteous and righteousness is also **NOT** primarily a word that has a **moral or ethical** meaning. The Hebrew word righteous (righteousness) has a **relational** meaning. Its primary meaning is **not an ethical behavior or moral sinlessness**, but of a **faithful** relationship to God or another person.

NOT ONCE is the Greek word, RIGHTEOUS, translated SINLESS in our English translations and versions of the New Testament.

Accordingly, the biblical expressions "Righteousness by Faith" and "Justification by Faith" mean exactly the same thing. And that is:

- **NOT to make us ethically, morally SINLESS OR RIGHTEOUS within, but**
- **TO JUSTIFY—TO ACCOUNT righteous, TO PUT right, TO PUT in a right relationship with God, and**
- **TO TREAT us as though we were perfectly righteous.**

ISSUE FIVE:

WHOSE RIGHTEOUSNESS IS IT THAT JUSTIFIES?

WHOSE righteousness is it that *justifies* us?

Is it solely the righteousness of the great *SECOND* member of the Godhead that *justifies?*

Or is it also the righteousness of the *THIRD* member of the Godhead?

ERRONEOUS PRESUPPOSITIONS

The author of the 48 page critique which we are considering in this reply teaches that God's justification of believers includes the Holy Spirit's converting, sanctifying work in them.

The **righteousness** that justifies believers must *not* be restricted to *Christ's atoning work* for sinners 2000 years ago.

The **righteousness** by which God justifies believers *must include THE HOLY SPIRIT'S converting, sanctifying, transforming work in us now—during this life on earth*.

Comments by The Author

The teaching above:

1. is an insult to Christ and His atoning work for sinners.
2. exalts the converting, sanctifying work of the Holy Spirit above the atoning, justifying work of Christ.
3. exalts the imparted righteousness of the Holy Spirit above the imputed righteousness of Christ.
4. exalts sanctification above justification.
5. leads us to take our eyes off of **Jesus** and His righteousness and to look within for the righteousness that justifies and saves us.
6. robs us of our assurance of forgiveness and heaven because we can never be quite sure that we have become good enough to pass the Judgment.
7. contradicts the clear teachings of the Bible and Mrs. White.

The Bible Teaches That:

The **righteousness** by which God justifies believers in Jesus is *never* the righteousness of the *Holy Spirit*—the righteousness of *repentance, conversion, sanctification, and transformation* of our nature, character or life!

The one and only righteousness by which God justifies believers is *Christ's atoning* work for them, *outside of them*, **2000 years ago!**

The Holy Spirit is not our Saviour! **Jesus is!**

We must *not fuse or confuse* the converting, *sanctifying* work of the Holy Spirit in us and the *atoning* work of Christ outside of us.

Jesus *redeemed* us—atoned for our sins—the Holy Spirit *converts and sanctifies* us.

We are justified *in order that* we might be sanctified.

We are not sanctified in order that we might be justified.

The Holy Spirit is not our Justifier; **Jesus is**.

We are *not* justified, forgiven, credited with Christ's righteousness, accepted by God unto adoption and eternal life, and treated by God as if we had not sinned on the *BASIS* of the converting, sanctifying, transforming work of the **Holy Spirit** *inside* of us, but on the *BASIS* of **Christ's** atoning work *outside* of us!

The above teaching guards us against being deceived by the seven errors mentioned above.

ISSUE SIX:
WHERE IS JUSTIFYING RIGHTEOUS?

WHERE does justification take place?

Does God's justification of sinners take place *in God* (Jesus) in heaven or *in Christians* on earth?

Where is the *righteousness* by which God justifies believers?

Is the righteousness by which God justifies us *objective* or is *it subjective*?

Is the righteousness that justifies us *always, in Jesus in Heaven*? Or is it also *in us on earth?*

ERRONEOUS PRESUPPOSITIONS

The righteousness that justifies believers in Jesus is **not only in Christ in heaven, it is also in us (believers) on earth.**

In the final analysis, God does not justify and take to heaven people who are **not righteous!** God justifies and takes to heaven *only perfectly righteous people.*
God cannot **call or treat** people who are **not** righteous—**righteous**! That would **be a lie!** And God cannot **lie!**

Therefore, when God justifies a person, He **imparts** Christ's righteousness to him or **infuses** Christ's righteousness into him and **makes** him **inwardly** righteous, pleasing and acceptable to Himself.

Those whom God justifies, He first makes righteous.

God justifies only righteous people.

Comments by The Author

(See the documentation throughout this reply to the author of the 48 page critique of the Campus Hill Church's statement of the gospel. The above is good Roman Catholic theology!)

Throughout his critique, our brother teaches all of the above. By doing so, he teaches that the righteousness by which God justifies believers is *inside* of them—that God *justifies* believers by *sanctifying* and *making* them *inwardly* righteous, pleasing, and acceptable to God.

The righteousness *by which God justifies* us is *never* a righteousness that is *inside* of us *on earth*!

FAITH IN JESUS puts us in a right relationship with God — a relationship in which God CAN CONVERT, SANCTIFY, AND TRANSFORM OUR CHARACTERS. Dear Reader, please stop and ponder this statement.

The Bible Teaches That:

The righteousness by which God justifies believers on earth *is always, in Jesus* in **Heaven!**

That is to say: The righteousness that justifies *is objective, never subjective!*

We are *never* justified by *an "in here"* righteousness!

We are *always* justified by *an "out there"* righteousness! Praise God!

We are *never* justified by the Holy Spirit's converting, sanctifying, transforming work *in us.*

We *are* justified solely by Christ's atoning work *for* us, *outside* of us, *2000 years before* we were born!

The righteousness of conversion, of sanctification, of Christ, and of the Holy Spirit in us, never, during this life on earth, makes us perfectly righteous in nature, character, or life.

The righteousness of the best Christians on earth is but "a dim reflection" of the **righteousness** of Christ's life, death and resurrection.

See pages **xiii, 16, 18, 107, 128-131, 136-139 of Volume One** for EGW statements confirming this statement.

The only righteousness that is *perfect enough to justify us* is the righteousness of *the atoning work of Christ* outside of us 2000 years ago!

All other righteousness, insofar as *justifying* us is concerned, is a mirage, shifting sand, a false hope, "another gospel", a cruel deception!

God's gift of Christ's *imputed* righteousness and of justification does not change *us!*

It changes God's *relationship* to us and our *relationship* to Him!

It changes the way God *regards* us and *treats* us.

In His gift of justification, God *regards* us as forgiven, as righteous, as adopted, as accepted unto eternal life, and *treats* us accordingly

**The ESSENCE OF CHRISTIANITY—
Justification by Faith (Righteousness by Faith)**

Is NOT a moral change in us.

**It is a change in
God's RELATIONSHIP to us
And our RELATIONSHIP To Him.**

●

*Righteousness by Faith—
is a Personal Faith-Love
RELATIONSHIP
With Jesus.*

FAITH puts us in a RIGHT RELATIONSHIP with God.

THE RIGHTEOUSNESS
of
Righteousness by Faith and Justification by Faith
●
WHAT it is, WHERE it is, WHAT it ACCOMPLISHES for Us,
In A Nutshell!

The RIGHTEOUSNESS of Righteousness by Faith:

1. **is NOT** the Righteousness that is **produced in us**!
2. **is NOT** the Righteousness that is **infused into, imparted to, or developed in us in sanctification**!
3. **is NOT** the Righteousness of **CHRIST IN US**!
4. **is NOT** the Righteousness of **THE HOLY SPIRIT IN US**!
5. **is NEVER IN US** on earth!
6. **IS always IN CHRIST** in heaven!
7. **NEVER MAKES** us inwardly righteous in nature, character, or life!
8. **IS** the **IMPUTED** righteousness of justification!
9. **IS** symbolized by **THE WEDDING GARMENT**! (SEE PAGE 143).
10. **IS OUR KEY, TICKET, TITLE, AND PASSPORT** to heaven!
11. **IS CHRIST'S DOING AND DYING for us, outside of us, 2000 years ago**!
12. **IS the OBJECTIVE** (outside–of–us) **BASIS** on which God justifies, forgives, and saves us!
13. **gives** us a righteous legal **STANDING** before God in our sinful moral **STATE**!
14. **is** the one and only meritorious **BASIS** on which God justifies us!
15. **is CREDITED** to our account in heaven!
16. is **the only Righteousness THAT IS GOOD ENOUGH TO:**
    - **atone for our sins**,
    - **perfectly satisfy** God's infinitely righteous law for us,
    - **get us through the Judgment**,
    - **secure for us** God's gifts of:
        (1) **justification**
        (2) **the knowledge of the Gospel—God's Plan of Salvation**
        (3) **faith**
        (4) **repentance**
        (5) **conversion**

(6) **forgiveness**

(7) **Christ's righteousness credited to us**

(8) **adoption** into God's spiritual family

(9) **eternal life**

(10) **heaven**

(11) **assurance** of salvation

(12) **peace** of mind

(13) **hope** for the future

(14) the great **JOY** of salvation

(15) **victory** over sin

(16) **perseverance** unto death or the Second Coming of Christ!

17. **HUMBLES THE PRIDE OF MAN IN THE DUST!**

18. The Righteousness of Righteousness by Faith **is received and rested in** by us personally **SOLELY BY FAITH, APART FROM OBEDIENCE AND GOOD WORKS!**

19. The Righteousness of Righteousness by Faith **INSPIRES** us **to truly believe** in God and in Jesus,

to truly love God,

to repent of our sins and to be **converted**,

to sanctify ourselves to God and **to live dedicated, sanctified Christian lives,**

to grow in grace, to perfect Christian character,

to sacrifice for God's cause,

to engage in Christian service,

to persevere faithful to the end!

20. is the only righteousness that completely **BREAKS SATAN'S POWER** OVER US!

21. **JUSTIFIES God in justifying us!**

22. **VINDICATES God in the great controversy between Christ and Satan!**

23. **ENABLES God to WIN the great controversy between Christ and Satan!**

24. **ENABLES God to SECURE the universe against a second uprising of sin!**

25. **MAKES POSSIBLE the redemption and restoration of the human race to its original perfection,**

the recreation of this earth, and

the inheritance of the NEW EARTH by a holy, healthy happy, righteous, redeemed people throughout the ceaseless ages of eternity!

PRAISE GOD! GLORY HALLELUJAH!

THE GREATEST DISCOVERY OF MY LIFE!

"I've discovered the way of GLADNESS!
I've discovered the way of JOY!
I've discovered, relief from sadness!
'Tis a happiness without alloy!"

Such love demands my heart, my will, my life, my ALL!

"WONDER O HEAVENS AND BE ASTONISHED O EARTH"

- the **RIGHTEOUSNESS** of **"Righteousness by Faith,"**
- the **RIGHTEOUSNESS** of **"Justification by Faith,"**
- the **RIGHTEOUSNESS** that **atoned** for our sins and legally **reconciled** us to God,
- the **RIGHTEOUSNESS** that perfectly **satisfies** God's infinitely righteous law for us,
- the **RIGHTEOUSNESS** that **gets us through** the Investigative Pre–Advent Judgment,
- the **RIGHTEOUSNESS** that **secures** for us God's gifts of forgiveness, Christ's righteousness credited to our account in heaven, adoption, eternal life, and heaven,
- the **RIGHTEOUSNESS** that gives us a righteous **legal standing before God** in our sinful **moral state**,
- the **RIGHTEOUSNESS** that **saves** us unto the uttermost,
- the **RIGHTEOUSNESS** that God **requires** of us for entrance into heaven,
- the **RIGHTEOUSNESS** that is our **key, ticket, title, and passport** to heaven,
- the **RIGHTEOUSNESS** in which **ALL** our hope of heaven resides,

IS NOT IN US! IT IS ALWAYS, ONLY IN CHRIST IN HEAVEN!

THEREFORE:

We must look **away from** our sinful selves **to Christ alone** for the righteousness which saves us!

ISN'T IT WONDERFUL?

The **RIGHTEOUSNESS** which God requires of us for entrance into heaven, **HE HIMSELF HAS ALREADY PROVIDED FOR US IN HIS SON JESUS CHRIST AS A FREE GIFT!**

The **sacrifice** which **ATONES** for our sins, which **RECONCILES** us to God, and which **SAVES** us to the uttermost was freely provided for us **by God Himself** in His Son as a free gift to **unworthy, sinful, sinning sinners 2000 years ago!**

"WHILE WE WERE YET SINNERS, CHRIST DIED FOR US." Rom. 5:8

God **KNEW** us before we knew Him! He **LOVED** us before we loved Him!
He **CHOSE** us while we were still **sinful sinning sinners!**
He **SOUGHT AND FOUND** us before we even knew we were **lost!**

"God justifieth **THE UNGODLY [sinners].**" Rom. 4:5. "Christ died for **THE UNGODLY [sinners].**" Rom. 5:6.

It is the **LOVE** of God, "the **goodness** of God," the **sacrifice** of God, "that **leads** us to **repentance.**" Rom. 2:4.

"We love HIM because He FIRST loved us." 1 John 4:19.

When we **LEARN** that God **TOOK** all our sins and **LAID** them all on **HIS** Son and dealt with (expiated) them all in Him and credited Christ's perfectly obedient life and His death to us 2000 years ago and treats us, during this life on earth, **AS IF** we were as righteous as Jesus, (2 Cor. 5:21) it **BREAKS OUR HEARTS WITH LOVE AND GRATITUDE AND REPENTANCE!** "God was in Christ, reconciling the world unto Himself, **NOT IMPUTING [NOT CHARGING] THEIR TRESPASSES UNTO THEM."** (2 Cor. 5: 19; Isa., Chapter 53). What an awesome God! What a wonderful salvation from Satan and sin and eternal death!

THE 1976 PALMDALE, CALIFORNIA CONSENSUS STATEMENT ON RIGHTEOUSNESS BY FAITH
Declared That: Strictly, Technically, Biblically Speaking, The Biblical Term, Righteousness by Faith, Refers to the **IMPUTED** righteousness of **JUSTIFICATION BY FAITH!**

At **Palmdale, both sides agreed that, technically** speaking, the term **Righteousness by Faith** refers to the **IMPUTED** righteousness of Christ–**to Justification by Faith Alone**.

The **TRADITIONAL** SDA view is that the term Righteousness by Faith includes **BOTH** justification and sanctification. See RH May 27, 1976.) Emphasis Mine.

THE 1976 PALMDALE
CONSENSUS STATEMENT
As it appeared in the Adventist Review

"We agree that when the words righteousness and faith are connected (by 'of ', 'by' *et cetera*) in Scripture, reference is to the experience of **JUSTIFICATION BY FAITH**.

"God, the righteous Judge, **DECLARES** righteous the person who **believes** in Jesus and repents.

"Sinful though he may be, he is **REGARDED** as righteous because in Christ he has come into **a righteous RELATIONSHIP** with God.

"This is the **GIFT** of God through Christ." RH May 27, 1976. (Bold face emphasis and CAPS added by this author)

●

"Christ was crucified, but in wondrous power and glory He rose from the tomb! He took in His grasp **THE [WHOLE] WORLD** over which Satan claimed to preside as his lawful territory, and by His wondrous work in giving His life, **HE RESTORED THE WHOLE RACE OF MEN TO FAVOR WITH GOD!**" YI April 16, 1903; Ms 50, 1900; QOD 680 and QOD 689; 1SM 343.

What God Does OUTSIDE of us and INSIDE of us

IMPORTANT DISTINCTIONS

It is extremely important for us to distinguish between that which God does **outside** of us and what He does **inside** of us.

There is absolutely NO justifying merit whatsoever in anything that we do, in anything that God does IN US or TO US, in anything He puts INTO US, or in anything He develops IN US!

ALL the merit that justifies us is in that which God did FOR us, OUTSIDE of us, IN JESUS, 2000 years ago!

These All Take Place
OUTSIDE of Us.

- **Jesus' INCARNATION**

- **Jesus' SINLESS LIFE**

- **Jesus' DEATH**

- **Jesus' RESURRECTION**

- **God's personal JUSTIFCATION of each individual sinner who believes in Jesus**

- **God's ADOPTION of believers**

- **God's promise of ETERNAL LIFE**

Note: All of the above constitute the OBJECTIVE, MERITORIOUS BASIS upon which God Justifies believers.

These All Take Place
INSIDE of Us.

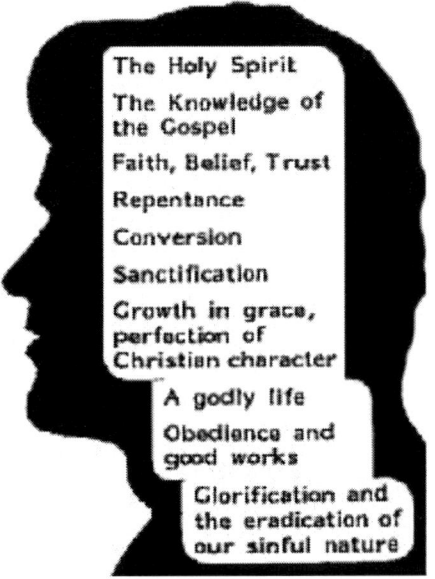

The Holy Spirit
The Knowledge of the Gospel
Faith, Belief, Trust
Repentance
Conversion
Sanctification
Growth in grace, perfection of Christian character
A godly life
Obedience and good works
Glorification and the eradication of our sinful nature

All of the above are the FRUIT of Justification

We must look **away from** our sinful selves, **TO JESUS ALONE**, for that **infinite** righteousness which perfectly fulfills and satisfies God's **infinitely** righteous law for us.
We must *DISTINGUISH* between *DIVINE* perfection (righteous) and *HUMAN* perfection (righteousness).

Human righteousness is the goal, *not divine* righteousness!

Christ's perfect righteousness is credited to us in God's gift of His IMPUTED righteousness of justification. We appropriate–believe, trust and rest in this righteousness personally solely by faith apart from anything else we may do.

The ONLY Righteousness that is GOOD ENOUGH TO Justify us:

THE RIGHTEOUSNESS THAT:

- Atones for our sins,
- Perfectly fulfills and satisfies God's infinitely righteous law for us,
- Reconciles us to God,
- Gets us through the Pre-Advent Judgment,
- Justifies us, secures God's forgiveness and acceptance of us,
- Is our TITLE to heaven,
- Reckons, accounts, and treats us as if we were righteous,
- Defeats Satan, vindicates God, and secures the universe against a second uprising of sin

IS CHRIST'S IMPUTED RIGHTEOUSNESS WHICH IS CREDITED TO US IN GOD'S FREE GIFT OF JUSTIFICATION!

These are always OUTSIDE of us — ALL, ALWAYS, ONLY IN CHRIST IN HEAVEN!

IN OURSELVES, even by the GRACE of God's help, we will never be good enough in nature, character or life to be saved. But IN CHRIST, we are NOW already good enough because God has CREDITED–IMPUTED–His righteousness to us in His gift of JUSTIFICATION which we receive solely by faith, apart from obedience and good works!

69

ISSUE SEVEN:
THE BASIS OF JUSTIFICATION

On what *BASIS* does God justify believers?

Does God justify believers solely on the *BASIS of His atoning* work *for* them, *OUTSIDE* of them, *in Jesus, 2000 years ago?*

Or, does God justify believers on the *BASIS* of the *Holy Spirit's* converting, sanctifying, morally transforming work *IN THEM* during this life?

ERRONEOUS PRESUPPOSITIONS

- *The basis* on which God *justifies* believers *includes* their faith, repentance, conversion, sanctification, prayers, obedience, good works, growth in grace, perfecting Christian character, living godly lives, and Christ living His perfectly righteous life in them.

- There can be *no* justification without all of the above.

- Page 19.10: "We are *justified* on the *two-fold basis* of the *imputed* and *imparted* righteousness of Christ."

  Our "*only ground* of hope is *two-fold*, [1] the righteousness of Christ *imputed* to us, *and* [2] the righteousness of Christ wrought *in* and through us by the Holy Spirit."

- This *bases* our justification partly on the imparted righteousness of sanctification inside of us.

- Pages 23 and 24: These two pages *base* justification on a righteousness *inside* of believers.

- Page 9.4" "…it is only by…a life of *obedience*, that men can hope to receive the favor of God."

- This is the same as saying that we are justified by faith plus conversion, obedience, sanctification, and by being made righteous.

- Page 26.4 "We are saved *BY* [emphasis mine] *faith*."*

- Page 28:10: Justification *includes sanctification*.
  Sanctification is *a part of* justification. Sanctification is the *basis* of justification. We are justified *by being sanctified*.

- Page 11.4: "It is by continual surrender of the will to, by *continual obedience*, that the blessing of justification is **RETAINED**. (1SM 397)."

- Page 12.0: "…in order to retain justification, we must be continually surrendered and continually *obey*."

- Page 12.10 and 13.2: "Having *made* us inwardly righteous…God *pronounces us just [justifies us]*, and treats us as just."

- Page 26.3: "…security (salvation) [justification, assurance] is guaranteed only as all specified conditions are met. This includes *obedience*."

- Page 26.7: "...by works a man is justified.

- Page 29.6: "...***Christ in you, the hope of glory [justification]."***

- Page 32.10: "He [God] prepares us to stand before Him [in the judgment] in the imputed ***and imparted*** righteousness of Christ."

---

* This is teaching that there is justifying **merit** in faith!

Comments by The Author

- This is precisely what the Roman catholic Church teaches and what the original Protestant leaders protested against.

- The Great Protestant Reformation was raised up by God to combat this false doctrine.

- This is contrary to the Bible, to the original Protestant leaders, and to the SDA statement of 28 Fundamental beliefs.

The Bible Teaches That:

We are justified on the ***basis*** of Christ's righteousness which is always, only ***in Him in heaven plus nothing!***

Insofar as there being any ***justifying merit*** in the obedience of sincere children of God is concerned, God says in **Isa. 64:6** *that even our righteousness [our obedience] of faith and love are "as filthy rags" to Him!*

To teach that a righteousness inside of us is a part of the ***basis*** on which God justifies us is an ***insult*** to God and a ***perversion*** of the truth concerning the ***objective, forensic*** nature of justification!

The basis on which God justifies believers is never in anything ***they*** may do, even though it is done ***by faith and love!***

Nor does God justify believers on the ***basis*** of anything ***He*** does ***in*** them, ***to*** them, ***puts into*** them or develops ***in them***.

In order for us to be justified on the ***basis*** of a righteousness ***in us, we would have to have never sinned;*** we would have to be ***perfectly obedient, perfectly righteous from birth to death.***

Since our faith, repentance, conversion, sanctification, obedience, good works, Christian living, and perfecting Christian character are never perfect, finished and complete during this life, ***none*** of these can be a part of the ***basis*** on which God justifies us.

Neither does Christ living His perfectly righteous life ***in us*** make us so sinless, so righteous, that we no longer come ***short*** of perfectly fulfilling God's infinitely righteous law.

Accordingly, the ***perfect righteousness***, or on the ***basis*** of which God can justly justify us ***is never in us on earth;*** it is always ***in Jesus in heaven!***

71

Note: We are *not* justified *by* or on the *basis* of faith!
- We are *justified by God through faith* in Jesus. Faith is not our Saviour; Jesus is.
- We are justified and saved by *Jesus*—the *object* of faith!

The best (most mature) Christians in the world still come SHORT of perfectly fulfilling the demands of God's infinitely righteous law!

The one and only objective, meritorious *basis* on which God justifies believers is in that which He did *for* us, *outside* of us, *in Jesus, 2000 years ago.*

We are justified *by* and on the *basis* of a righteousness that was wrought-out for us *by Someone Else 2000 years before we were ever born!*

We are justified on the basis of a righteousness that is *in Someone Else!*
Although we are *not perfect children of God*, we are *perfectly God's children* the moment we truly *believe* in Jesus!

The pure apostolic gospel proclaims the good news that: *Since* God took all our sins and "*laid*" them all on Jesus and *dealt with, atoned for, "punished" and expiated* them all *in Him*, and allowed *Him* to suffer the *consequences* of everyone's sins, He can *justly credit* His righteousness to us and *treat* us *as if* we were as righteous as *He!*

1. Isa. 53:6 "The Lord [the Father] hath *laid on Him* [the Son] the iniquity of us all."
2. Isa. 53:8: "for the transgression of my people was He stricken."
3. Isa. 53:10 "When Thou [God, the Father] shalt make His [the Son's] *soul an offering for sin…*"
4. Isa. 53:11: "My righteous servant [Jesus, shall] justify many; for He shall *bear* their iniquities."
5. Isa 53:12: "He *bare* the sin of many."
6. 2 Cor. 5:21: "For He [the Father] hath *made* [*reckoned*] Him [the Son] to be *sin* [*ful*] for us, who knew no sin: that we might *be made* [*reckoned*] the righteousness of God in Him."
7. 2 Cor. 5:21 actually says that: God took Jesus, who was infinitely righteous and charged all our sins to him and reckoned and treated Him as if He *were* sinful, in order to make it *just* for Him to take us who are exceedingly sinful and credit His perfectly righteous life to us and reckon and treat us as if we were righteous!

What a wonderful, but uneven exchange! Let us not *dishonor* Christ by teaching that a part of the *basis* on which God justifies us is *inside* of us!

Therefore, the one and only *objective meritorious basis* on which God justifies believers is *Christ's atoning work for sinners,* which consists of His *incarnation, sinless life, substitutionary death and resurrection* from the dead.

Is there anyone who is so arrogant or self-righteous as to think that he can *equal* what *God* has already done for him *in Jesus in order to justify Himself in justifying believing sinners?*

Jesus is *enough*, Dear Reader, *Jesus is enough!*

It is extremely important for Christians to *distinguish between* the *root and fruit (result, evidence)* of justification.

Although repentance, conversion, sanctification and the gift of the indwelling Holy Spirit *accompany* God's gift of justification, *none* of *these* is the *basis* on which God justifies us.

Jesus paid it all;
All to Him I owe;
Sin had left a crimson stain,
He washed it white as snow.

Page 23.4 (FLB 117.2 quoted):

"When in conversion the sinner finds peace with God through *[faith in] THE BLOOD of the atonement*, the Christian life has but just begun."

This EGW statement clearly makes the *blood (death) of Christ THE OBJECTIVE BASIS* on which God justifies believers.

The following Bible texts say that God justifies believers on the *BASIS* of Christ's *BLOOD* (death).

1. Heb. 9:22: "Without the shedding of *BLOOD [the BLOOD of Christ]* there is no *remission [forgiveness]."*

2. Ex. 12:13: "When I see *THE BLOOD*, I *will pass over* you."

3. Lev. 17:11: "It is *THE BLOOD* that maketh an *atonement* for the soul."

4. Matt. 26:28: "This is *MY BLOOD* of the new testament, which is shed for many for the *remission [forgiveness]* of sins."

5. Rom. 5:9: "Being now *justified by His BLOOD."*

6. 1 Peter 1:18,19: We were "*redeemed*…with the precious *BLOOD* of Christ."

7. 1 John 1: 7: "*THE BLOOD* of Jesus Christ …c*leanseth* us *[our record]* from all iniquity"

8. Rom. 3: 24-26 "Being now *justified freely by His grace through the redemption that is in Christ Jesus*, Whom God hath set forth to be the *propitiation [atoning sacrifice] through faith in His BLOOD*, to declare His righteousness *for the remission of sins*…that He might be just and the justifier of him which believeth in Jesus."

9. 1 Cor. 15:3: "*Christ DIED for our sins…*"

10. Eph. 1:7: "In Whom we have *redemption THROUGH HIS BLOOD* [on the *BASIS* of His *BLOOD*], *for the remission of sin…*"

11. Col. 1:14: "In Whom we have *redemption through [on the BASIS of His BLOOD], even the FORGIVENESS of sins…*"

12. Rev. 7:14: "And he said unto me, These are they which came out of great tribulation, and have washed their robes, and made them *white in the BLOOD of the Lamb*."

"What can take away my sins?
Nothing but the BLOOD of Jesus!"

"My *hope* is built on nothing less than
JESUS' BLOOD AND RIGHTEOUSNESS. "

*"*My only *hope*, my only *plea*,
That Jesus *DIED and DIED FOR ME!"*

"All my *sins* are *gone*,
All because of *CALVARY*;
Life is filled with song,
All because of *CALVARY!*"

"I hear the words of *LOVE*,
I gaze upon the *BLOOD*,
I *accept* the mighty sacrifice,
And I have *PEACE* with God."

"Therefore being justified *by FAITH [IN JESUS BLOOD], w*e have *PEACE* with God." Rom 5:1.

"Redeemed, how I love to proclaim it;
Redeemed by *THE BLOOD OF THE LAMB*."

In conclusion, *THE BASIS on which God justifies us is wholly CHRIST'S ATONING WORK FOR US, OUTSIDE OF US, 2000 YEARS AGO, PERIOD!*

How can this awesome, magnificent, transcendent truth be stated any more clearly of forcefully? Praise God for the precious blood of Jesus!

74

ISSUE EIGHT:
THE MEANS OF JUSTIFICATION: FAITH ALONE

How does God's gift of justification *become ours personally?*
By what *MEANS* does God's gift of justification become ours personally?
How is God's gift of justification *accepted, received, and appropriated by us personally?*
Is God's gift *received* and appropriated by us personally *by faith plus obedience and good works?*
Are we justified personally *solely by faith apart from anything else that we may do?*

ERRONEOUS PRESUPPOSITIONS

In order for us to be justified, Christ's atoning work and our faith are not enough.

We are *not* justified solely through faith apart from obedience and good works.

We *are* justified by faith *plus* obedience and good works.

In order for us to be justified, we must also be converted, and sanctified, and indwelt by Christ (The Holy Spirit) and made sinless within!

We are justified by being infused (filled) with Christ's righteousness and by being **made inwardly** righteous (obedient), pleasing and acceptable to God by the indwelling Holy Spirit.

We are justified *BY* "the faith that works by love and that purifies the soul."

God gives us a right standing with Himself by *imparting* Christ's goodness and virtue to us, by which He *makes* us into an innocent and virtuous person.

1. Page 2.0 line 24: "Justification can be *retained by works* of faith wrought in and through us by the Holy Spirit."

2. Page 2.0: "James balances out this truth. Was not Abraham our father justified *by works?*" James 2:21. "*By works* a man is justified and not by faith only." James 2:24.

3. Page 2.6: "Faith and *works* go together [as the *basis*] on which God justifies us, believing and *doing* are blended as God's *requirement* for justification."

4. Page 2.7: [For justification] "God requires of His child *perfect obedience.*"

5. Page 3.10: "All that man can do [with] Christ...which is wrought *through faith* is acceptable to God [as the *basis* on which He justifies believers.]"

6. Page 25.4: "It is *not enough* that we *believe* on Christ for the forgiveness of sin."
   The essence of this page (25 of the critique) teaches that we are not *justified* and saved solely through faith, but *by faith plus obedience.*

The Bible Teaches That:

We must not *co-mingle and confuse the basis* on which God justifies and the *means* by which we *appropriate* His wonderful gift of justification *to ourselves personally!*

Just as there is only *one objective, meritorious basis* on which God justifies us, so there is only one *subjective, instrumental means* by which believers *accept, receive, and appropriate* God's gift of justification to themselves personally.

There is only one subjective instrumental means by which we believe, trust, receive and appropriate God's gift of justification to ourselves personally, *and that is FAITH!*

And faith is *belief*, plus *trust*, plus *resting* in *Christ's completed work for our justification* outside of us 2000 years ago!

We are *not* justified *by faith!* We are justified by the *object* of faith (*Jesus!*).

We are justified by *God through* faith in Jesus. *Where there is true faith there will always be obedience. But that obedience is never perfect during this life on earth.*

We are justified *by* and on the *basis* of Christ's atoning work *for* sinners, *outside* of sinners, *2000 years ago!*

We repeat, we must *NOT* commingle, fuse and confuse the *BASIS* on which God justifies us, and the *MEANS* by which we *APPROPRIATE* His wonderful gift of justification to ourselves personally.

Faith is the empty hand that reaches up and receives God's gift of justification.

We are justified MERITORIOUSLY on the *BASIS* of Christ's atoning work for us outside of us 2000 years ago.

We are justified *EVIDENTIALLY* by our *obedience and good works and godly lives.*

Obedience is the "*acid*" test *of the genuineness* of our faith—the evidence that our faith is *genuine*.

Our obedience, good works and godly lives are the *fruit and result* of justification by faith, and *the validating evidence* that our faith is *genuine.*

We contribute nothing toward our justification.

We are justified by (through) faith plus nothing, period!

- James 2:21: "Was not Abraham our father justified [*evidentially*] by works, when he had offered Isaac his son upon the altar?"

- James 2:24: "Ye see then how that by works a man is justified [*evidentially*] and not by faith only."

- *James 2:23:* "Abraham *believed* [exercised *faith* in God], and it was *imputed [reckoned, credited]* unto him for righteousness."

- *Gen. 15:6, Rom. 4:3, and Gal. 3:6 say exactly the same thing as James 2:23.*

1. 1 SM 389: *"Faith is the ONLY condition upon which justification can be obtained."*

2. FW 100: *"Faith is the ONLY condition* upon which God has seen fit to promise *pardon* to sinners."

3. ST Mar. 24, 1890: "You are *justified by faith ALONE."*

4. OHC 52: "They [we] are *justified ALONE* through the *imputed* righteousness of Christ." This rules out imparted righteousness as having any part in our justification. (Imparted righteousness sanctifies us).

5. TIMK 82: "Man can be *justified ALONE* through the *imputation* of Christ's righteousness ."

6. AA 532: "Man's obedience can be made perfect *ONLY* by the incense of Christ's [*imputed*] righteousness ."

7. 1 SM 353: "Man can do *nothing, absolutely nothing* to commend himself to God."

8. 1SM 343: "ALL that man can possibly *DO* toward his own salvation is to *ACCEPT* the invitation."

Note: Christ's imparted righteousness never, during this life on earth, makes a person perfectly sinless—perfectly righteous.

Neither does Christ's *imputed* righteousness ever make anyone righteous within—in nature or character or life!

Christ's *imputed* righteousness of justification *credits* Christ's righteousness to us, *accounts us* righteous, and *treats* us *as if* we were righteous.

Faith is THE GIFT of God to unworthy sinners, undeserved, unmerited, unearned!

We repeat, we are justified through *THE INSTRUMENTAL MEANS OF FAITH PLUS NOTHING! PERIOD!*

When Abraham was about to plunge the knife into Isaac's heart, God shouted, "Stop Abraham! Now I know that you LOVE Me enough to OBEY ME. Unless we love God enough to obey Him we do not really love Him. Obedience is the acid-test of our love for God and our genuine Christian experience.

More Than 60 Bible Texts Teach That We Are JUSTIFIED SOLELY THROUGH FAITH!

Only the texts that have the words FAITH OR BELIEVE (BELIEF) are numbered.

Psalms 32:1,2: "Blessed is he whose **transgression is forgiven, whose sin is covered**. Blessed is the man unto whom the Lord **imputeth not iniquity**." God's **GIFT** of **FORGIVENESS** is received by us **solely by faith.**

Isa. 53:6,8,10,12: "**The Lord hath laid on Him the iniquity of us all...For the Transgression of my people was He stricken. ...when thou shalt make His soul an offering for sin**...because he hath poured out his soul unto death: and he was numbered with the transgressors; **and He bore the sin of many.**" [God's **gift** of **A Saviour, of forgiveness, of Christ's righteousness** and **of eternal life** is received by us **SOLELY BY FAITH.**

Jer. 23:6: "In his days Judah shall be **saved**, and Israel shall dwell safely: and this is his name whereby he shall be called, **THE LORD OUR RIGHTEOUSNESS**." We accept God's **gift** of a **Saviour** simply by **faith.**

1. **1 Cor. 1:21:** "It pleased God by the foolishness of preaching to save them that **BELIEVE**."
2. **1 Tim. 4:10:** "...the Saviour of all men, specially of those that **BELIEVE**."
3. **2 Tim. 3:15:** "And that from a child thou hast known the holy Scriptures which are able to make thee wise unto salvation through **FAITH** which is in Christ Jesus."
4. **Hab. 2:4:** "The just shall live by his **FAITH** [He who is **justified BY FAITH** shall live forever]."
5. **Gen. 15:6:** "And he [**Abraham**] **BELIEVED** in the Lord; and He **counted** it to him for **righteousness**." **Abraham** is God's classic example and illustration of how **we** are justified and saved. We are justified and saved at last in the same way Abraham was.
6. **Rom. 4:3:** "Abraham **believed** God, and it was **counted** to him for **righteousness**." This is Righteousness by Faith - Justitfication by Faith. **How Abraham** was **justified, forgiven,** and **saved** is God's classic example of how **we** are justified, forgiven, and saved.
7. **Gal. 3:6:** "Abraham **BELIEVED** God, and it was **accounted** to him for **righteousness**."
8. **James 2:23:** "Abraham **BELIEVED** God, and it was **imputed** to him for **righteousness**."
9. **John 1:12:** "As many as **received** him [**believed** in Him], to them gave He **power** [Greek: Authority, Right] to become **the sons of God**, even to them that **BELIEVE** on his name."
10. **John 3:14,15:** "As Moses lifted up the serpent in the wilderness, even so must the Son of man be lifted up: That whosoever **BELIEVETH** in Him **should not perish, but have eternal life.**"
11. **John 3:16:** "For God so **loved** the world, that **He gave** His only begotten Son, that whosoever **BELIEVETH** in Him **should not perish**, but **have everlasting life.**"
12. **John 3:18:** "He that **BELIEVETH** on Him **is not condemned.**"
13. **John 3:36:** "He that **BELIEVETH** on the Son **hath everlasting life.**"
14. **John 5:24:** "He that heareth my word, and **BELIEVETH** on Him that sent me, **hath everlasting life, and shall not come into condemnation; but is passed from death unto life.**"
15. **John 6:28,29:** "Then said they unto him, What shall we **DO**, that we might work the works of God? Jesus answered and said unto them, This is the **WORK** of God, that ye **BELIEVE** on Him whom He hath sent." This is how we attain to **a right relationship** with God.
16. **John 6:35:** "And Jesus said unto them, 'I am the bread of life: he that cometh to me [truly believe in me] shall **never hunger**; and he that **BELIEVETH** on me shall **never thirst.**"

17. **John 6:40:** "And this is the will of Him that sent me, that everyone which seeth the Son, **and BELIEVETH on Him, may have everlasting life: And I will raise him up at the last day.**"
18. **John 6:47:** "Verily, verily, I say unto you, he that **BELIEVETH** on me **hath everlasting life.**"
19. **John 11:25:** "Jesus said unto her, I am the resurrection, and the life: he that **BELIEVETH** in me, though he were dead, **yet shall he live.**"
20. **John 11:26:** "And whosoever liveth and **BELIEVETH in me shall never die.**"
21. **John 20:31:** "But these are written, that ye might **BELIEVE** that Jesus is the Christ, the Son of God; and that **BELIEVING ye might have life** through His name."
22. **Acts 10:43:** "To Him give all the prophets witness, that through His name whosoever **BELIEVETH** in Him **shall receive remission of sins.**"
23. **Acts 13:38,39:** "Be it unknown unto you therefore, men and brethren, that through this man is preached unto you the **forgiveness** of sins: and by Him all that **BELIEVE** are **justified** from all things, from which ye could not be **justified** by [obedience to] the law of Moses."
24. **Acts 16:30,31:** "The jailer asked Paul and Silas, '**What must I do to be saved?**' And they said **BELIEVE** on the Lord Jesus Christ, **and thou shalt be saved.**"
25. **Rom. 1:16**–"For I am not ashamed of the gospel of Christ: for it is the power of God unto **salvation** to every one that **BELIEVETH.**"
   Rom. 3:20,21: "Therefore by the **deeds** of the law there shall **no** flesh be **justified** in his sight: for by the law is the knowledge of sin. But now the **righteousness** of God **without the law** [apart from our obedience to the law] is manifested, being witnessed by the law and the prophets."
26. **Rom 3:22:** "Even the **righteousness** of God which is **by FAITH** of Jesus Christ unto all and upon all them that **BELIEVE.**"
   Rom. 3:24: "Being **justified** freely by his **grace** through the **redemption** that is in Christ Jesus."
27. **Rom. 3:25:** "Whom God hath set forth to be a propitiation **through FAITH** in his blood, to declare **His righteousness** for the **remission of sins** that are past, through the forbearance of God.
28. **Rom. 3:26:** "To declare, I say, at this time his **righteousness:** that he might be just, and the **justifier** of him which **BELIEVETH** in Jesus."
29. **Rom. 3:28:** "Therefore we conclude that a man is **justified by FAITH without the deeds of the law.**"
30. **Rom. 3:30:** "Seeing it is one God, which shall **justify** the circumcision **by FAITH,** and uncircumcision **through FAITH.**"
31. **Rom. 4:5:** "But to him that **worketh not,** but **BELIEVETH** on him **that justifieth** the ungodly, his **faith is counted** for **righteousness.**"
32. **Rom. 4:6-9:** "Even as David also describeth the **blessedness** of the man, unto whom God **imputeth righteousness without works,** Saying, Blessed are they whose iniquities are **forgiven,** and whose sins are **covered.** Blessed is the man to whom the Lord **will not impute sin.** Cometh this blessedness then upon the circumcision only, or upon the uncircumcision also? for we say that **FAITH** was **reckoned** to Abraham for **righteousness.**"
33. **Rom. 4:11:** "And He received the sign of circumcision, a seal of the **righteousness of the FAITH** which he had yet being uncircumcised: that he might be the father of all them that **BELIEVE,** though they be not circumcised: that **righteousness** might be **imputed** unto them also [**that believe**]."
34. **Rom. 4:13:** "For the promise, that he should be **the heir of the world**, was **not** to Abraham, or to his seed, **through the law**, but through **the righteousness of FAITH.**" If **right standing** with God is **not** obtained by obedience or works of the law, then it must be **solely by faith.**
35. **Rom. 4:14:** "For **if** they which are of **the law be heirs, FAITH is made void**, and the **promise** made of **none effect**."
36. **Rom. 4:16:** "Therefore it [God's promise to Abraham of **heirship** and **righteousness**] is **of FAITH,** that it might be **by grace...**to that also which is of the **FAITH** of Abraham [like Abraham's faith]."
37. **Rom. 4:20-22:** "He staggered not at the **promise** of God through unbelief; but was strong in **FAITH,** giving glory to God; And being fully persuaded that, what He had **promised,** He was able also to perform. And therefore **it** [**Abraham's FAITH**] was **imputed** to him for **righteousness.**"

38. **Rom. 4:23-25:** "Now it was not written for his [Abraham's] sake alone, that it [**Abraham's faith**] was **imputed** to him; But for us also, to whom it [**righteousness**] shall be **imputed** if we BELIEVE on Him that raised up Jesus our Lord from the dead; Who was delivered for [Greek, Because of] our offenses, and was raised again for [Greek, Because of] our **justification**."

39. **Rom. 5:1:** "Therefore being **JUSTIFIED BY FAITH, we** have **peace** with God through our Lord Jesus Christ."

40. **Rom. 5:2:** "By whom also **we have access by FAITH into this grace** wherein we **stand,** and rejoice in hope of the glory of God." By the **grace** of God, through **FAITH in Jesus,** we have **right standing** with God.

41. **Rom. 5:9:** "Much more then, being **now justified by His blood,** we shall be **saved** from wrath through Him [Jesus]." This **blanket, universal justification** of the entire world of lost sinners **collectively** 1963 years ago becomes ours **personally** the moment we truly **believe** in Jesus and accept it by **FAITH.**
Rom. 5:10, 11: "For if **when we were enemies,** we were [**legally**] **reconciled** to God by the **death** of His Son, much more, **being reconciled,** we shall be **saved by his life.** And not only so, but we also joy in God through our Lord Jesus Christ, by whom we have now received **the atonement** [margin, reconciliation]." This atonement — reconciliation — is received by us solely **by faith.**
Rom. 5:12-17: These verses declare that just as sin, guilt, condemnation, and death came upon everyone in the world because of the first Adam's sin, so righteousness, pardon and life come to everyone because of the Second Adam. This righteousness of the Second Adam is called A GIFT five times in Rom. 5:15-17. If we had to work for it, it would not be A GIFT. This gift of Christ's righteousness and eternal life is received by us **solely by faith.**
Rom. 5:18: "Therefore as by the offense of **one** judgment came upon **all** men to condemnation; even so by the righteousness of **One, the free gift** came upon **all** men unto **justification** of life.
Rom. 5:19-21: As sin and death have come by the first Adam, so righteousness and eternal life come by the grace of God by the Second Adam. This grace and righteousness and eternal life are received solely by faith."
Rom. 6:23: "For the wages of sin is death; but the **gift** of God is eternal life **through [faith in] Jesus Christ** our Lord."
Rom. 8:1: "There is therefore **now no condemnation** to them which are **in [which believe in]** Christ Jesus, who walk not after the flesh, but after the Spirit."

42. **Rom. 9:30:** "The Gentiles, which followed [sought] not after righteousness, have attained to **righteousness, even the righteousness which is of God by FAITH.**"

43. **Rom. 9:33:** "Whosoever BELIEVETH on Him [Jesus] **shall not be ashamed** [lost—shall be justified and saved]."

44. **Rom. 10:4:** "For Christ is **the end of the law** for [as a way or means of obtaining] **righteousness** to every one that **BELIEVETH.** "

45. **Rom 10:6: "The righteousness which is of FAITH** [the righteousness which is imputed to sinners by the grace of God and which is received by them by faith]."

46. **Rom. 10:9:** "If thou. . .shall **BELIEVE** in thine heart that God raised Him [Jesus] from the dead, **thou shalt be** saved."

47. **Rom. 10:10:** "For with the heart man **BELIEVETH** unto **righteousness.**"

48. **Rom. 10:11:** "For the Scripture saith, Whosoever **BELIEVETH** on Him **shall not be ashamed** [shall not be lost, but shall, instead, be saved]."
Rom. 10:13: "For whosoever shall **call** upon the name of the Lord [in faith - whosoever believeth in Jesus] **shall be saved.**"

49. **Rom. 11:20:** "Because of unbelief they [the unbelieving Jews] were broken off [lost], and **thou STANDEST BY FAITH.**"
2 Cor. 5:19: "God was in Christ, reconciling the world unto himself **not imputing** their trespasses unto them." This is RIGHT STANDING with God which we receive solely by faith.
2 Cor. 5:21: "For He [God] hath made Him [Jesus] to be sin for us, who knew no sin; that we might be made the **righteousness** of God in Him." God treated Christ, who was **righteous, AS IF** He were **sinful**

in order that He might treat us, who are **sinful, AS IF** we were **righteous**. God's gracious gift is received by us **SOLELY BY FAITH**.

50. **Gal. 2:16:** "Knowing that a man is **not justified** by the **works** of the **law**, but by the **FAITH** of Jesus Christ, even we have **BELIEVED** in Jesus Christ, that we might **be justified by the FAITH** of Christ, and not by the works of the law: for by the works of the law shall no flesh be justified."

51. **Gal. 3:7-9:** "Know ye therefore that they which are **of FAITH**, the same are the children of Abraham. And the Scripture, foreseeing that God would **justify** the heathen **through FAITH**, preached before the gospel unto Abraham, saying, In thee shall all nations be blessed. So then they which be **of FAITH** are blessed with faithful Abraham."

52. **Gal. 3:11:** "But that **no man is justified by the law** in the sight of God, it is evident: for, **the just shall live by FAITH**." This verse can be correctly translated - "those who are **justified by faith** shall live!"

53. **Gal. 3:14:** "That the **blessing** of Abraham might come on the Gentiles through Jesus Christ; that we might receive the **promise** of the Spirit **through FAITH**."
Gal. 3:18: "For if the inheritance [the new earth and eternal life] be of the law, it is no more of promise: but God gave it to Abraham **by promise**."

54. **Gal. 3:24:** "Wherefore the law was our schoolmaster to bring us unto Christ, that we might be **justified by FAITH**."

55. **Gal. 3:26:** "For we are all **children of God by FAITH** in Christ Jesus."
Gal. 3:29: "And if ye be Christ's, then are ye Abraham's seed, and heirs according to **the promise**." God's promise of heirship is received by us **solely by faith**.

56. **Gal. 5:5:** "For we through the Spirit wait for the hope of **righteousness by FAITH**."
Eph. 1:6: "To the praise of the glory of his grace, wherein he hath made us **accepted in the beloved**." All that remains is for us to accept our acceptance. And we do that solely by faith.
Eph. 1:7: "In whom we have **redemption** through his **blood, the forgiveness of sins,** according to the riches of his grace." We accept God's gift solely by faith.
Eph. 2:5: "Even when we were dead in sins, hath quickened us together with Christ, (**by grace ye are saved**)."

57. **Eph. 2:8:** "For by **grace** are ye saved **through FAITH**; and that not of yourselves, it is the **gift** of God."

58. **Phil. 3:9:** "And be found in him, not having mine own **righteousness**, which is of the law, but that which is **through the FAITH of Christ, the righteousness which is of God by faith**."
Col. 1:14: "In whom we have **redemption through his blood, even the forgiveness of sins**." All that remains, is for us to accept God's gift by faith.

59. **Col. 1:20-23:** "**And having made PEACE through the blood of his cross, by him to reconcile all things unto himself,** by him, I say, whether they be things in earth, or things in heaven. And you, that were sometimes alienated and enemies in your mind by wicked works, yet now hath he **RECONCILED**. In the body of his flesh through death, to present you **HOLY AND UNBLAMABLE AND UNREPROVABLE [righteous]** in his sight. If ye continue in the **FAITH** grounded and settled, and be not moved away from the hope of the gospel."

60. **2 Thess. 1:10,11:** "When he shall come to be glorified in his saints, and to be admired in all them that **BELIEVE** (because our testimony among you is **believed**) in that day. Wherefore also we pray always for you, that our God would **count you worthy** of this calling, and fulfill all the good pleasure of his goodness, and the work of **faith** with power."

61. **2 Thess. 2:13:** "God hath from the beginning chosen you to **salvation** through sanctification [consecration] of the Spirit and **BELIEF** of the truth." This is Righteousness by Faith - Justification by Faith.

62. **1 Tim. 4:10:** "For therefore we both labor and suffer reproach, because we trust in the living God, who is the Saviour of all men, specially of those who **BELIEVE**."

63. **2 Tim. 3:15:** "And that from a child thou hast known the Holy Scriptures, which are able to make thee wise unto **salvation through FAITH** which is in Christ Jesus."

64. **Heb. 10:38: "Now the just shall live by FAITH** [those who are **justified by faith** shall live]."

65. **Heb. 10:39:** "But we are not of them who draw back unto perdition: but of them that **BELIEVE to the saving of the soul**."

66. **Heb. 11:7:** "**By FAITH** Noah, being warned of God of things not seen as yet, moved with fear, prepared an ark to the **saving** of his house; by the which he condemned the world, and became **heir of the righteousness which is by FAITH**."

67. **James 2:23:** "And the Scripture **was** fulfilled which saith, Abraham **BELIEVED** God, and it was **imputed** unto him for **righteousness;** and he was called the Friend of God."
    1 John 5:11,12: "And this is the record, that God hath given to us **eternal life,** and this life is in His Son. He that **hath [believes in] the Son hath life**."

68. **1 John 5:13:** "These things have I written unto you, that **BELIEVE** on the name of the Son of God; **that ye may know that ye have eternal life,** and that ye may **BELIEVE** on the name of the Son of God."

THE WHOLE TRUTH
The Great Presbyterian Protestant Reformer John Calvin, had it right! John Calvin said,
- **"We are justified MERITORIOUSLY by Christ's Atoning Work.**
- **We are justified INSTRUMENTALLY by Faith.**
- **We are justified EFFICACIOUSLY by Grace.**
- **We are justified EVIDENTIALLY by Works."**

This is a great statement and truth. Every SDA Christian in the world should memorize these four statements.

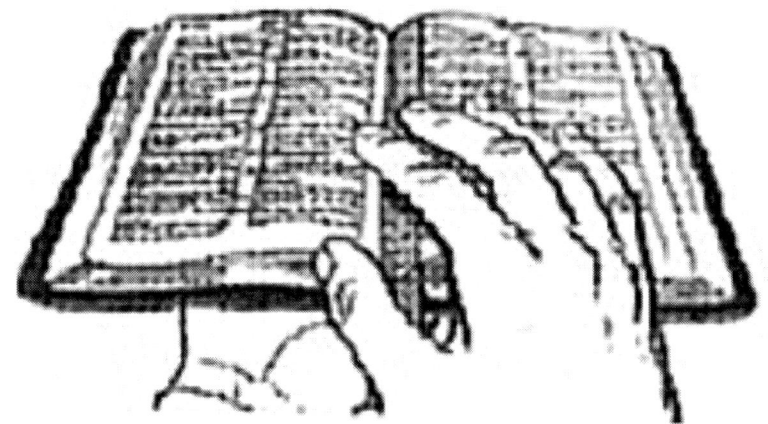

In his CLASSIC SUPLEMENT To HIS SYLABUS ON RIGHTEOUSNESS BY FAITH, Dr. Herppenstall said that Justification by Faith is GOD'S UNIVERSAL AMNESTY OF THE ENTIRE HUMAN RACE AT CALVARY.

18 BIBLE TEXTS Which Declare That We Are Justified SOLELY THROUGH FAITH APART FROM OUR OBEDIENCE AND GOOD WORKS.

1. **Acts 13: 38, 39** — "Be it known unto you therefore, men and brethren, that through this man is preached unto you the **forgiveness** of sins: And by him all that **believe** are **justified** from **all** things, from which ye could **not be justified by the law of Moses**."

2. **Rom. 3:20** — "By the **deeds** of the law shall **no flesh be justified** in His sight."

3. **Rom. 3:21** — "But now the righteousness of God **without the law** is manifested."

4. **Rom. 3:28** — "Therefore we conclude that a man is **justified by faith without the deeds of the law [apart from obedience and good works]**."

5. **Rom. 4:5** — "But to him that **worketh not,** but believeth on Him that **justifieth the ungodly,** his **FAITH** is **COUNTED** for righteousness."

6. **Rom. 4:6** — "God **imputeth** righteousness **without works [apart from obedience and good works]**."

7. **Rom. 4:14** — "For if they which are of the **law** be heirs, faith is **made void,** and the promise of **none effect."**

8. **Rom. 6:14** — "For sin shall **not** have dominion over you: for ye are not under the **law [as a way of becoming righteous or of securing God's forgiveness and acceptance of us],** but under grace."

9. **Rom. 9:30** — "What shall we say then? That the Gentiles, which followed not after righteousness **[by their obedience to the law],** have attained to righteousness, even the righteousness which is of faith."

10. **Rom. 10:4** — "For Christ is **the end of the law** for righteousness **[as a way of becoming righteous]** to every one that believeth."

11. **Gal. 2:16** — "Knowing that a man is **not justified by the works of the law,** but by the **FAITH** of Jesus Christ, even we have **BELIEVED** in Jesus Christ, that we might be justified by the **FAITH** of Christ, and **not by the works of the law: for by the works of the law** shall no flesh be justified."

12. **Gal. 2:21** — "I do not frustrate the grace of God: for if righteousness come by **the law,** then Christ is dead in vain."

13. **Gal. 3:10** — "For as many as are of the **works of the law** are under the curse."

14. **Gal. 3:11** — "**No man is justified by the law [by obedience and good works]** . . . for the just shall live **by faith**."

15. **Gal. 3:21** — "Is **the law** then against the promises of God? God forbid: for **if there had been a law given which could have given life,** verily righteousness should have been by the law."

16. **Gal. 5:4, 5** — "Christ is become of no effect unto you, whosoever of you are justified **by the law;** ye are fallen from grace. For we through the Spirit wait for the hope of righteousness by faith."

17. **Eph. 2:8, 9** — "By grace are ye saved through faith; and that **not of yourselves** [not by **the best obedience** of the best Christian on earth]: it is the gift of God: **Not of works, lest any man should boast**."

18. **Phil. 3:9** — "And be found in Him, **not having mine own righteousness, which is of the law,** but that which is through the faith of Christ, the righteousness which is of God **by faith**."

Every one of these 18 Bible texts teaches that we are justified **solely through faith APART FROM WORKS**.

1. **1ST March 24, 1890.** "Let not the fallacies of Satan deceive you; **you are justified by faith ALONE.**"

2. **FW 12.** "The plan for the salvation of lost mankind is based on man's acceptance **by faith ALONE** of Christ's substitutionary death."

3. **1SM 330.** "You will then understand that **justification** will come **ALONE through faith** in Christ."

4. **OHC 52.** "They are **justified ALONE through the imputed** righteousness of Christ."

5. **TIMK 82; RH Nov. 11, 1890.** "Man can be **justified ALONE through the imputation** of Christ's righteousness."

6. **1SM 389; TIMK 110. "Faith is the ONLY condition upon which justification can be attained,** and faith includes not only belief but trust."

7. **PP 524.** "It is **ONLY by faith** in Christ that they could secure **pardon** of sin."

8. **IHP 51.** "**ONLY through faith** in Christ's name can the sinner be saved."

9. **SC 60, 61.** "It is **faith and faith ONLY** that makes us partakers of the grace of Christ."

10. **FILB 107.** "It is **ONLY through faith** in His blood that Jesus can **justify** the believer [personally]." (Also 6BC 1071).

11. **4T 27.** "It is **ONLY through faith** that we can reach heaven."

12. **ST Aug. 22, 1892.** "You will then understand that **Justification can come ALONE through faith.**"

13. **1SM 389.** "The sinner can be **justified ONLY through faith** in the atonement made through God's dear Son [on the cross] who became a sacrifice for the sins of the guilty world."

14. **1SM 367; FW 101.** "The law demands righteousness, and this the sinner owes to the law; but he is incapable of rendering it. *The ONLY way in which he can attain to righteousness is through faith.* [**How** is this accomplished?] **By faith** he can bring to God the merits of Christ, and the Lord **places [credits]** the obedience of His Son to the sinner's account." See also SC 62.

15. **1SM 389.** "The sinner can be **justified ONLY through faith** in the atonement made through God's dear Son, who became a sacrifice for the guilt of the world. **No one can be justified by any works of his own.**"

16. **FW 72.** "Salvation is gained by **looking** at the cross. . . . Man can be saved through Jesus Christ, if we **ONLY have faith** in Him."

17. **1SM 395.** "In order to be candidates for heaven, we must meet the requirements of the law . . . We can do this **ONLY** as we grasp **by faith** the righteousness of Christ [which is **imputed** [credited] to us in God's gift of **justification**].

18. **1SM 343.** "Jesus' righteousness **alone** can avail . . . **ALL** that man can possibly do toward his own salvation is to **ACCEPT [by faith]** the invitation."

19. **FW 100. "Faith is THE CONDITION** upon which God has seen fit to promise **pardon** to sinners."

20. **St May 23, 1895.** "In Him, through Him **ALONE, we have forgiveness of sins. Through faith** in his blood we have **justification** in the sight of God."

21. **1SM 396.** "By His perfect obedience He [Jesus] has satisfied the claims of the law, and **my ONLY hope** is found in **looking [by faith]** to Him as my **Substitute and surety**, who obeyed the law perfectly for me."

22. **FW 19.** "Salvation is **through faith in Christ ALONE."**

23. **FW 37.** "If you are conscious of your sins, do not devote all your powers to mourning over them, but **LOOK to Jesus and live."**

    (All we have to do in order to be saved is to "LOOK AND LIVE." See John 3:14,15.)

24. **FW 100, 101. "Faith is THE CONDITION** upon which God has seen fit to promise **pardon** to sinners; not that there is any virtue in faith whereby salvation is merited, but because faith can **lay hold of** the merits of Christ, the remedy provided for sin. **Faith** can present Christ's perfect obedience instead of the sinner's transgression and defection.

    "When the sinner **believes** that Christ is his personal Saviour, then according to His unfailing promises, God **pardons** his sin and **justifies** him freely. The repentant soul realizes that his **justification** comes because Christ, as his **Substitute and Surety**, has died for him, is his atonement and righteousness."

    (This is **Justification solely by faith, apart from works!**)

25. **1SM 296.** "In the prophecy of Daniel it was recorded of Christ that He shall 'make reconciliation for iniquity, and . . . bring in everlasting righteousness'" (Dan. 9:24).
    "Every soul may say: 'By His perfect obedience He has satisfied the claims of the law, and **my ONLY hope is found in looking** to Him as my **substitute and surety**, who obeyed the law perfectly for me.'"

    "**By faith** in His merits I am free from the condemnation of the law. He clothes me with His righteousness, which answers all the demands of the law. I am complete in Him who brings in everlasting righteousness.
    "He presents me to God in the spotless garment of which no thread was woven by any human agent. **All** is of Christ, and **all** the glory, honor, and majesty are to be given to the Lamb of God, which taketh away the sins of the world." 1SM 396.

26. **RH May 23, 1899.** "Through the **imputed** righteousness of Christ, the repentant sinner **stands justified** before the law."

The Pre-Advent Judgment is GOOD NEWS For Christians!

O Blessed Judgment Day! Hasten On, O Blessed Judgment Day!
Why?
Because Christ stands in for us in the Judgment!
It is HIS character that gets us through the Judgment! Not Ours!

THANK GOD!

All our sins are under the blood!

Christ STANDS IN for us in the Judgment! It is HIS character that perfectly satisfies God's infinitely righteous law for us! God CREDITS HIS DOING AND DYING TO US AND WE STAND BEFORE GOD AND HIS INFINITELY RIGHTEOUS LAW AS IF WE WERE AS RIGHTEOUS AS HE!

"We are not to be anxious about what Christ and God think of US, but about what God thinks of CHRIST OUR SUBSTITUTE." 2SM 32, 33. "Ye are COMPLETE IN HIM!" Col. 2:10; Eph. 1:6,7; 1 Cor. 1:30.

Even in THE JUDGMENT we are justified, forgiven, and accepted by the GRACE of God through FAITH in Jesus.

14 EGW Statements Which Declare That We Are Justified SOLELY THROUGH FAITH APART FROM OBEDIENCE AND GOOD WORKS

1. **1SM 389:** *"No one can be justified by any works of his own."*

2. **FW 23:** *"No work of man* can merit for him the pardoning *love of God."*

3. **FW 48:** *"Works will never save us;* it is the merit of Christ that will avail in our behalf."

4. **1SM 343:** *"All that man can possibly do* toward his own salvation is to *accept the invitation."*

5. **FW 39; 1SM 353, 354:** "We [Christians] can *do nothing, absolutely nothing* to commend ourselves to divine favor. We must *not trust at all to ourselves or to our good works."*

6. **FW 20:** "Justification [forgiveness and acceptance of God] is wholly of grace and *not procured by any works that fallen man can do."*

7. **FW 24:** *"Any works* that man [Christians] can render to God [even with His help] will be far less than *nothingness."*

8. **1SM 364:** "He who is trying to reach heaven by *his own works in keeping the law, is attempting an impossibility."*

9. **FW 36":** We must learn in the school of Christ. Nothing but *His [imputed] righteousness can entitle* us to one of the blessings of the covenant of grace."

10. **1SM 377:** *"While good works will not save even one soul,* yet it is impossible for even one soul to be saved *without good works."*

11. **1SM 343:** "Let no one take the limited, narrow position that *any of the works of man* can help in the least possible way to liquidate [cancel] the debt of his transgression. This is **A FATAL DECEPTION.."**

12. **FW 24:** "If you would gather together everything that is good and holy and noble and lovely in man [born-again, Spirit-filled Christians] and then present the subject to the angels of God as acting a part in the salvation of the human soul or in merit, the proposition *would be rejected AS TREASON."*

13. **1SM 184:** "You cannot gain an entrance by penance nor by any *works that you can do.* No, God Himself has the honor of providing a way, and is so complete, so perfect, that *man cannot, by any works he may do, add* to its perfection. It is broad enough to receive the greatest sinner if he repents."

14. **1SM 363:** "We have transgressed the law of God, and *by the deeds of the law shall no flesh be justified. The best efforts that man [including the Christian] in his own strength can make, are valueless to meet the holy and just law* that he has transgressed; but through faith in Christ he may claim the *[Imputed]* righteousness of the Son of God as all-sufficient." (Nor do obedience and works of faith justify)!

ISSUE NINE:
ROOT AND FRUIT

What is the *root* of justification? The *fruit* of justification?

Is it important for us to distinguish between:

**The *root (basis)* of justification and
The *fruit (result)* of justification?**

Erroneous Presuppositions

Throughout his 48 page document, our friendly critic teaches the following errors:

1. The *root* and the *fruit* of justification are *one* and the *same* thing.

2. The *same* faith *and works* that *sanctify* us *also always justifies* us.

3. We *are* justified by the *indwelling* Holy Spirit and the *imparted* righteousness of conversion and sanctification.

4. The *root* and the *basis* of justification are conversion, sanctification, obedience, good works, a godly life, growing in grace, perfection of character, and Christ living His righteous life *in us*.

5. It is "Christ *in you*, the hope of glory—heaven." The righteousness that *justifies* and *saves* is **inside** of believers

Comments by The Author

The False Roman-Catholic doctrine above leads some of its adherents:

1. to take their eyes off of *Jesus above*, and to look *within* for that righteousness that justifies and saves them.

2. to work real hard to become good enough *to pass* the Judgment.

3. to *question* whether or not they are righteous enough to be saved.

4. to become *discouraged* and to give up being Christians altogether!

•

We must distinguish between the root and fruit, the basis and the result of Justification!

Justification and sanctification are distinct, but never separate! We must never fuse the two into one and the same thing!

The Bible Teaches That:

It is imperative that we *distinguish* clearly and decisively between *Christ's* righteousness that *justifies* and *the Holy Spirit's* righteousness that *converts, sanctifies and transforms.*

If we do not, we are in danger of *fusing* the two and therefore of *confusing* them and making them both the *bases* on which God justifies us.

This is *the basic Roman Catholic* error concerning justification.

We must *distinguish* between the righteousness that is *outside* of us and the righteousness that is *inside* of us—the righteousness that *justifies and saves*, and the righteousness that *sanctifies*, but does *not* justify and save!

We must *not* make the *Holy Spirit* our *justifier and Saviour*. It is *not* the righteousness of the Holy Spirit in us that *justifies* and *saves*, but the righteousness of *Christ outside of us*.

Jesus is our *one and only* justifier. The Holy Spirit is our *sanctifier*.

The Bible *distinguishes* between the *root* and the *fruit* of justification.

Jesus' righteousness is the *root* and the Holy Spirit's righteousness is the *fruit, result, and evidence* of justification.

Jesus' atoning work outside of us 2000 years ago is the ROOT of our justification; and the Holy Spirit's converting, sanctifying, morally transforming work in us is the FRUIT of our justification.

Those who are teaching that we are justified by the converting, sanctifying, transforming work of the Holy Spirit are teaching that the Holy Spirit is our *Co-Redeemer*. This is good **Roman Catholic** and "Certain SDA Independent ministries" doctrine!

It is extremely important for Christians to *distinguish between* the *root and fruit (result, evidence)* of justification.

Although repentance, conversion, sanctification and the gift of the indwelling Holy Spirit *accompany* God's gift of justification, *none* of *these* is the *basis* on which God justifies us.

"Jesus paid it all;
All to Him I owe;
Sin had left a crimson stain,
He washed it white as snow."

FLB 117.2 quoted:
"When in conversion the sinner finds peace with God through [*faith in*] THE BLOOD of the atonement, the Christian life has but just begun."

This EGW statement clearly makes the *blood (death) of Christ THE OBJECTIVE BASIS* on which God justifies believers.

The following Bible texts say that God justifies believers on the **BASIS** of Christ's **BLOOD** (death).

1. Heb. 9:22: "Without the shedding of **BLOOD [the BLOOD of Christ]** there is no *remission [forgiveness]."*

2. Ex. 12:13: "When I see **THE BLOOD**, I *will pass over* you."

3. Lev. 17:11: "It (is) **THE BLOOD** (that) maketh *atonement* for the soul."

4. Matt. 26:28: "This is **MY BLOOD** of the new testament, which is shed for many for the *remission [forgiveness]* of sins."

5. Rom. 5:9: "Being now *justified by His BLOOD."*

6. 1 Peter 1:18,19: We were "*redeemed*…with the precious **BLOOD** of Christ."

7. 1 John 1: 7: "**THE BLOOD** of Jesus Christ …*cleanseth* us *[our record]* from all iniquity."

8. Rom. 3: 24-26: "Being now *justified freely by His grace through the redemption that is in Christ Jesus*, Whom God hath set forth to be the *propitiation [atoning sacrifice] through faith in His BLOOD*, to declare His righteousness *for the remission of sins*…that He might be just and the justifier of him which believeth in Jesus."

9. 1 Cor. 15: 3: "*Christ DIED for our sins*…"

10. Eph. 1: 7: "In Whom we have *redemption THROUGH HIS BLOOD* [on the **BASIS** of His **BLOOD**], *for the remission of sin*…"

11. Col. 1: 14: "In Whom we have *redemption through [on the BASIS of] His BLOOD, even the FORGIVENESS of sins*…"

12. Rev. 7: 14: "And he said unto me, These are they which came out of great tribulation, and have washed their robes, and made them *white in the BLOOD of the Lamb*."

"What can take away my sins?
Nothing but the BLOOD of Jesus!"

•

"My *hope* is built on nothing less than
JESUS' BLOOD AND RIGHTEOUSNESS."

•

"My only *hope,* my only *plea,*
that Jesus **DIED and DIED FOR ME!"**

•

"All my *sins* are *gone,*
All because of **CALVARY**;

Life is filled with song,
All because of *CALVARY!*"

•

"I hear the words of *LOVE*,
I gaze upon the *BLOOD*,
I *accept* the mighty sacrifice,
And I have *PEACE* with God."

•

"Therefore, being *justified by FAITH [IN JESUS' BLOOD,]* We have *PEACE* with God." Rom 5:1

"Redeemed, how I love to proclaim it;
Redeemed by *THE BLOOD OF THE LAMB*."

In conclusion, THE BASIS on which God justifies us is wholly CHRIST'S ATONING WORK FOR US, OUTSIDE OF US, 2000 YEARS AGO, PERIOD!

How can this awesome, magnificent, transcendent truth be stated any more clearly or forcefully? Praise God for the precious blood of Jesus!

The TRUE, and the FALSE Doctrines of:
1. The BASIS 2. The MEANS and 3. The FRUIT of
JUSTIFICATION by FAITH

The TRUE Doctrine

1. The ONE Meritorious BASIS of JUSTIFICATION

GOD'S ATONING
WORK FOR US,
OUTSIDE OF US, IN JESUS,
2000 YEARS AGO.

2. The ONE Instrumental MEANS of JUSTIFICATION

FAITH Believes, Trusts, and Rests,
Securely in God's GIFT of
JUSTIFICATION

3. The Inevitable FRUIT

THE EVIDENCE & RESULT OF
JUSTIFICATION

FORGIVENESS, MORE OF THE HOLY
SPIRIT'S PRESENCE IN US,
CONVERSION, SANCTIFICATION,
MORE FAITH FOR VICTORY OVER SIN,
OBEDIENCE, A GODLY LIFE, GOOD
WORKS, PERFECTING CHRISTIAN
CHARACTER

NOTE:
This chart shows that the FALSE doctrine (right column) requires TWO BASIES PLUS FOUR CONDITIONS WHICH WE MUST MEET BEFORE GOD WILL JUSTIFY US! The TRUE doctrine (left column) SHOWS that there is ONLY ONE BASIS on which God justifies us-CHRIST'S ATONING WORK FOR US OUTSIDE OF US 2000 YEARS AGO!

The FALSE Doctrine

The TWOFOLD BASIS OF JUSTIFICATION

1
CHRIST'S
ATONING
WORK
FOR
US
OUTSIDE OF US,
IN JESUS,
2000 YEARS AGO

2
THE HOLY
SPIRIT'S
RIGHTEOUS,
CONVERTING,
SANTIFYING,
TRANSFORMING
PRESENCE
IN US NOW

3
ADDITIONAL CONDITIONS
WHICH WE MUST MEET
BEFORE GOD WILL
JUSTIFY US

OBEDIENCE, GOOD WORKS,
LIVING A GODLY LIFE, AND
DEVELOPING A PERFECTLY
RIGHTEOUS (SINLESS)
CHARACTER, ETC.

JUSTIFICATION

ISSUE TEN:
THE ONLY CONDITION OF JUSTIFICATION

What must we *DO in order* to be justified?

How many *CONDITIONS* must we *fulfill before God will justify us?*

Is there only one? Or are there many?

**Does the Bible ever *fuse* or *blend* justification and sanctification
into one and the same *BASIS OR CONDITION* on which God *justifies* believers?**

Erroneous Presuppositions

Our friendly critic teaches the following:
Faith is not the only condition which we must meet in order to be justified, forgiven and saved at last.

There are **many** *conditions* which we must meet before God will forgive and take us to heaven.

Before God will justify, forgive, accept and take us to heaven, we must first *repent* of our sins, we must be *converted*, *sanctified*, *filled* with *the Holy Spirit* and *the righteousness of Christ.*

Only those who *are converted, sanctified and perfectly obedient*, who perform *good works*, who *live godly lives*, and who *perfect Christ-like Characters can* be *justified*.

Justification is *retained* by faith **AND** obedience.

Since Jesus told Nicodemus that unless a person is *converted* he cannot be saved; conversion is a part of *the basis or condition on* which God justifies believers.

Conversion and sanctification and our being *made* inwardly righteous must *precede* justification.

God justifies only those whom He has *converted* and *sanctified* and *made* righteous by the indwelling of Christ or the Holy Spirit.

Before God will justify us, He must *make* us inwardly righteous by *imparting* Christ's righteousness to us and *converting* and *sanctifying* us.

Those whom God *justifies*, He must first *make* righteous by *infusing* Christ's righteousness into them.

God justifies us by sanctifying us.

Since we are not justified and saved at last unless we have *perfectly obeyed* God, obedience is a part of the *basis* on which God justifies us.

Justification is:
1. By faith,
2. By baptism,
3. By repentance,
4. By conversion,

5. By sanctification
6. By "Christ in you,"
7. By our living a godly life,
8. By Obedience and good works,
9. By perfection of Christian character.

All of the above are firmly believed and taught by *right-wing Seventh-day Adventists*—"**Certain Independent Ministries.**"

Now, let us read our critic's 21 statements which teach that there are MANY CONDITIONS which we must meet before God will justify us.

This is also *good Roman Catholic doctrine!*

Accordingly, many SDA's are *Roman Catholic* in their understanding of *the Gospel*!

1. Page 2.3: "The imputed righteousness of Christ by faith...*there are conditions* to our receiving justification...and the righteousness of Christ."
2. Page 2.7: "*God requires of His child perfect obedience* [for justification]."
3. Page 7.7: "...there are *conditions* that have to be met before forgiveness *can be granted.*...There are *conditions* that have to be met in order for justification...*to be retained.*"
4. Page 8.8: "But the sinner nevertheless, must comply with the *conditions* [*plural*] in order to [take?] full advantage of it [justification] and to retain its benefits."
5. Page 9.5 "It is only...*a life of obedience*, that man can hope to receive the favor of God [*justification*]. Only the *perfectly obedient* are justified."
6. Page 10.6: God can be just, and the *justifier* of him which *believeth* in Jesus *[and in whom]* the very righteousness of the law *is fulfilled*...[who perfectly *obeys* the law]."
7. Page 11.4: "It is by continual *obedience* that the blessing of justification is *retained*." (In other words, our justification *rests* (not on faith, but) on our *obedience of faith*).
8. Page 12.0: "In order to *retain* justification, we must...continually *obey*. [In other words, only those who perfectly obey will be justified]."
   (See also page 12.7).
9. Page 12: This entire page is on *conditions* we must meet before we can be justified. Some of which are: obedience, full surrender, prayer, repentance, victory over sin, and being "made" inwardly righteous.
10. Page 41.3: "All that man can do [in obedience and good works, etc.] *without* Christ is polluted with selfishness and sin but that which is *wrought through faith is acceptable* to God."
11. Page 48.3: "Our claim to Christ's 'righteousness' [justification] is without a flaw, *IF* we meet the *conditions* upon which it is promised." (Youth's Instructor, July 12, 1894, par. 1).
12. Page 34.5: "Let us *keep* His law and then He can *TRUST* us, for He has a law and He will reward obedience to the law; He will give us a crown of glory." (1888 Ms. p128.4) In other words, God justifies us and takes us to heaven, *not* because Jesus *died* to save us, but because of, or on the basis of our being *SAFE to save.*
13. Page 26.3: "We are to turn from sin to   *obedience*…man must *cooperate* with these saving agencies…he must…*believe and obey* all the divine requirements."
14. Page 26.4: "[salvation] is guaranteed only as all specified *conditions* are met. This includes *obedience.*"
15. Page 30.6: "It is not faith that claims the favor of Heaven without complying with the *conditions* on which mercy is to be granted." (DA 126.1)
16. Page 28.10: " '*Fruit in Sanctification*' are *components* of [parts of, conditions of] 'Justification by Faith alone.' So when someone says, 'Justification by Faith alone' they *are including 'Fruit in Sanctification.'* "

17. Page 19.9: "Our only **ground** [*basis*] of hope is in the righteousness of Christ imputed to us **and** in that wrought by His Spirit working **in** and through us."

18. Page 23.0: "Now, if *justification* is our title to heaven (MYP 35) can our title alone get us into heaven? If not, then justification does not save us. Apparently it takes something else."
    The rest of this page teaches that our justification rests at least partly on: our **"conversion," "being born from above," "the new birth," "a new creation," "A new heart," "a new creature," "a new mind."**

19. Page 24.2: : *"renewed* in the Spirit of our mind," *"A new heart."*

20. Page 30.6: *"There is no justification without complying with the conditions!"*

21. Page 48.4: On his last page, the author of the 48 page critique of the Loma Linda Campus Hill church statement on the gospel returns to *"the conditions"* which we must meet before we can be justified.

The above erroneous statements **teach** that, for justification to take place there must first be *"perfect obedience."* (Page 2.7)

BLESSED ASSURANCE!

Dear Reader, you can **NOW** have the calm assurance that God has forgiven all your sins and that you are **NOW** His child and that you **NOW** have eternal life.

- John 3:18: "He that believeth in Him **HAS** [present tense] eternal life."
- Rom. 8:1: "There is…**NOW NO CONDEMNATION** to them which" believe "in Christ Jesus…"
- John 5:24: "He that believeth…**HAS** eternal life, and shall **not** come into condemnation, but **IS** passed from death unto life."

The Bible Teaches That:

We will be justified **SOLELY BY FAITH, APART FROM WORKS,** because there is only *one gift* of God that enables a sinner to *believe, trust, accept, receive, appropriate, and rest* in Christ's perfect, finished, completed, all-sufficient atoning work, and that is *FAITH.*

There is nothing else that will enable us to do all the above.

It is *Christ's doing and dying* that justifies and saves us, *not our doing and trying*!

It is Christ's *atonement* that justifies us, not our *attainment!*

It is NOT God's great *ACT in us* that justifies and saves, but His great *ACT in Jesus!*

Faith is the empty hand that reaches up and *accepts* God's free gift of Christ's righteousness that covers our unrighteousness.

Justification is *not retained* by faith plus obedience!

Justification is *retained* in exactly the same way it is originally *received—solely through faith apart from obedience and good works.*

Obedience is *not* a part of the *basis* or condition on which God justifies believers.

God does not justify us *because of* or on the *basis* of what He does *in us*, but on the *basis* of what He did *for us outside of us in Jesus nearly 2000 years ago!*

The Bible teaches that believers are justified solely through faith apart from obedience and good works. (See ISSUES 7 and 8.)

Of course, the same faith that *justifies* also, always, at the same time, *sanctifies*!

•

"Jesus paid it all;
All to Him I owe
Sin had left a crimson stain;
He washed it white as snow."

•

"Nothing in my hand I bring,
Simply to Thy cross I cling!"

•

"I would not work my soul to save,
For that my Lord hath done.
But I would work like any slave
For the love of God's dear Son!"

The fact that no one will be saved at last who does not *repent* of his sins, who is *not converted*, who is not *sanctified* and who does not *obey* God *does not mean* that these are *prerequisites* for justification or a part of the *basis* on which God justifies people.

Repentance, conversion, sanctification, and obedience are all the *fruit, result, and evidence* of God's justification of believers.

We are not justified *by* these, but neither will we be justified if we *refuse* to do these things. True faith which enables us to accept God's gift of justification will always lead to repentance, conversion, sanctification, obedience, and to a godly life.

Christ's atoning work for sinners and God's justification of believers always *precede* repentance, conversion, sanctification, and obedience.

We are *justified* in order that we may be *sanctified*.

The same faith that justifies us also, always, at the same time, *empowers* us to obey. Justification and sanctification are *distinct, but never separate*.

We are justified solely by FAITH because faith enables and leads us to repentance, conversion sanctification, obedience, good works and a godly life.

No other gift of God can do any of these things for us.

Accordingly, THERE IS ONLY ONE CONDITION which we must meet in order for God to justify us personally, individually, effectually, and savingly; and that is FAITH!

See Volume One, pages 36 - 40 and Volume Two pages 74 to 86.

1. Romans 3:28: "Therefore we conclude that a man is justified by faith *without [apart from]* the deeds of the law."

2. Romans 5:1: "Therefore, *being justified by [through] faith,* we have peace with God."

3. Eph. 2:8, 9: "For by *grace* are ye saved *through faith*; and that [faith] not of yourselves: it [faith] is the gift of God: *not of works*, lest any man should boast."

4. 1 SM 389: *"Faith is the only condition upon which justification can be obtained."*

5. PW 100: *"Faith is the only condition* upon which God has seen fit to promise *pardon* to sinners."

6. ST Mar. 24, 1890: "You are *justified by faith alone!"*

7. OHC 52: "They [we] are *justified alone* through the *imputed* righteousness of Christ." This rules out imparted righteousness as having any part in our justification."

8. TIMK 82: "Man can be *justified alone* through the *imputation* of Christ's righteousness."

9. AA 532: "Man's obedience can be made perfect only by the incense of Christ's *[imputed]* righteousness."

   Note: Christ's imparted righteousness never, during this life on earth, makes a person perfectly sinless—perfectly righteous.

   Neither does Christ's *imputed* righteousness ever make anyone righteous in nature or character or life! Christ's *imputed* righteousness of justification *credits* Christ's righteousness to us and *treats* us *as if* we were righteous.

10. 1 SM 353; 354: "We can do *nothing, absolutely nothing* to *commend* ourselves to divine favor."

All that a person can *do* in the way of obedience and good works through faith in Christ is *acceptable* to God, but never as a part of the **condition or basis** on which God justifies him.

The statements in the **ERRONEOUS PRESUPPOSITIONS SECTION** must not be interpreted to mean that *obedience or sanctification* is a *condition or basis* on which God *justifies* us (forgives and accepts us unto eternal life).

Although we are not justified on *the condition or basis of our obedience and good works, etc.* we will not be saved at last if we *refuse* to be obedient.

The *condition*, *ground*, *basis*, on which God grants mercy, justification, forgiveness, eternal life and heaven is always, only *Christ's atoning work for sinners.*

Statement number 16 in the Erroneous Presuppositions above:

Sanctification is *not a part, ground, cause, basis, or component* of justification. Sanctification is always the *fruit*.

There is *only one condition or ground or basis* on which God *justifies* believers which we must meet, and that *one basis* is Christ's atoning work for sinners. All that takes place *in believers* is *the result, fruit and evidence* of justification by faith.

MRS. WHITE SAYS: "NO CONDITIONS!"

"But you cannot enjoy His blessing without any action on your part. Salvation is a gift offered to you free; *ON NO OTHER CONDITION can you obtain it, than as A FREE GIFT."* RH 8-25-91

"The Lord specifies *NO CONDITIONS* except that you hunger for His mercy, desire His counsel, and long for His love. 'Ask.' The asking, makes it manifest that you realize your necessity; and if you ask **in faith** you will receive." MB 130

"The question will come up, How is it? Is it by *CONDITIONS* that we receive salvation*?—NEVER BY CONDITIONS* that we come to Christ. And if we come to Christ, then what is **the condition?** THE CONDITION is that by living **faith** we lay hold wholly and entirely upon the merits of the blood of a crucified and risen Saviour." MR Vol. 6 p. 32

CONCLUSION

Dear Reader,

Can we not see that the one and only CONDITION (BASIS) on which God justifies , forgives, and saves believers is Christ's atoning work for sinners which we receive solely BY MEANS OF FAITH in Jesus?

ISSUE ELEVEN:
STANDING AND STATE

Does God justify *SINNERS?* Or does He justify only those He has *made* righteous?

Does God's gift of Justification—God's Gift of Christ's *imputed* righteousness—give us *a righteous legal STANDING* before Him and His law in the judgment in our *sinful moral STATE?*

Or does God's gift of Justification *change* our *STATE* (inner sinful moral nature) from being *sinful* to being *righteous?*

Is our sinful nature ever really *DEAD* during this life on earth? Or, is it only *SUBDUED* through watchfulness and a personal devotional life?

WHEN will our sinful nature be *REMOVED* from us forever?
WHEN will we be perfectly righteous in nature, character and life?

Erroneous Presuppositions

God's gift of the *imputed* righteousness of Christ *makes* us inwardly righteous, pleasing and acceptable to God.

Having *made* us inwardly righteous, pleasing and acceptable to Himself by *infusing* Christ's righteousness into us, God then justifies us, forgives us, and *accepts us unto eternal life.*

God cannot, will not, justify, forgive, and accept us until He has *made* us inwardly righteous.
God cannot forgive, accept, justify or treat anyone as righteous who is not actually righteous. That would be A LIE, and God will not lie!

1. Page 12.10: "Having *MADE* us [*inwardly morally*] righteous through the *IMPUTED* righteousness, God pronounces us just [*inwardly righteous*] and treats us as just [*inwardly righteous*]."

2. Page 13.2: "Having *MADE* us [*inwardly*] righteous through the *IMPUTED* righteousness of Christ."

3. Page 15.7: God "has brought His people to the *STATE* where they will reflect His glory perfectly."

4. Page 19, entire page including boxes [19.4] and 19.10 teaches that Christ's IMPUTED righteousness MAKES us inwardly morally righteous and DEAD to sin! (page 21.2). See also page 23 of the 48 page critique.

Comments by The Author

Notes one, two and three above are a misuse of the word IMPUTE!

Erroneous Presuppositions Concluded

5. Page 24.2: "To be *pardoned* [*justified*] in the way that Christ *pardons* [justifies] is *not* only to be *forgiven* [justified], but to be *renewed* in the spirit of our mind. The Lord says, '*A NEW HEART* will I give unto thee.' "

6. Page 24.6: "God's *forgiveness* [*justification*] is *not* merely a *judicial* act by which He sets us free from condemnation…It…is the outflow of redeeming love that *transforms the heart*."

7. Page 40.2: "…Christ who was hanged upon the cross that He might be able to **IMPART** His righteousness to fallen, sinful man and thus present men to His Father IN HIS [PERFECTLY] righteous character!

(1 SM 341.2).

(Emphasis mine)

Comments by The Author

- Romans 4:5: God "justifieth the ungodly [sinners]."
- Romans 5:6: "Christ died for the ungodly [sinners]."

My Jesus, I Love Thee
"I love Thee because
Thou hast first loved me,
AND PURCHASED MY PARDON
ON CALVARY'S TREE;

I love Thee for wearing
The thorns on Thy Brow
If ever I loved Thee,
My Jesus, tis now."
William Ralf Featherstone
Church Hymnal, page 321

•

Many hymns and gospel songs, like the above, teach that God expiated all our sins when Jesus died on the cross, which **provided** forgiveness for everyone in the world. (See old Church Hymnal, page 123.)

All that remains is for us to *respond* to God's wonderful love and accept His gift of *justification*—forgiveness, Christ's righteousness imputed to us, acceptance unto adoption, eternal life, and treatment of us during this life *AS IF* we had never sinned.

The Bible Teaches That:

We must *distinguish* between our *righteous legal standing* before God and our *sinful state* (inner moral *condition, sinful nature and character.)*

> God's gift of justification gives us a righteous legal *STANDING* before *Him* and His infinitely righteous law in the judgment in our sinful moral *STATE (SINFUL NATURE).*

Although our inner moral *state* before God is *sinful*, He *credits* Christ's perfectly obedient life, death and resurrection to believers and *accepts and treats them as if* **they were actually righteous!**

That is to say: although we (Christians) *continue to have the sinful moral nature*, although we all have *sinned* times without number, and, although the best Christians in the world *CONTINUE to come short* of perfectly obeying and satisfying God's infinitely righteous law, (Romans 3: 23—Greek), God *credits* Christ's perfect life, death and resurrection to us and *accepts* us unto eternal life!

The *new heart, mind, will*, which we receive when we are *converted* is *not yet 100% new or perfect*. It is *a partially* converted heart, will, mind.

Conversion, sanctification, is the transforming work of the Holy Spirit *throughout* the entire life of the Christian!

The *imparted* righteousness of conversion and sanctification do *not* make us *100%* righteous in nature or character during this life!

Our physical, mental, and spiritual transformation and restoration are not complete until glorification.

May God haste that glad day!

Page 27.4: Our *"FITNESS"* for heaven *is never perfect or 100%* during this life.

It is Christ's *imputed* righteousness alone that *"qualifies"* us for heaven. Our *"qualification"* for heaven is *never* in us; it is always, *only in Christ in heaven!*

Christ's IMPARTED righteousness never makes a person perfectly righteous within—as righteous as Adam and Eve were before they sinned or as righteous as Jesus was in the flesh when He was on earth!

This Is A Marvelous Truth!
Let us repeat it and glory in it.

Although our *STATE*—inner moral condition—is still *sinful*, God's gift of Christ's perfectly obedient life which He *CREDITS* to us in His gift of *justification*, gives us an absolutely sinless (Righteous) *STANDING* before Him and His infinitely righteous law in the Judgment!

That is to say:

although we all *retain* the *sinful* moral nature for as long as we live or until glorification,

although we all have *sinned* times without number,

and although we all *continue* to come *SHORT* of perfectly obeying God,

He *credits* Christ's perfectly righteous life, death, and resurrection to us, which gives us a righteous legal *STANDING* before Him in our sinful moral *STATE (CONDITION)*—

We *STAND* before God *AS IF* we had never sinned—*AS IF* we were as righteous as Jesus was in human flesh when He was on earth.

"We are not to be anxious about what God and Christ think of us, but about what God thinks of CHRIST OUR SUBSTITUTE. 'Ye are complete IN THE BELOVED.'"
2SM 32, 33.

Nine Very Important
Bible Truths About Righteousness

If every professing Christian in the world UNDERSTOOD the answers to these seven questions:

- The Christian world would experience **a second Pentecost!**
- The world would quickly be **enlightened** by the angels of Revelation 14:6-12 and 18:1–4!
- The gospel would soon be carried to **everyone** in the world!
- Jesus would **soon return** in His glorious, triumphant **Second Coming!** (Matt. 24:14).

QUESTION 1

HOW MANY Different **ASPECTS** of Righteousness Are There?

ANSWER

There Are **TWO** Different Aspects of Righteousness.

QUESTION 2

WHAT ARE the Two Different Aspects of Righteousness?

ANSWER

The TWO Different Aspects of Righteousness Are:

- **CHRIST'S** righteousness which consists of His **incarnation**, sinless **life**, substitutionary, reconciling **death** on the cross, and His **resurrection** from the dead.
- **THE HOLY SPIRIT'S** converting, sanctifying, empowering and transforming presence in believers.

●

- The righteousness of **JUSTIFICATION BY FAITH (Righteousness by Faith)** which God **IMPUTES (CREDITS)** to us in His gift of **justification**.
- "The righteousness of **THE LAW**" which is the Christian's obedience and godly life which are enabled by the **IMPARTED** righteousness of the Holy Spirit and of sanctification.

QUESTION 3

WHERE ARE the Two Different Aspects of Righteousness?

ANSWER

- The righteousness of **JUSTIFICATION BY FAITH** (Righteousness by Faith) **is never in us on earth**. It is not even the righteousness of Christ or the Holy Spirit **IN US**! It is always only **in Christ in heaven**! We must look **away from** our sinful selves, **to Christ alone** for **THAT RIGHTEOUSNESS** which **justifies and saves us.** (The righteousness of **sanctification** makes us righteous only in a **relative** sense).

- The righteousness of **THE LAW**, the righteousness which is the result of the **imparted** righteousness of the Holy Spirit and of **sanctification**, the obedience and good works and godly lives of Christians is, of course, **IN THEM.** This righteousness makes us righteous only in a **relative** sense, never in an absolute sense.

QUESTION 4

WHAT DOES Each of These Two Different aspects of Righteousness **ACCOMPLISH** for Christians?

ANSWER

- **The righteousness of "RIGHTEOUSNESS BY FAITH" (Justification by Faith) is CHRIST'S righteousness (Christ's doing and dying and resurrection) which :**
  1. **atoned** for our sins 2000 years ago.
  2. **expiated** our sins.
  3. **reconciled** us to God in a **legal** sense, 2000 years ago.
  4. **is the BASIS** on which God justifies, forgives, accepts, and saves us into eternal life.
  5. **gives us** a righteous legal **STANDING** before God in our sinful moral **STATE.**
  6. **God credits** to our account in heaven and which gives us the righteousness we need for **entrance** into heaven and into God's hallowed presence.
  7. **perfectly satisfies** and fulfills God's infinitely righteous law for us.
  8. **get us through** the Investigative Judgment.
  9. **justifies God** in justifying and forgiving sinners.
  10. **secures for us** all of God's gifts of justification, which are all the above plus His gifts of **adoption, eternal life, and heaven**.
  11. **gives us the assurance** and the **joy** of salvation, **hope** for the future, and the **peace** of mind which passes all understanding.
  12. **vindicates God** and enables Him **to win** the Great controversy between Christ and Satan and to **secure** the universe against a second uprising of sin.

- **The righteousness of "THE LAW" (of the Holy Spirit and of sanctification), which is the Christian's obedience, good works, and godly life of faith and love accomplishes all the following for us:**
  1. helps us to remain **faithful** to God.
  2. helps us to **resist** temptations to sin.
  3. helps us to **grow** in grace and to **develop** Christian character.
  4. is the **validating evidence** to us, to all who know us, and to God, that our faith, repentance, conversion, sanctification, and Christian experience are **genuine**.
  5. helps us **to become more and more like Jesus in character**—more and more like what God **accounts** us in justification.
  6. helps us to **rightly represent** the character of Christ (God) to others.
  7. helps us to **win souls** to Christ, to **build up** the kingdom of God, and to **hasten** the Second Coming of Christ.
  8. helps us to **vindicate** the character of God, to **prove** Satan a liar, and to **defeat** Satan.
  9. helps God to **win** the Great Controversy between Christ and Satan.
  10. helps God to **secure** the universe against a second rebellion.
  11. makes us **easier** and more pleasant to live with.
  12. makes for a much **happier** and more **successful** Christian life on earth.

QUESTION 5

HOW Does Each of These Two Different Aspects of Righteousness
BECOME OURS PERSONALLY?

ANSWER

- The righteousness of Righteousness by Faith (Justification by Faith) becomes ours personally **solely by faith, apart from works**.

- The righteousness of **The Law**—the righteousness of our sanctification, obedience, and of our Christian character—becomes ours and is developed in us by the Holy Spirit and **by our faith AND OUR COOPERATION with God (obedience, good works, and godly lives)**. **God NEEDS our knowledge, consent and cooperation** in our sanctification and growth in grace

QUESTION 6

WHY Is it IMPORTANT for us to **Understand** the Answers to These Five Questions Above?

ANSWER

It is important for us to understand the answers to these questions because those who do not understand the answers to these questions **are in danger of being deceived by the false** system of salvation by which perhaps 95 percent of the people of the world are deceived. As the result they may be **eternally lost** unless they come to this knowledge! (Those who rely on **their** obedience, sacrifices and good works are in danger of being **lost forever!**)

QUESTION 7

HOW Does This Righteousness which Saves Become **OURS** Personally and Savingly?
What Then Must **I DO** to Be Saved?

ANSWER

- "BELIEVE on the Lord Jesus Christ, and thou shalt be saved." Acts 16:31.
- "For by GRACE are ye saved, **through faith**; and that not of yourselves: it is the **gift** of God: **Not of works**, lest any man should boast." Eph. 2:8, 9.
- plus 68 New Testament texts. See pages 78 to 82.

**"If you are RIGHT with God today,
you are READY if Christ should come today."**
1HP 227

QUESTION 8

Again, is This Righteousness Which Justifies and Saves Us **Ever INSIDE of Us?**

ANSWER

NO!

- The righteousness which **justifies and saves us**,
- the righteousness which **perfectly satisfies** God's infinitely righteous law for us,
- the righteousness which **atones** for our sins,
- the righteousness which **gets us through** the Judgment,
- the righteousness which **brings to us** all of God's gifts of adoption, eternal life, immortality, and heaven, **IS NEVER IN US on earth. It is always IN CHRIST IN HEAVEN!**

QUESTION 9

Does the Righteousness Which **Justifies** and Saves us **MAKE** us
Perfectly Righteous in Nature, Character, or Outward Life?

ANSWER

NO! **The righteousness which justifies and saves us does NOT MAKE us inwardly righteous.**

- "There is **NONE** righteous, **NO NOT ONE**." Rom. 3:10.
- "ALL have sinned, and **ALL CONTINUE to come SHORT (Greek) [of perfect obedience]**." Rom. 3:23.
- "If we say that we have **NO SIN**, we deceive ourselves, and the truth is not in us." 1 John 1:8.
- In God's eyes, apart from Jesus, **"NO MAN LIVING IS RIGHTEOUS."** Ps. 143:2 (NASB).
- **Insofar as there being any JUSTIFYING MERIT in our obedience and good works, all our righteousness are as "filthy rags" to God!** "All our [Christians] righteousness are **AS FILTHY RAGS** [to God]." Isa. 64:6.
- "There is **NOT** a just [righteous, sinless] man upon earth that doeth good [and only good all the time] and **sinneth not**." Eccl. 7:20.

I Will Sing of My Redeemer

"I will sing of my Redeemer,
    And His wondrous love to me,
On the Cruel Cross He suffered
    From the curse to set me free.

"I will sing of my Redeemer,
    And His heavenly love to me;
He from death to life hath brought me,
    Son of God, With Him to be."

"I will tell the wondrous story,
    How my lost estate to save,
In His boundless love and mercy,
    He the ransom freely gave.

Chorus:
"Sing, Oh sing of my Redeemer,
    With His blood He purchased me;
On the cross He sealed my pardon,
    Paid the debt and made me free,
    [from the condemnation of sin]."

Philip P. Bliss,
SDA Church Hymnal, p. 343

Dear Reader, in this and the two preceding chapters, we have considered: 1. the BASIS, 2. the MEANS, 3. and the FRUIT of Justification. We now visualize on a chart these three aspects of Justification by Faith—Righteousness by Faith.

THE BASIS, MEANS AND FRUIT OF JUSTIFICATION

1	2	3
BASIS	MEANS	FRUIT
CHRIST'S RIGHTEOUSNESS AND ATONING WORK for sinners	FAITH in Christ's righteousness and atoning work for sinners	The Christian's OBEDIENCE and GOOD WORKS of faith and love
This righteousness is INFINITELY MERITORIOUS, PERFECT, COMPLETE, AND FINISHED	NO JUSTIFYING MERIT WHATSOEVER in this, CONTINUALLY GROWING AND STRENGTHENING	NO JUSTIFYING MERIT WHATSOEVER in this, NEVER PERFECT— Continually Increasing
We are SAVED to the uttermost by this imputed (reckoned, credited) righteousness	We APPROPRIATE Christ's imputed Righteousness SOLELY BY FAITH	We are NOT saved BY this, but neither are we saved WITHOUT this
This is NEVER IN US.	This (FAITH) IS IN US	This too IS IN US

Let Us Now Consider

The TWO Different Aspects of RIGHTEOUSNESS

1		2	
The RIGHTOUSNESS of "RIGHTEOUSNESS BY FAITH", "JUSTIFICATION BY FAITH" The righteousness of Jesus.		The RIGHTEOUSNESS of "THE LAW" The Rightousness of the Holy Spirit and of our Obedience and Good Works of Faith and Love.	
1. Rom. 3:22	12. Jas. 2:23	1. Rom. 2:26	12. Rom. 10:4
2. Rom. 4:11	13. Acts 13:38,39	2. Rom. 3:20	13. Rom. 10:5
3. Rom. 4:13	14. Rom. 3:20-31	3. Rom. 3:21	14. Gal. 2:16
4. Rom. 9:30	15. Rom. 4:6-9,11,13	4. Rom. 3:27	15. Gal. 2:21
5. Rom. 10:6	16. Rom. 5:16-18	5. Rom. 3:28	16. Gal. 3:5
6. Gal. 5:5	17. Rom. 9:30-33	6. Rom. 4:5	17. Gal. 3:10
7. Phil. 3:9	18. Rom. 10:4-6;9-13	7. Rom. 4:6	18. Gal. 3:11
8. Heb. 11:7	19. 2 Cor. 5:19-21	8. Rom. 4:13,14	19. Gal. 5:4
9. Gen. 15:6	20. Gal. 2:16,21	9. Rom. 8:4	20. Eph. 2:9
10. Rom. 4:3	21. Gal. 3:6-11;11-24	10. Rom. 9:30	21. Eph. 3:6
11. Gal. 3:6	22. Gal. 5:4,14	11. Rom. 9:32	22. Phil. 3:9
This is the IMPUTED RIGHTEOUSNESS of Justification/Righteousness by Faith		This is the IMPARTED RIGHTEOUSNESS of Sanctification	

(See page 36-38)
1SM 353, 354

"We can do nothing, absolutely nothing to commend ourselves to divine favor."

TWO DIFFERENT ASPECTS OF RIGHTEOUSNESS
Explained Clearly, Simply, Biblically

- **There is the perfect, absolute, infinite MORAL (ETHICAL) righteousness of GOD (Christ) which is *IMPARTED* to and developed in Christians in a relative sense in sanctification.**

- And there is the perfect, absolute, infinite MORAL (ETHICAL) righteousness of God (CHRIST) which is **CREDITED** to sinners' account in heaven in Justification.

AN HONEST CONFESSION

For the first 25 years of my ministry as a pastor–evangelist of the Seventh–day Adventist Church, I did not really understand this most important subject. Like most Seventh–day Adventists of that day and of today, I could not give a clear, decisive, Biblical explanation of these two different aspects of righteousness. I could not have told you that Righteousness by Faith and Justification by Faith **are exactly the same thing! (I paid a terrible price for believing that Righteousness by Faith is MY right-doing by Faith!)**

Like Most Seventh-day Adventists Then and Today, I Believed the Following four ERRORS:

1. At conversion, and more and more throughout life, God **imparts to us** and **develops in us** Christ's righteousness by which He converts us and sanctifies us and **MAKES** us more and more righteous within and that **this is the righteousness of Righteousness by Faith.**

2. The righteousness of Righteousness by Faith includes **sanctification**. Righteousness by Faith is **our obedience** by faith, **our right doing** by faith, **our becoming inwardly righteous** by faith. (This too is a very serious error!)

3. The way we become **acceptable** to God and are saved at last is for us to be **converted**, to have Christ's righteousness **IN US,** and for us to become **perfectly righteous within.** (This is good **JESUIT** and rightwing "certain Independent SDA ministry" theology!)

4. We **HAVE to become perfectly righteous** in character and life in order to be saved when Jesus returns.

   Most Seventh–day Adventists still believe these four errors. How tragic! (This too is contrary to the Bible. The best Christians on earth still come **SHORT** of perfectly fulfilling God's infinitely righteous law.

(No Christian is perfectly righteous within. We all continue to have **sinful natures**, and we all continue to come **SHORT of perfect, continuous, unbroken obedience** to God's infinitely righteous law all the time.)

TWO DIFFERENT ASPECTS OF RIGHTEOUSNESS
Explained Clearly, Simply, Biblically

THE TWO DIFFERENT ASPECTS OF RIGHTEOUSNESS

The Righteousness of SANTIFICATION	The Righteousness of JUSTIFICATION
WHAT It Is	WHAT It Is
WHERE It Is	WHERE It Is
Its PURPOSES	Its PURPOSES
Its ACCOMPLISHMENTS	Its ACCOMPLISHMENTS

THE TWO DIFFERENT ASPECTS OF RIGHTEOUSNESS

God's INNATE MORAL (ETHICAL) RIGHTEOUSNESS	THE CHRISTIAN'S LEGAL, JUDICIAL, FORENSIC RIGHTEOUSNESS
1. **CHRIST'S** perfectly righteous moral (ethical) nature, character **which is imparted and developed IN US by the Holy Spirit in SANCTIFICATION.** 2. **CHRISTIANS,** by the grace of God, through faith in Jesus, and by repentance, conversion, sanctification, and growing in grace become **MORALLY (ETHICALLY) RIGHTEOUS ONLY IN A RELATIVE SENSE—NEVER, during this life on earth, in an ABSOLUTE sense.**	THE CHRISTIAN'S TITLE TO HEAVEN—CHRIST'S DOING AND DYING WHICH IS IMPUTED (CREDITED) TO OUR ACCOUNT IN GOD'S GIFT OF JUSTIFICATION. 1. **CHRIST'S** perfect righteousness, which is the meritorious **BASIS** of our justification, is put to our account in heaven and we are accepted and treated by God **AS IF** we were righteous. 2. **CHRIST'S IMPUTED (CREDITED)** righteousness is the righteousness of **Justification by Faith (Righteousness by Faith).** 3. **CHRIST'S imputed** righteousness which **justifies** and saves us **IS NEVER INSIDE of us. It is always only in Christ in Heaven.** 4. **This imputed (credited)** righteousness of Christ **NEVER MAKES** us inwardly righteous; it simply accounts us righteous. It gives us a righteous legal **STANDING** before God's infinitely righteous law in our sinful moral **STATE.** 5. It is **THIS** righteousness—**CHRIST'S** doing and dying—the righteousness of Justification by Faith (Righteousness by Faith) which perfectly **fulfilled** God's infinitely righteous law for us, **atoned** for our sins, **gets us through** the Investigative Judgment, **secures for us** God's gifts of forgiveness, Christ's imputed righteousness, adoption, eternal life, and heaven and **puts** us in a right relationship with God.

There are TEN TRUTHS we need to understand about JUSTIFICATION BY FAITH (RIGHTEOUSNESS BY FAITH):

1. Justification by Faith and Righteousness by Faith **are exactly the same thing.**
2. The righteousness of Justification by Faith is **NOT** the righteousness of the Holy Spirit; it is **Christ's** righteousness!
3. Justification by Faith (Righteousness by Faith) is a **relational** term. It is not a creating, converting, sanctifying, transforming act of God in believers!
4. The **righteousness** of Justification by Faith (Righteousness by Faith) **IS NOT IN US.** The righteousness of Justification by Faith and of Righteousness by Faith **is always in Jesus in heaven.**
5. The **righteousness** of Justification by Faith (Righteousness by Faith) does **NOT MAKE us actually, personally, inwardly, morally righteous.**

TEN TRUTHS ABOUT JUSTIFICATION BY FAITH – RIGHTEOUSNESS BY FAITH (Continued)	THE CHRISTIAN'S LEGAL, JUDICIAL, FORENSIC RIGHTEOUSNESS (Continued)

6. In Justification by Faith (Righteousness by Faith), God forgives all our sins, **CREDITS** Christ's righteousness to us, **accounts** us righteous, and **treats** us, during this life on earth, **AS IF** we were perfectly righteous.

7. The righteousness of Justification by Faith (Righteousness by Faith) gives believers **a righteousness legal STANDING** before God in our **sinful moral STATE (NATURE).**

8. **The one and only MERITORIOUS BASIS** of Justification by Faith (Righteousness by Faith) is **CHRIST'S atoning work** for sinners 2000 years ago.

9. **The one and only INSTRUMENTAL MEANS** by which we appropriate God's gift of Christ's righteousness to ourselves personally is **FAITH. Faith is belief, plus trust, plus resting in Christ's completed atoning work for us 2000 years ago.**

10. **The inevitable FRUIT** of Justification by Faith is repentance, conversion, sanctification, obedience, good works, a godly life, and growing in grace.

The same **FAITH** that justifies us personally also, always, at the same time, converts and sanctifies us. God justifies no one whom he does not also, at the same time sanctify. But sanctification is not the **basis** of justification.

Justification and sanctification are **distinct, but never separate**. He who is not sanctified is not justified! The righteousness of Justification by Faith **never** makes us **perfectly** righteous within. It only **accounts** us righteous! Sanctification always accompanies justification by faith. The righteousness of sanctification makes us relatively righteous – never absolutely righteous.

---

6. **CHRIST'S IMPUTED** righteousness alone is our **key, ticket, title, and passport to heaven and our assurance of salvation!**

7. Christians simply **BELIEVE, TRUST, AND REST IN Christ's imputed** righteousness solely by faith, apart from their obedience and good works. Rom. 3:28.

8. The Christian's obedience **is never so perfect** that it no longer comes **SHORT** of perfectly satisfying God's infinitely righteous law.

- **MRS. WHITE SAYS: "NO ONE IS PERFECT BUT JESUS."** TIMK 136.
- "The **ONLY** righteousness I have is **IN CHRIST** [in heaven]." 1SM 392.
- "The **ONLY** way we become [perfectly] righteous is by the **IMPUTED [CREDITED]** righteousness of Christ." YI Aug. 10, 1893; RH Sept 3, 1901. (We become *relatively* righteous by sanctification).
- "In ourselves we are **sinners [sinful]**; but in Christ we are **righteous**." 1SM 394.

Mrs. White declares that Christians will **NOT** be perfectly righteous until the **Second Coming of Christ**. Christ will then **remove** our sinful natures from us and fill us with the **fullness** of the Holy Spirit. **Then**, and not until then, will we be as **righteous** as Adam and Eve were before they sinned and our **obedience** be of the same **quality** as theirs was before they sinned. (See pages 98, 102–104).

We Seventh-Day Adventist Christians need to **MASTER these ten important truths and FIX** them in our minds forever! The righteousness which justifies and saves **IS NOT IN US and it DOES NOT MAKE US inwardly righteous!** The righteousness which justifies and saves us—the righteousness of Justification by Faith and of Righteousness by Faith—is in the **OBJECT** of our faith—**solely in CHRIST** in heaven! **Praise God! O how wonderful, how thrilling, is the good news of the gospel!**

STANDING AND STATE
●
OUR PROBLEM
●
GOD'S SOLUTION

The superabundance of Biblical and EGW evidence presented in this **REPLY** declares unequivocally that: it is **NOT** the **IMPARTED** righteousness of **SANCTIFICATION** that gives believers **a righteous legal STANDING** before God and His infinitely righteous law in the Judgment in their *sinful moral STATE*, but that it is instead the **IMPUTED** righteousness of **JUSTIFICATION**!

FOR THIS TRUTH WE WILL DIE!

OUR PROBLEM

- **SINCE** all human beings **are born APART FROM GOD and APART FROM RIGHTEOUSNESS,**
- **SINCE** all human beings have **SINNED** innumerable times, and
- **SINCE** all human beings, during this life on earth, **continue to come SHORT** of perfectly fulfilling God's infinitely righteous law (Romans 3:23–Greek), we need a righteousness **outside, above and beyond** ourselves to secure for us God's acceptance of us unto eternal life!

GOD'S SOLUTION

And that righteousness, God Himself has already provided for us in His Son, Jesus Christ, as a free gift!

Christ's perfect, transcendent, infinite righteousness which God credits to us in His gift of justification consists of four, mighty, historic, unrepeatable, cosmic acts in Jesus Christ of Nazareth—in His:

- **Incarnation,**
- **Absolutely sinless life,**
- **Substitutionary, atoning death, and**
- **Resurrection from the dead!**

Wonder, O, Heavens! And be astonished, O, earth! God Himself hanging on a tree! Apparently cursed both by earth and by heaven, suffering in the sinner's place the penalty, the results, the natural, inevitable consequences of our sins so we will not have to suffer them ourselves, but **GO FREE AND LIVE FOREVER!**

Christ's incredible incarnation, sinless life, substitutionary, reconciling death and resurrection from the dead **JUSTIFY** God in **JUSTIFYING** sinners! Since we sinful human beings have no inherent righteousness of our own, and never will have, God provides it for us in Jesus, unearned, unmerited, undeserved!

Thus, God's gift and imputation of Christ's righteousness to us in Justification gives us a righteous legal *STANDING* before Him in our sinful moral *STATE*!

WHAT A GIFT! WHAT A DELIVERANCE! WHAT A GREAT AND WONDERFUL GOD WE SERVE!

SUCH LOVE, SUCH SACRIFICE, SUCH SUFFERING DEMANDS OUR HEARTS, OUR WILLS, OUR DEVOTION, OUR LIVES, AND OUR ALL!

Consequently, we must look **away from ourselves–beyond, outside of and above ourselves**–for that perfect righteousness which perfectly **fulfills** and satisfies God's infinitely righteous law for us, which **atones** for our sins, which **gets us through** the Judgment, which **secures** God's forgiveness of all our sins, and which **secures** God's acceptance of us unto eternal life!

That is the only righteousness in God's vast universe which is good enough, great enough and efficacious enough to justify us during this life on earth and to save us eternally in the world to come!

THERE IS NO OTHER!

**IF WE INSIST ON TRUSTING IN CHRIST'S RIGHTEOUSNESS
IN OURSELVES TO SAVE US, WE WILL PERISH FOREVER!**

"There is LIFE in a LOOK at the Crucified One;

"There is LIFE at this moment for thee;

"Then, LOOK, friend, LOOK unto HIM and be saved;

Unto Him Who was nailed to the tree."

"**LOOK UPON JESUS, SINLESS is He;**
        Father **IMPUTE** His life unto me.
My life of scarlet, my sin and woe,
        COVER with His life, whiter than snow.

"Reconciled by His death for my sin,
        JUSTIFIED by His life pure and clean,
Sanctified by obeying His word,
        Glorified when returneth my Lord.

"**COVER** with His life, whiter than snow;
        Fullness of His life then shall I know;
My life of scarlet, my sin and woe,
        COVER with His life, whiter than snow."

F. E. Belden, Church Hymnal, page 412.

111

ISSUE TWELVE:
SANCTIFICATION

What is sanctification? Are justification and sanctification essentially the *same thing?*

That is to say, is sanctification *a part of* justification?

Is sanctification a part of the BASIS on which God justifies believers?

Or is sanctification the FRUIT of justification?

When God justifies believers, does He, *IN THAT ACT, also sanctify them?*

Are justification and sanctification DISTINCT BUT NEVER SEPARATE?

**Does sanctification *MAKE* believers *perfectly righteous within*—
in nature or character or life during this life?**

IS THERE ANY *JUSTIFYING MERIT* IN ANY OF THE FOLLOWING?

- **Faith in Jesus—in the faith that works by love and that purifies the soul.**
- **Repentance,**
- **Conversion,**
- **Sanctification,**
- **Obedience by faith and love,**
- **Our living a godly life by faith,**
- **Our growing in grace by faith,**
- **Our perfecting Christian character by faith,**
- **Sacrificing our lives for God (in God's cause) by faith,**
- **"Christ in you [us, me] the hope of glory"?**

The answer to the questions above is **a resounding NO!**

Erroneous Presuppositions

- Page 3.2: "The genius of Wesley was...*an integration of justification and sanctification* within [**inside**] the Christian life."

Sanctification *is a part of justification.*

Sanctification is a part of the ***basis*** on which God Justifies believers.

Sanctification is a part of God's ***act*** of justifying believers.

Sanctification and justification ***are never separate or distinct*** from each other.

We are justified by first being ***sanctified.***

By His ***imparted (infused)*** righteousness of ***sanctification***, God purposes to make us perfectly—100%—righteous in heart, will, mind, character and life during this life on earth.

God **sanctifies** us in order to **justify** us.

112

God justifies those *only* whom He has *converted and sanctified and made* inwardly righteous by the indwelling Holy Spirit.

Our justification is *based* on our sanctification.

There is no justification until we are sanctified.

Comments by The Author

The above is the same as saying that Christ's sinless life, substitutionary death and resurrection are *not enough to justify us.*

Something *more* must be added to justify God in justifying sinners.

It is extremely important for Seventh-day Adventist Christians to distinguish between two things:
- The *ATONING* work of the *SECOND* member of the Godhead *OUTSIDE* of us 2000 years ago, which is the *BASIS* on which God *justifies* us, and
- the *CONVERTING* work of the *THIRD* member of the Godhead *INSIDE* of us now by which God sanctifies us which is the *FRUIT, RESULT*, and *EVIDENCE* that our faith is genuine.

Recently, I asked an 85 year old lady who had been an SDA all her life, WHY God should forgive her and take her to heaven. She replied, "Because *I'M safe to save*; *God can trust me in heaven*."

Also I asked another SDA over 80 the same question recently, and she said, "Because I *LOVE* Jesus."

Others have answered:
- "Because *I BELIEVE* in Jesus."
- "Because *I* have *REPENTED* of my sins."
- "Because *I* have been *CONVERTED*."
- "Because *I* have been *BAPTIZED AND JOINED* the Church."
- "Because *I am A CHRISTIAN* and *KEEP* God's commandments."

The moment they answered, "Because *I*..." I knew that they did not understand the gospel.

They should have answered, "Because JESUS died for me in my place . . ."

It is *Jesus'* righteousness *OUTSIDE* of us that justifies us, *not* His righteousness *INSIDE* of us!

The Bible Teaches That:

Sanctification is *not* a part of justification.

Sanctification is *not* a part of the *basis* of justification. Sanctification is the *fruit (result)* of justification.

God's *act* of *justifying* believers *does not include* His act of *sanctifying* them.

Justification and sanctification *are distinct (different), but never separate.*

113

We must *never fuse* justification and sanctification into one and the same thing!

Like forgiveness which it includes, *justification* is always *outside of us*.
Sanctification is always *inside* of us.

The same faith that justifies us also, always, at the same time, sanctifies us.

God **justifies** us in order to **sanctify** us.

Sanctification is an extremely important doctrine, absolutely indispensable, for our Christian experience to be a genuine, successful, growing one.

Sanctification never, during this life, makes anyone perfectly—100%—righteous within.

We are not justified by being sanctified.

Christ's doing and dying is the *root* of justification.

Conversion, sanctification, obedience, good works; and a godly life are the *fruit of justification*.

(God justifies us *apart from our sanctification*.)

God's *act* of *justifying* us *does not make* us inwardly righteous; it *credits* Christ's righteousness to us, *accounts* us righteous and *treats* us *as if* we were actually righteous within.

God's *act* of justifying us gives us a righteous legal *standing* before Him in the judgment in our sinful moral *state*.

That is, although we remain *sinful* moral human beings:
- Who have *sinned*,
- Who continue to have a sinful moral nature,
- Who continue to come short of perfectly fulfilling God's infinitely righteous law,

God *imputes (credits)* Christ's perfectly righteous life, death and resurrection to us—to those who continue to exercise true faith in Jesus—and treats us *AS IF* we were already perfectly righteous within.

And God can *SAFELY* credit Christ's perfectly righteous life to us because Christ atoned for our sins and justified us, and because we truly believe in Jesus and desire and purpose, by His grace, to live a perfectly righteous life.

So, while we are growing up into Christ and *overcoming our besetting sins*, and perfecting Christian character, *forgiveness (justification) is always available to us!*

The same faith that justifies also always at the same time sanctifies.

If we are not *sanctified*, we are not *justified*.

Justification is outside of us and sanctification is inside of us. The same is true with forgiveness. Forgiveness is outside of us.

The Righteousness
of
"JUSTIFICATION BY FAITH"
and of
"SANCTIFICATION BY FAITH"

There are TWO views in the Seventh-day Adventist Church concerning the WHAT and the WHERE of the RIGHTEOUSNESS of "Justification by Faith" and of "Sanctification by Faith" and what each ACCOMPLISHES for us.

The ERRONEOUS view includes some elements of BOTH the TRUE view (left column below) and the FALSE view (right column). Satan's doctrine is a MIXTURE of truth and error—a "knowledge of both good and evil."

The Righteousness of "Justification by Faith"
and
The Righteousness of "Sanctification by Faith"
The Righteousness of "Righteousness by Faith"

	THE TRUE BIBLICAL VIEW:	THE FALSE JESUIT VIEW:
1	**The righteousness of "Justification by Faith" and of "Righteousness by Faith" is restricted to CHRIST'S** infinitely righteous life, death, and resurrection. There is no justifying merit in the Christian's faith, repentance, conversion, obedience, good works or godly life.	Justification by Faith is **NOT** restricted to Christ's doing and dying, but **also includes the CHRISTIAN'S** conversion, sanctification, obedience, good works, and righteous life. In order for us to be **justified**, we must **first be converted, sanctified, and MADE inwardly righteous**.
2	**Righteousness by Faith IS restricted to Christ's IMPUTED** righteousness which God **CREDITS** to our account in heaven in His gift of **justification**.	**Righteousness by Faith** is **NOT** restricted to Christ's **imputed** righteousness, but **also includes** the righteousness which God **IMPARTS to us and DEVELOPS in us in sanctification.**
3	**The righteousness of Righteousness by Faith IS NEVER IN Christians** on earth, but is **always objective** to Christians—**always outside** of Christians—**always** only **in Christ** in heaven.	**The righteousness of Righteousness by Faith IS NOT only IN Christ** in heaven, but is also **subjective—IN Christians** on earth. We **have** to become inwardly righteous **before** God will accept and **treat** us as righteous.
4	**Righteousness by Faith** does **NOT MAKE** Christians morally righteous within; but **accounts** them as righteous and **treats** them, during this life on earth, **AS IF** they were perfectly righteous. God forgives and accepts us not because of **OUR** doing and trying, but because of **JESUS'** doing and dying.	**The Righteousness of Righteousness by Faith DOES MAKE** Christians morally righteous within. We must have **perfect** characters in order to **pass** the Judgment and to **live** without an Intercessor after Probation closes. God forgives and accepts us **BECAUSE He has MADE us** inwardly righteous.

The Righteousness of "Justification by Faith" and The Righteousness of "Sanctification by Faith"

	The Righteousness of "Righteousness by Faith"	The Righteousness of "Righteousness by Faith"
	THE TRUE BIBLICAL VIEW:	**THE FALSE JESUIT VIEW:**
5	**Righteousness by Faith** does **NOT include** the Christian's best obedience, living a godly life, or becoming inwardly righteous. These are the **FRUIT** of Justification by Faith. Christians always come short. . .	**Righteousness by Faith DOES include** the Christian's perfect obedience, living a godly life, and becoming inwardly righteous. God cannot forgive and accept anyone who is not perfectly righteous.
6	We **ARE** justified, forgiven, accepted by God, and saved to the uttermost solely on the **BASIS** of Christ's **imputed** righteousness of **justification, solely through faith** in Jesus, **apart from** our obedience and good works. (See pages 75 to 77).	**NO! Faith is NOT enough! We must also obey God, perform good works, live godly lives, and develop perfect characters.** No one will be saved when Jesus returns who does not **perfectly obey** God and who has **not developed a perfectly righteous character**.
7	The righteousness of **Righteousness by Faith IS infinitely meritorious.** There is absolutely **NO** justifying **MERIT** whatsoever in **OUR** faith, repentance, conversion, sanctification, obedience, good works, godly lives, or perfecting of Christian character. **ALL** the merit that justifies and saves us is **SOLELY IN CHRIST in heaven—never in us on earth!**	Although there is no justifying merit in anything we do, we **MUST** perfectly **obey** God, **live** perfect lives, and **develop** perfect characters in order to be **approved** by God in **the Investigative Judgement.** The righteousness which **justifies** and saves us when Jesus returns, **must be IN US** or we will be **LOST!**
8	**Only CHRIST'S** righteousness which is **credited** to us in **Justification by Faith** (Righteousness by Faith) is **good enough** to atone for our sins, **perfectly satisfy** God's infinitely righteous law for us, **get us through** the Judgment, and **secure** for us God's gifts of adoption, eternal life, and heaven.	Christ's righteousness, which is **imparted** to us and developed in us in **sanctification**, and which **IS inside** of us, **IS also necessary** to perfectly **satisfy** God's infinitely righteous law for us, **get us through** the Judgment and **secure for us** God's gifts of justification, forgiveness, Christ's righteousness credited to us, adoption, eternal life, and heaven.

Justification by Faith (Righteousness by Faith) does not refer to a creative, converting, morally transforming act of God in us. God's gifts of justification and faith put us in **a right RELATIONSHIP** with God. When God justifies us, He sets us right with Himself solely through faith, apart from obedience and good works.

Although we sincere, born–again Christians **are not sinless**, God **loves** us, **forgives** us, **credits** Christ's righteousness to us, **accepts** us, and **treats** us, during this life on earth, **AS IF we had never sinned. This is the Good News of the Gospel.** Of course, no one who **continues** to **willfully** sin or to **practice** sinning will be saved!

God **took everybody's sins and put them all on Jesus** on the cross and dealt with them all in Him 2,000 years ago! Because of Christ's atoning work for sinners, God **credits** Christ's perfect obedience and His death to us and treats us, during this life on earth, **AS IF we were perfectly righteous!** That is to say, God's justification of sinners is good only for as long as they live. God's gift of justification must be accepted by us by the time we die. If we truly believe in Jesus by the time we die, we will be saved. If we do not, we will be lost forever! Of course, true faith in Jesus will always lead the true Christian to live a godly life.

The gospel proclaims the good news that:
- Christ's victory over sin is our victory over sin.
- Christ's victory over death is our victory over death.
- Christ's resurrection from the dead is our resurrection from the dead.
- Christ's perfect life, death, and resurrection are all credited to our account in heaven; and we are accepted by God just as if we had lived His perfectly righteous life, and suffered His death.
- **Christ's imputed** righteousness of **justification ALONE** makes us acceptable to God. **All that remains,** is for us to **respond** to God's love, to **trust** Him, and to **rest** in His finished work for us **in Jesus! And we do that by faith and by faith alone, apart from obedience, good works, and godly lives.**

RECAPITULATION

The righteousness that is imputed to us in God's gift of justification by faith (righteousness by faith) is Christ's righteousness which, in turn, is His perfectly obedient life, death, and resurrection.

In His act of justifying us, God forgives our sins and imputes (credits) Christ's perfectly obedient life, death and resurrection to us and treats us AS IF we were as righteous as He was when He was on earth.

- His perfect obedience is our obedience; so we are no longer considered guilty and condemned and rejected!
- His death is our death; so we will never suffer the second death, but live forever!
- His resurrection is our resurrection from the dead; so we will rise in the resurrection of the righteous when Christ returns.

This is what it means to be justified! This is what the **GIFT** of Justification by Faith secures for us!

THE FACTS ARE THESE:

1. There is a righteousness of "Righteousness by **FAITH.**"
   And there is a righteousness of **Sanctification by Faith and WORKS.**

2. The first is **PERFECT AND COMPLETE.**
   The second is **NEVER** perfect and complete during this life on earth.

3. The first **CREDITS** Christ's perfect righteousness to our account in heaven.
   The second **DEVELOPS** Christ's righteousness in us in a **relative** sense.

4. The first **ACCOUNTS** us perfectly righteous.
   The second **MAKES** us relatively righteous — never absolutely righteous within!

5. The first accounts us **LEGALLY** righteous.
   The second makes us **MORALLY** righteous within, in a relative sense.

6. The first is **Christ's** atoning work.
   The second is **The Holy Spirit's** converting work.

117

7. The first is in **Christ in heaven**.
    The second is in **us on earth**.

8. The first is the **BASIS** on which God justifies us.
    The second is the **FRUIT (RESULT)** of our justification.

9. The first gives us a **righteous legal STANDING** before God and His infinitely righteous law in the Judgment in our **sinful moral STATE**.
    The second helps us to become more and more **Christ-like** in character—more and more like what God **accounts** us in **justification**.

10. The first is our **TITLE** to heaven.
    The second is our **FITNESS** for heaven (in a relative sense).

*   We are NOT justified by faith in the righteousness of the Holy Spirit which is in us on earth!
*   We ARE justified by faith in the righteousness of Christ which is OUTSIDE of us in heaven!

My Dear Seventh-day Adventist Brother, Sister, "HOW READEST THOU?"

---

*   The righteousness of Justification **is perfect, but it is not in us.**
*   The righteousness of Sanctification **is in us, but it is not perfect.**
*   The righteousness of glorification **is both in us and is perfect.**

●

*   **In Roman Catholic** theology, God sanctifies us in order that He might **justify** us.
*   **In biblical theology,** God justifies us in order that He might **sanctify** us.

ISSUE THIRTEEN:
BIBLICAL (CHRISTIAN) PERFECTION—WHAT IS IT?

1. For *entrance* into Heaven, *what* does God *require* of us*?* Since for entrance into heaven, God requires "perfect obedience, perfect righteousness" from birth till death, (SC 62), *how many* human beings have that perfect righteousness in themselves to present to God? *Not one!* What then? Is there no hope? **Ah, yes! There IS hope! What is that hope?**

2. Is the best *obedience (righteousness)* that Christians can attain to *by the grace of God through faith in Jesus, absolute or relative?*

3. During this life on earth, do the best, most mature, most righteous Christians on earth become so righteous, so sinless within themselves, by the grace of God through faith in Jesus, that they no longer come *short* of being as righteous as *Adam and Eve* were before they sinned, or as righteous as *Jesus* was in the flesh when He was on earth 2000 years ago, or as righteous as *God's infinitely righteous law* requires?

4. Once a human being has *sinned*, is there anything he can *do*, by the *grace* of God through *faith* in Jesus, *to cancel or atone for* his sins, *remove* his guilt, *change* his sinful moral nature from sinful to righteous, or *become perfectly righteous, fit for, or worthy of heaven?*

5. *Does* the *imputed* or *imparted* righteousness of Christ *make* believers *inwardly perfectly* righteous in nature or character or life?

6. *Will* the best Christian in the world become *absolutely free from selfishness* during this life on earth?

7. Does anything that the best Christians on earth can **DO**, by the grace of God through faith in Jesus, ever become so good, so sinless, so righteous that his obedience and good works and character development are *acceptable* to God as *a part of the basis* on which God can justly or mercifully *justify* them and take them to heaven?

8. *Can* fully dedicated, fully mature, fully victorious Christians who continue to possess *the sinful nature* (the bent bias, inclination, tendency and propensity to sin), *"crucify"* it so fully that they become *"dead"* to it before the Second Coming of Christ?

9. Do Christians at last become so perfectly sinless and righteous *in nature, character or life* by being *"baptized with the Holy Spirit,"* and *"Christ formed within, the hope of glory"* that they are *righteous enough to be translated?*

10. Throughout the entire history of the world, from the fall of Adam and Eve, to the close of probation, *how perfect (sinless)* must human beings become *within* in order to be justified—forgiven and accepted by God unto eternal life?

11. Must *the last generation* Christian become sinless or righteous in nature or character or life in order to be saved at last?

12. Does the *imputed or imparted* righteousness of Christ prepare, enable and *QUALIFY US INWARDLY to stand in the judgment without an Intercessor?*

13. What does the *BIBLE* say about Christian perfection?

14. What does *EGW* say about Christian perfection?

15. Does the Bible or EGW teach that we can or must become so righteous, so sinless in nature or character or life, that we no longer come **SHORT** of perfectly fulfilling or satisfying God's infinitely righteous law?

16. Does Christ's *imputed* righteousness of justification give believers a righteous legal **STANDING** before Him and His law in the Judgment in their sinful moral **STATE**?

17. On what **BASIS** does God justify sinners?

18. Although sincere, born again, mature Christians are not **perfect** children of God, are they **perfectly** God's children as soon as they truly believe, trust and exercise faith in Jesus as their personal Saviour?

19. How many **conditions** are there that believers must meet and fulfill before God will *justify* them and take them to heaven?

20. Is **FAITH** enough? Or is there something more that we must do or become before God will *justify* us and take us to heaven?

Erroneous Presuppositions

The perfect righteousness which God requires of us for entrance into heaven, He Himself graciously provides for us by **INFUSING** Christ's grace and righteousness into us by the indwelling Holy Spirit by which He *converts*, *sanctifies*, and *makes* us inwardly righteous, pleasing, and acceptable to Himself.

Having *made* us righteous within, God *justifies* us, *forgives* our sins, and *accepts* us unto eternal life.

So our justification is **not a "legal fiction."** It is *a reality*. God actually *makes* us righteous enough *within* to pass the judgment—*to live without a mediator* in the Heavenly Sanctuary.

We *retain* this righteous *state by faith and obedience*, by living a godly life, growing in grace and perfecting a perfect character until we are finally good enough to live without a mediator in the heavenly sanctuary and to pass the Judgment.

We ultimately come to the place where we are "*dead*" to the sinful nature with which we were born.

The result of this teaching is that we can look *within ourselves* for a part of the righteousness by which we are justified and saved.

Thus, by being "*baptized with the Holy Spirit*" and by "*Christ formed within, the hope of glory*," we become righteous enough to be translated to heaven and into God's hallowed presence.

Christian (biblical) perfection teaches that we *can* and that we *must* become *perfectly righteous* (sinless in character and action) in order to live without an intercessor in the heavenly sanctuary and to be saved when Jesus returns.

1. Page 3.2: "Wesley restored the doctrine of biblical *perfection*."

Christ's perfectly righteous life which God both imputes and imparts to us *makes* us perfectly, inwardly, morally righteous before the close of probation.

2. Page 14.4: "There will be a final generation that will stand before God without an intercessor, without a mediator before they are glorified." (EW 280.2, GC 614.1, and others.

3. Page 3.5, 3.8 and 3.10: "Everything that we ourselves can do [apart from faith] is defiled by sin."...*but that which is wrought through faith is acceptable to* God."

4. Page 15.7: "They will reflect His glory *perfectly*."

5. These statements are interpreted to mean that In order to be saved when Jesus returns, we must and will be absolutely sinless, absolutely righteous, as righteous as God's law requires, without ever coming short of perfectly fulfilling God's infinitely righteous law!

6. ***Page 28.5: The obedience of faith brings into our lives "the righteousness and perfection that was seen in the life of Christ." (1 BC 1118.4)***

This statement in number 6 just above is interpreted to mean that we become *as righteous as Christ!*

7. Page 38.4-38.7: To be "*clothed*" with Christ's righteousness is to receive *the "perfect obedience"* (*righteousness* of Christ *inside* of us!).

Note: All of these statements put the righteousness that justifies and saves *inside* of us.

8. Page 21.1: "Sinful flesh will remain until glorification, but we will be *DEAD TO IT*."

9. Page 21.2: "We can come to the place where we *fully reflect* His image."

10. Page 21.3: "The saints will *fully* reflect the image of Christ and will stand without a mediator."
    Page 21.3: "They no longer need *forgiveness* [*justification*]."

11. Page 21.4: "…but continuous *forgiving* is no longer needed."

12. Page 21.9: "My flesh is sinful, but I am *DEAD* to it." Pages 23 and 24 are more of the same issue we are dealing with here.

13. Page 27.3: Through the Holy Spirit and sanctification "the believer becomes *fitted* for the courts of heaven." "We would not enjoy heaven unless *qualified* for its holy atmosphere by the influence of the Spirit and the righteousness of Christ [*inside* of the believer]."

14. Page 22.4: "Christ *in us* the hope of glory."

15. Page 22.9 "Making justification into something that is *purely forensic, outside of a person, in heaven only, a declaration* that changes nothing except the records in heaven *[is a false doctrine]*." *(Emphasis mine.)*

16. Pages 23 and 24. Justification is not *forensic*. Justification *includes* our repentance, conversion, sanctification, obedience and Christ living His perfectly righteous life *in us*!

17. Page 27.4 and 27.5: It is Christ's "imparted" righteousness, His righteousness inside of us that "*fits*" us for heaven and that "*qualifies*" us for heaven.

18. Page 34.4: "Our lives *may measure [equal in righteousness]*, with the life of God."

19. *Conclusion:* Christian perfection *is not relative, but absolute.* The last generation Christian must be so righteous that he no longer comes *SHORT* of *perfectly* obeying and fulfilling God's infinitely righteous law

The Bible Teaches That:

Bible perfection is *not absolute, but relative.*

Nowhere does the Bible teach that we must become actually, *inwardly* perfectly righteous *(sinless)* in order to be justified, forgiven and saved!)

1. Rom. 3:10: "**THERE IS** *NONE RIGHTEOUS, NO, NOT ONE.*"
2. Rom. 3:23: (The original Greek of this verse says:) "*All* have sinned, and *all CONTINUE* to come *short* of
3. 1 John 1:8: "If we say that we have *no sin*, [or that we *have not sinned*, or are *not sinful* creatures] we deceive ourselves, and the truth is not in us."
4. Ps. 143:2 (NASB): "*No man* living is righteous."
5. Isa. 64:6: "*All* our righteousnesses are *as filthy rags* [to God]." (This verse is speaking of God's sincere converted children.)
6. Eccl. 7:20: "There is *no man* upon the earth that doeth good and *sinneth not.*"
7. Jer. 17:9: "The heart is *deceitful* above all things, and desperately *wicked*: who can know it?"
8. Ps. 14:3: "There is *none* that doeth *good* [all the time without ever coming short], *no not one.*"
9. 1 Kings 8:46: "There is *no man* that sinneth not."
   TMK 136: **"No one is perfect but Jesus"** (This is an EGW quote).
   See pages 105, 109—129, 146—149 and 161 for many Bible and EGW statements which strongly support the above 9 Bible statements.

Reader, How readest thou?

1SM 344.2 to bottom of page: "The religious services, the prayers, the praise, the penitent confession of sin ascend from true believers as incense to the heavenly sanctuary, but passing through the corrupt channels of humanity, they are so defiled that unless purified by blood, they can never be of value with God.

"They ascend not in spotless purity, and unless the Intercessor, who is at God's right hand, presents and purifies all by His righteousness, it is not acceptable to God."

"All incense from earthly tabernacles must be moist with the cleansing drops of the blood of Christ. He holds before the Father the censer of His own merits, in which there is no taint of earthly corruption.

"He gathers into this censer the prayers, the praise, and the confessions of His people, and with these He puts His own spotless righteousness. Then, perfumed with the merits of Christ's propitiation, the incense comes up before God wholly and entirely acceptable. Then gracious answers are returned.

"Oh, that all may see that everything in obedience, in penitence, in praise and thanksgiving, must be placed upon the glowing fire of the righteousness of Christ. The fragrance of this righteousness ascends like a cloud around the mercy seat."

1. For entrance into heaven, God requires of us perfect obedience, perfect righteousness from the cradle to the grave. But no human being on earth has that perfect righteousness to present to God. So, is there no hope? Ah, yes! There is hope! What is that hope?

> That righteousness which God requires for entrance into heaven, He Himself has already provided for us in His Son Jesus Christ as a sheer gift! And that transcendent gift is received by us sinful sinners solely through faith apart from works.

2. Christian perfection is *never absolute*; it is *always relative* to Adam's and Eve's righteousness before they sinned. The best, most mature Christians on earth still come *short* of perfectly fulfilling God's infinitely righteous law.
3. Once a person has sinned, no amount of "perfect" obedience can cancel or atone for his sins, remove his guilt, change his sinful nature from sinful to righteous, or make him fit for or worthy of heaven.
4. Neither the imputed nor imparted righteousness of Christ makes a person inwardly righteous. Justification *credits* Christ's righteousness to us, and accepts and treats us *as if we were righteous!*
5. The best Christians in the world will never, this side of glorification, be free from selfishness.
6. The best that Christians can do by the grace of God through faith in Jesus can never be a part of *the basis* on which God justifies us because, even that which is done by faith (see number 3 in the Erroneous Presuppositions section) is permeated by selfishness and is not acceptable to God unless it is covered by Christ's righteousness.
7. The sinful nature cannot, during this life on earth, be eradicated from us or "*crucified*" so fully that we become *dead* to it. **WE ARE TO "*RECKON*" OURSELVES TO BE *DEAD* TO SIN** and "*make no provision*" to fulfill the lusts of the flesh.
8. God's requirement for heaven has always been perfect obedience (perfect righteousness from birth to death.) God does not require a more perfect character of the *last* generation Christian than He did of the first. The standard for the last generation is the same as for *all preceding generations.*
9. We may keep our sinful nature *subdued* and *as if* it were dead through a personal devotional life. If we neglect our personal devotional life, our sinful nature will rise up and reassert itself.
10. No one, including the 144,000, will become so righteous *within* that they will be able to stand in the judgment without an intercessor.
11. The "*baptism* of the Holy Spirit" and "Christ *in you* the hope of glory" do not make one righteous enough to be translated on the *basis* of this righteousness. It is the *imputed* righteousness of Christ that *qualifies* us for translation, not His imparted righteousness.

Thank God! He has *already* provided that perfect righteousness in His Son, which He generously *credits* to our account in the judgment.

This is the good news of the judgment! The last generation Christian does not have to be absolutely sinless (righteous) in nature, character or life in order to live without a mediator in the heavenly sanctuary. Christ's imputed righteousness covers us to the very end. Praise God!

We are to be diligent to obey God and to perfect Christian character. But we are to be just as diligent NOT to trust in our obedience and perfecting of Christian character for our assurance of justification. We must trust alone in Christ's righteousness.

Although the last generation Christian will desire and purpose and strive earnestly by the grace of God and faith in Jesus to live without sinning:

1. He will still have a *sinful* nature.
2. He will still be a *sinner* because he has sinned in the past, and
3. He will still come *short* of being as sinless (righteous) as the law requires.

It is *not* the "*Christ IN YOU*" that justifies and saves, but **THE CHRIST ON THE CROSS***!—The Christ FOR you!*

We will always, during this life on earth, **need the robe** of Christ's righteousness (His **imputed** righteousness) to cover our sins of a lifetime and our sinful nature.

We will never come to the place, during this life, where we will "**fully**" (**perfectly**) reflect the **infinitely** righteous character of Christ.

In order to "fully" (perfectly) reflect the infinitely righteous character of Christ, we would have to be **as righteous** as He is.

As long as we (Christians) live on this earth, we will need God's **forgiveness** and Christ's **imputed** righteousness to cover our sinful lives.

We will **NEVER**, during this life be "**DEAD**" to our sinful nature. Our flesh is not sinful. **Sin lies in the mind!** (Comment on **numbers 8 and 12** on page 121)!

Selfishness and a coming **short** of Christ's character will be the lot of the best Christians in the world until our change from mortality to immortality.

Was there ever any act by us which was inspired by the Holy Spirit and performed by faith in Jesus and love for God that was **perfectly free from selfishness?**

Christ's imputed righteousness is our only "**FITNESS**" and "**QUALIFICATION**" for heaven. There is absolutely no justifying merit in "**Christ in us!**" Our **qualification** for heaven is **always outside of us!**

"**Christ in us**" is **not** the **basis** on which God forgives us and accepts us unto eternal life.

"**Christ in us**" is the **fruit, result, and evidence** that we have been **converted** and are in **a right relationship** with God.

"**Christ in us**" by the indwelling Holy Spirit is the "**earnest,**" "**assurance**" "**title deed**" to heaven. 2 Cor. 1:22; 5:5 and Eph 1: 14.
Number **14** in the Erroneous Presuppositions above **is a straw-man argument.** When we are justified, we are also changed, but it is **not justification** that changes us, but the Holy Spirit, faith, repentance, conversion and sanctification!

The faith by which we are justified always leads to repentance, conversion, sanctification, obedience, a godly life, and to the perfecting of Christian character.

The teaching that the righteousness that justifies us is **inside** of us **is a pagan and Roman Catholic doctrine**—the essence of every false religion in the world.

Such a doctrine is **the greatest insult** to God and to Jesus and is **blasphemous**.

Paul said, "If anyone preaches any other gospel, let him be **anathema (cursed)!**"

In order for our obedience and good works to justify us:

1. We would have to have an unfallen nature (not have a sinful nature) **and,**
2. Our obedience and good works would have to be perfect and unspotted from birth until death!

Since the above is impossible, **let us cease teaching perfectionistic** doctrine!

We repeat: Once a human being has **sinned one time**, no amount of perfect obedience and good works can **cancel** his sin, **atone** for his sin, **secure** God's justification and forgiveness of him, **make him righteous** in nature, character or life, or make him **pleasing and acceptable** to God!

Perfectionism is bankrupt!

It can only give a person false hopes, and deceive and discourage people!

In reference to **number two**, page 14.4 in the Erroneous Presuppositions section of this chapter, page 121, at this time, the saints will be free from the **domination**, but not from the **inner presence of sin. We will still have the help of the Holy Spirit and the angels after the close of probation!**

(Of course, the saints will not sin **willfully** after they are sealed.)

EGW STATEMENTS

1. 6T 60: "The life of Christ revealed **an infinitely perfect** [righteous] character."
2. 5T 739: "He [Christ] stands before us as the embodiment of **divine perfection**."
3. Col. 2: 9: "In Him dwelleth **all the fullness** of the Godhead bodily."
4. 2T 549: "He [Jesus] is a **perfect** and holy example, given us to **imitate**. We **CANNOT EQUAL** the Pattern: but we shall not be approved of God if we do not **copy** it, and according to the ability God has given, **resemble** it."
5. CT 365: "God is perfect **in His high [divine] sphere** of action, so man may be perfect in **his human sphere.**"
6. CDF 133; CT 71; 4T 455: "We may be perfect in our **[human]** sphere as God is perfect in His **[divine]** sphere."
7. 7BC 904: "...the excellence of character found in Him, which **NEVER** had been found, **NEITHER COULD BE**, in another."
8. MB 49: "... the divine beauty of the character of Christ, of whom the noblest and most gentle among man are but **a faint reflection.**" (We are to reflect the character of Christ as the moon reflects the light of the sun.)
9. RH Mar. 15, 1888: "There are many, especially among these who compare themselves to Christ, as though they were **EQUAL** with Him in **perfection of character**. This is **BLASPHEMY.**"
10. TMK 136: **"NO ONE IS PERFECT BUT JESUS."**
11. 5T 48: "Are you [abiding] in Christ [by faith]? Not if you do not acknowledge yourselves **erring [sinning] helpless, condemned sinners.**"
12. 1SM 394: **"In ourselves**, we are sinners, but [abiding] **in Christ** [by faith] we are **[accounted] righteous**."
13. RH. Sept. 3, 1901: "That which God required of Adam in Paradise before the fall, He requires in this age of the world from those who would follow Him—**perfect obedience, perfect righteousness" [SC 62]** to His law. But righteousness **without a blemish** can be obtained only through the **IMPUTED** righteousness of Christ."
14. PP 353: Christ's **"perfect righteousness**, which through faith is **imputed [credited]** to His people and which can **alone** make the worship of sinful beings **acceptable** to God."
15. Ministry (Magazine) June 1988, p. 27: "I loathe myself. I would clothe myself in sackcloth and ashes and cry **'unclean, unclean'. The only cleanness [righteousness]** I have is that which is **in Christ Jesus [which He imputes, reckons, credits to me in His gift of justification].**"

Praise God! Although we are not **perfect children of God**, we are **perfectly God's children** the moment we truly believe in Jesus and continue to accept Him as our personal Saviour and Lord of our lives!

NOT SINLESS UNTIL GLORIFICATION

EGW Statements Which Teach That Sin REMAINS In Believers Until
Glorification–That We Will NOT BE Sinless or Perfectly Righteous in Nature,
Character or Life Until Our "Probation Closes."
(See numbers 1 to 6 below)

1. (May 16, 1895): "When the saints have been *GLORIFIED,* then and then only will it be safe to claim that we are *SAVED AND SINLESS.*"

2. 4T 367: "Man may grow up into Christ, his living head. It is not the work of a moment, but that of *a life-time*. By growing daily in the divine life, he will not *attain* to the *full* stature of a *perfect* man in Christ *UNTIL HIS PROBATION CLOSES*. The growing is a continuous work."

3. TIMK 361: [SDA Christians] "We *cannot* say, *'I am sinless'* till this vile body is *CHANGED* and fashioned like unto His *GLORIOUS [GLORIFIED]* body. But if we constantly seek to follow Jesus, the blessed hope is ours of standing before the throne of God without spot, or wrinkle, or any such thing, complete in Christ, robed in His righteousness and perfection."

4. RH Aug. 18, 1971: "*REPENTANCE* [a godly sorrow for coming short of perfect obedience] is a *daily* continuous exercise, and must be so *until mortality is swallowed up in IMMORTALITY*. *REPENTANCE* and humiliation, and sorrow of soul must be our daily meat and drink, *till we cease* to carry with us so many imperfections and failures [sinning]."

5. AA 560, 561: "*SO LONG AS SATAN REIGNS* [until Probation closes or Christ returns], we shall have self to subdue, *besetting SINS to overcome*; so long as life shall last, there will be no stopping place, no point which we can reach and say, I have fully attained. Sanctification is the result of lifelong obedience."

6. 15M 363: "IF you would stand through *THE TIME OF TROUBLE*, you must know Christ, and appropriate the gift of His righteousness which He *IMPUTES* to the repentant sinner."

7. MLT 250: "When it is in the heart [faith] to obey God, when efforts are put forth to this end, Jesus accepts this disposition and effort as man's best service, and He *makes up for the* deficiency with His own divine merit [which is *imputed* to us in God's gift of *Justification*]."

8. 5T 744: "Through the merits of Christ, through His righteousness, which by faith is *IMPUTED* unto us, we are to attain to the *perfection* of Christian character."

9. EW 107: "Jesus stands in the holy of holies, now to appear in the presence of God for us. There He ceases not to present His people moment by moment, *complete in Himself* [*complete in His IMPUTED righteousness*.]"

10. RH Sept. 3, 1901: "*Righteousness without a blemish* can be obtained *only* through the *IMPUTED* righteousness of Christ."

11. 1SM 394: "*In ourselves* we are *SINNERS*; but *in Christ* we are *RIGHTEOUS*."

12. TIMK 136: "*NO ONE IS PERFECT [SINLESS] BUT JESUS*."

13. 1SM 367: "Righteousness is obedience to the law. The law demands [perfect] righteousness, and this the sinner owes to the law; but he is *incapable* of rendering it. The *only* way in which he can attain to *righteousness* is *through faith*. *By faith* he can bring to God the *merits of Christ*, and the Lord *places [credits]* the obedience of His Son to the sinner's *account*. Christ's righteousness is accepted *in place of* man's failure, and God *receives, pardons, justifies* the repentant, believing soul, treats him *as though* he were righteous and loves him as He loves His Son. This is how faith is *accounted* righteousness; and the *pardoned* soul goes on from grace to grace, from light to a greater light." See also SC 62.

14. MINISTRY, June 1988, p.27: Mrs. White, 50 years a Christian, at age 66, said to some students, "I loathe myself. I would clothe myself in sackcloth and ashes and cry, 'unclean, unclean.' The *only* cleanness [righteousness, sinlessness] that I have is that which is *in Jesus Christ*."

15. AA 532: *Our "obedience can be made perfect ONLY* by the incense of Christ's *[imputed]* righteousness which fills with divine fragrance every act of obedience."

16. 1SM 398: *"The believer is justified [forgiven and accepted by God] without any merit of his own."*

17. 2 RH 437 (Nov. 11, 1890, right col., line 19): "Christ **ONLY** is the way, the truth, the life; and man can be *JUSTIFIED ALONE* through the *IMPUTATION* of Christ's righteousness. Man is justified freely by God's grace through faith, and *not by works*, lest any man should boast. Salvation is the *GIFT* of God through Jesus Christ our Lord."

18. TIMK 82: "Man can be *JUSTIFIED ALONE* through the *IMPUTATION* of Christ's righteousness. Man is justified freely by God's *grace* through faith, and *not by works*, lest any man should boast. Salvation is the *GIFT* of God through Jesus Christ our Lord."

FIVE statements by Mrs. White declare that the Christian's *ONLY* hope of justification, forgiveness, acceptance by God, and heaven is in the "*IMPUTED*" righteousness of Christ! (See numbers 6, 8, 10, 17 and 18 above).

CONCLUSION

Although sin does not REIGN in believers, it DOES REMAIN IN THEM until Glorification.
(Martin Luther).

Mrs. White said:
"The only righteousness I have is in Christ [in heaven]." 1SM 392

For statements which teach that the only way Christians become perfectly righteous during this life on earth is by the IMPUTED righteousness of Christ. Please see the following pages of this book: 26—31, 52—57, 68, 69, 76, 77, 84, 111, 116, 123—126, 140, 143, 147, 149, 150.

ISSUE FOURTEEN:
THE ATONEMENT

What are the *TWO ASPECTS* OF CHRIST'S ATONING WORK FOR sinners?
- **His past, objective, sacrificial phase**
- **His present, subjective, dispensing-the-benefits phase.**

Often MISSUNDERSTOOD E. G. W. Statements

The following ten statements by Mrs. White are being interpreted by many SDAs to mean that Christ's *atoning* work for us now as our Great High Priest, in the heavenly sanctuary consists of *making* us perfectly righteous, pleasing, and acceptable to God so He can fully *justify* us and take us to heaven.

1. Page 33.0: "We are now in the great day of **atonement**."
2. Page 33.3: "Solemn are the scenes connected with the closing work of the **atonement**."
3. Page 33.7: "Christ is in the heavenly sanctuary. And what is He doing? Making **atonement** for us."
4. Page 33.8: "He [Christ] will make an **atonement** for all who will come with confession.
5. Page 35.9: "…while this work of **atonement** is going forward [in the heavenly sanctuary]…"
6. Page 38.5: "Christ in His humanity wrought out a perfect character, and this character He offers to *impart* to us."
7. Page 38.7: "Then as the Lord looks upon us He sees…[His] *perfect* obedience to the law of Jehovah." (COL 311.4).
8. Page 39.8: "God requires of His *child perfect obedience.*"
9. Page 39.10: "The Holy Spirit…we can be fitted for heaven…we must have Christ's righteousness *[inside of us]* as our *credentials* [in order to be saved]."
10. Page 40.2: "That He [Christ] might be able to *impart* His righteousness to fallen, sinful man and thus [through the *infused* righteousness of Christ *into* believers] present men to His Father *in His righteous character.*"

Jesus is *now atoning* for our sins in the heavenly Sanctuary which consists of all the following:
- Imparting, infusing, putting the Holy Spirit into us,
- Converting us,
- Sanctifying us,
- Perfecting our character,
- Making us inwardly righteous, pleasing and acceptable to Himself **in nature and character and life**.

Comments by The Author

The above statements are speaking of sanctification. They are interpreted to teach that Christ's "**atoning**" work in heaven includes His work of *making us righteous within so we can become good enough to pass the judgment, to be justified, and to go to heaven.*

The Bible Teaches That:

Christ is not now *atoning* for our sins in the heavenly sanctuary. Both the Bible and Mrs. White say that the atonement was *completed 2000 years ago.*

The erroneous teaching takes all the honor and *glory* of justifying and saving us *from Jesus* and makes *the Holy Spirit* our co-redeemer (co-Saviour).

The Roman Catholic church makes Mary, the mother of Jesus, their co-redeemer!
The *sacrificial* atoning sacrifice of Christ *outside* of us *2000 years ago* was perfect, finished and complete, and is all-sufficient to *justify* us.

Nothing else is necessary as the perfect all-sufficient *basis* on which God *justifies* believers. We cannot add to it, we cannot improve upon it! God Himself cannot *add* to or *improve* upon it.

All we can *do* is to *respond* to it in faith, love, and thanksgiving, and accept and appropriate it to ourselves personally.

> **Christ is now *dispensing* to us the *benefits* of His atoning sacrifice and *making effectual in us* His atoning work for us outside of us 2000 years ago.**

Christ's atoning work for us 2000 years *ago was and is eternally sufficient to justify us! It does not need our obedience* to help or to complete it.

His work *in us now* does *not* justify us, but *sanctifies* us. It is the work of sanctification to enable us to grow in grace.

Christ, by His atoning work for us, outside of us, 2000 years before we were born, *justifies* us.
The Holy Spirit's converting sanctifying, transforming work in us now *helps us to* overcome our besetting sins, and to perfect Christian character.

What a wonderful deliverance from Satan and sin and death! What a wonderful Deliverer is Jesus our Saviour, Substitute, Sinbearer, Surity, and soon-coming King of Kings and Lord of Lords!

Dear Reader, "If you are RIGHT with God TODAY, You are READY if Christ should come TODAY!" 1 HP 227.

129

THE GREAT ETERNAL AT – ONE – MENT

	THE TWO CHRONOLOGICAL PHASES OF THE ATONING WORK OF CHRIST	
1	The **first** Phase	The **second** Phase
2	The **earthly** Phase	The **heavenly** Phase
3	The **cross** Phase	The **heavenly sanctuary** Phase
4	The **sacrificial death** Phase	The **intercessory mediation** Phase
5	The **forensic, legal, judicial** Phase	The **personal, experiential** Phase
6	The **objective** (outside of us) Phase	The **subjective** (inside of us) Phase
7	The **perfect, complete, finished** Phase	The **imperfect, incomplete, unfinished, ongoing** Phase
8	The **past** Phase	The **present ongoing** Phase
9	The **for-us** Phase	The **in-us** Phase
10	The deliverance from **guilt and condemnation** of sin Phase	The deliverance from the **power and dominion** of sin Phase
11	The **rescue** Phase	The **restoration** Phase
12	The **justifying** Phase	The **sanctifying** Phase
13	God **reconciled** us to Himself **forensically** Phase	God is now **reconciling** us to Himself **experientially** more and more Phase
14	Reconciliation **provided** Phase	Reconciliation **applied** Phase
15	The **Godward** Phase	The **manward** Phase
16	The **vindication-of-God** Phase	The **salvation-of-man** Phase
17	The **meritorious-basis** Phase	The **instrumental-means** Phase
18	The **sin** Phase (to expiate sin)	The **sinner** Phase (to save sinners)
19	The **atoning, satisfaction** Phase	The **reconciling** Phase
20	The **salvation** Phase	The **judgment** Phase
21	The **one, once-for-all, all sufficient** Phase	The **continuing, progressive** Phase
22	The **victim** Phase	The **great high priest** Phase
23	The **justice** Phase	The **mercy** Phase
24	The **atoning** Phase	The **morally perfecting** Phase
25	The **ransom** Phase	The – **dispensing** – the – **benefits** Phase

ISSUE FIFTEEN:
THE JUDGMENT IS GOOD NEWS

Is the judgment good news or bad news?
Can Christians become good enough within—
in nature, character, or life—to pass the judgment?
How do Christians become good enough to pass the judgment?

Erroneous Presuppositions

1. Page 32.2: "In order to be prepared for the *judgment*, it is necessary that men should *keep the law of God.*" *[Perfectly, without ever coming short].*

2. Page 32.10: "He [God] prepares us to stand before Him in the *investigative judgment* in the imputed *and imparted* righteousness of Christ. We get no credit, it's all Christ's righteousness [inside of us.]!"

Comments by The Author

(This is salvation *by* and on the *basis* of a righteousness that is *inside* of us!)

This is a very common false presupposition. The reasoning goes something like this: "Because it is *not my* righteousness, but *Christ's* that is inside of me, I get no credit for it."

"Because it is *Christ's* perfect obedience and righteousness *in me*, *He* gets all the credit."

This fallacious reasoning puts the righteousness that justifies and saves *inside* of us!

This is good Roman Catholic theology. Many sincere SDA's are somewhat Roman Catholic in their understanding of the gospel!

The Bible Teaches That:

Many Christians who do not understand the judgment *fear* it and *are working real hard, trying to become good enough to pass "the awful assize!"*

But those who *understand* the judgment look forward to it with eager anticipation and exclaim, **"O Blessed Judgment Day! Hasten on, O Blessed Judgment Day!"**

They rejoice in the knowledge that Jesus *stands-in* for them in the judgment, that it is *His* character that gets them through the judgment, *not their own.*

> They glory in the good news that: "He that believeth in Him is not [now] condemned." John 3:18
>
> And Romans 8:1 is particularly comforting to them: "There is therefore now no condemnation to those who are in Him."
>
> The words of Jesus in John 5:24 give them great assurance: "Verily, verily I say unto you, He that heareth My words and *believeth* in Him that sent Me *HAS* everlasting life, and shall *not* come into judgment, [Greek], *but IS passed from death unto life."*

Our hope of heaven is not in the great *ACT* of God *IN US*! All our hope of heaven is in the great *ACT* of God *IN JESUS*!

All our hope of heaven is not in *OUR ATTAINMENT*, but in *CHRIST'S ATONEMENT*! "My hope is built on nothing less than Jesus' blood and righteousness."

Hasten on, O Blessed Judgment Day!

In the Judgment, CHRIST STANDS-IN FOR US! God does not charge (hold) our sins against us. Instead He charges them against Christ and He imputes, credits, Christ's righteousness to us, and we are accepted "IN THE BELOVED." It is His character that gets us through the Judgment, not our own! It is Christ's IMPUTED righteousness that justifies us! Praise God!

The imparted righteousness of the Holy Spirit never makes us sinless in nature, character of life. It never cancels our sins, atones for our sins, gets us through the Judgment or secures God's justification of us.

"We are not to be anxious about what Christ and God think of US, but about what God thinks of CHRIST OUR SUBSTITUTE." 2SM 32,33.

Christ STANDS IN for us in the Judgment! It is His character that perfectly satisfies God's infinitely righteous law for us!

Even in THE JUDGMENT we are justified, forgiven and accepted by the GRACE of God through FAITH in Jesus ALONE! IT IS JUSTIFICATION BY FAITH, AND A JUDGEMENT ACCORDING TO WORKS! We are JUDGED AND CONDEMED by the LAW and JUSTIFIED and SAVED by GRACE THROUGH FAITH.

ISSUE SIXTEEN:
PAUL AND JAMES

Are there two aspects of justification?

Are Christian believers justified *MERITORIOUSLY* on the *basis* of
Christ's atoning work for sinners, *outside* of sinners *2000 years ago,*
and *EVIDENTIALLY* by their *obedience and good works and godly lives?*

Erroneous Presuppositions

1. We are justified by faith plus obedience, sanctification, good works, a godly life and a perfect character.
2. James 2:21 says that Abraham was *"justified by works."*
3. "Was not Abraham our father justified by works, when he offered Isaac his son upon the altar?"
4. James 2:24 says: "Ye see then how that by works a man is justified and not by faith only."

Comments by The Author

Paul and James were two soldiers of Christ fighting back to back against two opposite extremes. Paul was fighting against **legalism**—salvation by works. So he was emphasizing salvation by the grace of God through faith in Jesus, apart from obedience and good works.

On the other hand, James was fighting against **antinomianism**—"the law was nailed to the cross."

•

Like Abraham, we are justified by faith. "Abraham believed God and God credited it to him for righteousness." Gen. 15:6; Rom. 4:3; Gal. 3:16; James 2:21 and 24; Phil. 3:9; Rom. 3:28.

•

Conservative Seventh-day Adventists, who are in the legalistic, perfectionistic right wing of the church, believe that they are justified by faith plus obedience, good works, character development, and Christ in them!

This is a serious deception! Those who believe this error are trying real hard to become good enough to pass the Judgment!

Instead of looking away from their sinful selves to Christ alone, they are looking within for that perfect righteousness which satisfies the law for them, and gets them through the Judgment!

Grace as the method of salvation does not abolish the law as the standard; the standard **remains!**

The Bible Teaches That:

The biblical answer to the two questions above is a resounding *YES!*

Abraham was justified *meritoriously* by *faith* and *evidentially* by *works*.

Abraham's obedience was the *evidence* that his faith was real (genuine).

James 2:17 says: "Even so faith, if it hath not works, is dead, being alone."

133

True faith, true repentance, true conversion, true sanctification always leads to a growing love for righteousness, obedience, good works, a godly character and to a growing hatred for sin and disobedience.

James 2:18 says: "Yea, a man may say, Thou hast faith and I have works: shew me thy faith without thy works, and I will shew thee my faith *by my works.*"

True faith is revealed by a person's willingness to be obedient to God's every command.

Obedience is *"the acid test"* of the **genuineness** of our faith and conversion. Perfectionists love James 2:21 and 24.

But verse 23 says: "Abraham ***BELIEVED*** God, and it was ***RECKONED*** to Him as ***RIGHTEOUSNESS.***" James 2:23 NASB.

●

This is worth repeating – We are justified:
- *meritoriously* by **Christ's ATONING WORK** AND IMPUTED RIGHTEOUSNESS,
- *instrumentally* by **FAITH**,
- *efficaciously* by **GRACE**,
- *evidentially* by **WORKS**.

JUSTIFICATION is not a creative , converting, sanctifying, transforming act of God in believers. Justification is RELATIONAL! God's gift of Justification puts us in a right relationship with Him.

Jesus is seeking a personal love-RELATIONSHIP with us.

WILL WE RESPOND?

There Was One Who Was Willing

"There was One Who was willing
    To die in my stead,
That a soul so unworthy might live
    And the path to the cross
He was willing to tread.
    All the sins of my life to forgive.

"They are nailed to the cross,
    They are nailed to the cross,
O how much He was willing to bear!
    With what anguish and loss,
Jesus went to the cross!
    But He carried my sins with Him there.

Mrs. Frank A. Breeck

Erroneous Presuppositions

1. The *assurance* of our justification, forgiveness and acceptance with God is *not alone Christ's atoning work for us?*

2. *Our assurance of justification INCLUDES* our faith, repentance, conversion, sanctification, the indwelling Holy Spirit, obedience, good works, a godly life and perfecting a perfectly sinless character.

3. Our *assurance* of justification is our being *filled* (infused) with Christ's righteousness and being *MADE* inwardly righteous, pleasing, and acceptable to God in nature, character and life.

4. Our assurance of justification is "**CHRIST IN YOU**," the hope of eternal life.

5. Our assurance of justification is **not** solely in Christ's righteousness and atoning work for us, outside of us, 2000 years ago, but is also in the Holy Spirit's converting, sanctifying work and presence inside of us now!

6. Instead of our assurance of heaven being solely in Christ's atonement, it is also in our attainment.

7. Our assurance of acceptance by God is not alone in His great ACT IN JESUS, but is also in His great ACT IN US.

Comments by The Author

Those who look **within** for the righteousness that justifies and saves them can never have the full assurance of salvation because they can never be quite sure that they are good enough or have done enough to be approved by God.

Those who are looking within for the assurance of their salvation are trusting in a false righteousness and will certainly be lost!

(See Page 131, shaded area, for three tremendously encouraging texts).

The Bible Teaches That:

"BLESSED ASSURANCE, Jesus is mine!

O, what a foretaste of glory divine!

Heir of salvation, purchase of God,

Born of His Spirit, washed in His blood!

"This is my story, this is my song,

Praising my Saviour all the day long;

This is my story, this is my song,

Praising my Saviour all the day long."

Fanny Crosby

"There's *sunshine* in my soul today,

More glorious and bright,

That glows in any earthly sky,

For Jesus is my light."

E. E. Hewitt

"What a *blessedness*, what a *peace* is mine,

Leaning on the everlasting arms."

E. A. Hoffman

"Safe in the arms of Jesus,

Safe on His gentle breast-

Here by His love o'er shaded,

Sweetly my soul doth *rest*."

Fanny J Crosby

"Peace! Peace! Wonderful peace,

Coming down from the Father above;

Sweep over my spirit forever I pray,

In fathomless billows of love."

W. D. Cornelli alt.

The above is the exuberant testimony of the saints of all ages who **KNEW** Christ as a personal Saviour, who had *a personal faith-love relationship* with God, and a calm, steadfast assurance that their sins were forgiven by God.

1. Rom. 8: 16: "His Spirit testifieth with our spirit that *we are* **the children of God."**

2. Job. 19:25-27: "I *KNOW* that my Redeemer liveth, and that He shall stand at the latter day, upon the earth: and though after my skin worms destroy this body, yet in my flesh shall I see God: whom I shall see for myself…"

3. 2 Tim. 1:12: "I *KNOW* whom I have believed, and am persuaded that He is able to keep that which I have committed unto Him against that day."

4. 1 John 5: 10, 11: "He that *believeth* on the Son of God *hath the witness in himself*…[that he has eternal life]."

5. 1 John 5: 13: "These things I have written unto you that *believe* on the name of the Son of God; that ye may *KNOW* that ye have eternal life, and that ye may *believe* on the name of the Son of God."

6. Our assurance of salvation comes, not from what God does in us, but from what He did for us in Jesus 2000 years ago!

7. Jesus Christ and His sinless life, His substitutionary atoning death, and His resurrection from the dead are the solid rock-bottom basis of our salvation from Satan and sin and death.

"J. C. Ryle gave a beautiful, brief description of assurance. He wrote that a true Christian may reach a comforting degree of faith in Christ "that in general he shall feel *entirely confident* as to the pardon and safety of his soul—shall seldom be troubled with doubts—seldom distracted with fears—seldom be distressed by anxious questionings—and, in short, though vexed by many an inward conflict with sin, shall look forward to death without trembling, and to judgment without dismay!"
Go Free, by Robert R. Horn, page 76

●

"Those who know that they are justified, know that their most important need is secure, can therefore endure passing troubles, no matter how severe." Ibid. 76.

●

"I've been adopted; my name's written down."

Hattie E. Buel

●

Faith, conviction, certainty, assurance come by reading, hearing, pondering, singing the Word of God. John 17:17.

If you doubt, if you want faith in God, read His word prayerfully every day.

Faith will grow in direct proportion to the time we spend with God's Word.

●

1. We have Christ's atoning work for us,

2. We have God's promises in the Bible to forgive all our sins, and

3. We have the inner witness of the indwelling Holy Spirit as **THE BLESSED ASSURANCE** of God's adoption and acceptance of us unto eternal life.

●

"I'm a child of the King,

A child of the King!

With Jesus, my Saviour,

I'm a child of the King."

—Hattie E. Buel

ISSUE EIGHTEEN:
OFTEN MISUNDERSTOOD BIBLE TEXTS

Comments by The Author

1. Matt. 5:48 is interpreted by some: "Be ye therefore *sinless* or *perfectly righteous* all the time without ever coming *short* of perfectly fulfilling God's infinitely righteous law."

2. 1 John 3:2: "When He shall appear, we shall be like Him." This text is interpreted to mean that we shall be as righteous as Christ when He appears.

3. 1 John 3:3: "And every man that hath this hope in him purifieth himself, even as He is pure." This text is erroneously interpreted the same as above—perfectly sinless.

4. 1 John 3:6: "Whosoever abideth in Him sinneth not." This text is wrongly interpreted as follows: "whosoever abideth in Him never sins:" But that is not what this text says in the original Greek. In the original Greek this text says: Whosoever abideth in Him does not **practice** sin—does not **habitually** sin—does not **keep on** sinning **continually** throughout life.

5. 1 John 3:9: "Whosoever is born of God doth not commit sin." This text is understood by many as saying: "Whosoever is born of God never sins." Like 1 John 3:6, **"sinneth not"** and **"does not commit sin"** in the Greek are in the present indicative active voice, which means continuous action—**does not keep on sinning habitually**.

6. 1 John 5:18: "We know that whosoever is born of God sinneth not." The same comments on 1 John 3:6, 9 above apply here as well—does not continue to **practice** sin.

7. Col. 1:27: "**Christ in you, the hope of glory**" is interpreted to mean that our justification, acquittal, forgiveness and acceptance by God at last depends upon and is **based** upon **our** being surrendered to and **indwelt by Christ** instead of exclusively upon Christ's atoning work for us, outside of us, 2000 years ago. This is interpreted to mean:

   We are justified, made righteous, pleasing and acceptable to God on the **BASIS of Christ's dwelling in us by the Holy Spirit**.

The teaching above makes the Holy Spirit our Justifier and Saviour instead of Jesus.

8. **Rev. 12:17**: "And the dragon was wroth with the woman, and went to make war with the remnant of her seed, **which keep the commandments** of God," is interpreted by many SDAs as: "which **perfectly** keep all of God's commandments all of the time without ever sinning."

This text is speaking of a **relative** righteousness, not an absolute righteousness.

9. **Rev. 14:12** is interpreted by many SDAs as: "Here is the patience of the saints: here are they that [perfectly] keep [obey] the commandments of God [all of the time, without ever coming short]."

10. **Rev. 22:14**: "Blessed are they that **do [obey] His commandments**, that they may have right to the tree of life and may enter in through the gate into the city."

This text is interpreted by some to say, "Blessed are they that **perfectly obey** His commandments all the time without ever sinning."

But this is a mistranslation since it is contrary to what the rest of the Bible and Ellen White teach.

Neither the Bible nor Mrs. White teach that God's people must be perfectly sinless in nature or character or life in order to be saved when Christ returns!

We must not be selective in formulating our doctrines.

We must take all of the Bible and Mrs. White's writings to arrive at a balanced truth.

Dear Reader, let us be balanced Christians; let us not go to extremes!

We must take into consideration ALL of the Biblical and Ellen G. White's balancing, complementary statements on every subject.

The Bible Teaches That:

The original Greek word in Mt. 5:48 which is translated, perfect is *telos* which means, *mature*. **It does not mean sinless**.

Accordingly, what Jesus is actually saying in Matt 5:48 is, "***Become mature Christians***."
We are to "***grow up***" into Christ, into *mature* men and women in Christ.

Nowhere does the Bible teach that we have to become perfectly sinless in nature, character, or outward life in order to be saved.

The Bible teaches over and over again that "There are none righteous, no not one." Rom. 3:10.
"All have sinned and come short of the glory of God [Greek: continue to come short of perfect righteousness—perfect obedience]." Rom. 3:23.

"If we say that we have no sin, we deceive ourselves, and the truth is not in us." 1John 1:8.

"No man living is righteous." Psalm 143:2. NASB.

"All our [God's people] righteousness is as filthy rags." Isa. 64:6.

Insofar as our best obedience is concerned, as forming any part of the **basis** on which God justifies us, they are utterly repugnant to God. God is pleased with our efforts, by His grace, to live sinless lives, but we always come short of perfect obedience—perfect righteousness, perfect sinlessness! There is absolutely no justifying merit in them. (see SC 62; 1SM 344; 367; 389)

Many well-meaning SDAs place an extreme interpretation on Rev. 12:17; 14:12; 22:14 and Matt. 12:37.

In the original Greek text of 1 John 3:6 and 9 the word which is translated "sinneth not" is in the present indicative active tense which, literally, is "does not practice sin," or "does not habitually sin," or "does not keep on sinning with a high hand."

The original Greek text requires this verse to be translated, "whosoever is born of God does not keep on practicing sinning."

"Sinneth not" in 1 John 5:18 is also in the present (linear tense) which should be translated, "whosoever is born of God does not practice sin" or does not keep on habitually sinning."

Christ in us is not the basis on which God justifies us. The basis on which God justifies us is Christ's atoning work for us, outside of us, 2000 years ago!

"Christ in you" is **the result and assurance and pledge** of our justification and acceptance by God, not the basis!

In comparison to Adam's and Eve's obedience before they sinned, the obedience of the best Christian on earth is always relative—never absolute, never perfect. **See pages 126–127.**

The best Christians on earth, although they desire and purpose and strive to perfectly obey God, always come **short** of perfect obedience.

Our so-called "perfect" obedience is not our **title** to heaven; Jesus' perfect obedience is. (MYP 35). Generally speaking, God's people desire and purpose to be obedient Christians. True faith in Jesus never leads anyone to become careless and permissive about sin.

There is no excuse for sinning. "God's grace is sufficient for us." We **CAN** live above conscious, known, willful sin.

We are to be diligent to obey God and to perform good works, but we are to be just as diligent not to trust in our obedience and good works for our justification, forgiveness and acceptance by God at last!

Conclusion

The best Christians in the world still come short of being as perfect as Jesus was in nature. The belief that we can or that we must become as sinless as Jesus was when He was on earth in order to be saved is a delusion!

THE BELIEF IN A "SINLESS LAST GENERATION" IS A MYTH!

1. **TMK 136:** "**No one is perfect, but Jesus.**"
2. **1 SM 394:** "In ourselves we are sinners: but **in Christ we are righteous**."
3. **1 SM 192:** "The only cleanness [righteousness] that I have is that which is **in Christ**."
4. **YI 8/10/93:** "[During this life on earth] The only way we become perfectly righteous is by the **imputed** righteousness of Christ."
5. **TIMK 361:** "We cannot say, 'I am **sinless**,' till this vile body is changed and fashioned like His glorious body [**at the Second Coming of Christ**]."
6. **AA 532:** "Our obedience can be made **perfect** [and acceptable to God] only by the incense of Christ's [**imputed**] righteousness."
7. **4T 367:** "Man may grow up into Christ, his living head. It is not the work of a moment, but of a lifetime. By growing daily in the divine life, he will not attain to the **full** stature of a perfect man in Christ **until his probation ceases**."
8. **1SM 353, 354:** "We can do **nothing, absolutely nothing** to commend ourselves to divine favor."
9. **RH 9/3/1901:** "Righteousness without a blemish can be obtained **only** through the **imputed [credited]** righteousness of Christ."
10. **1HP 227:** "If you are **right** with God today, you are **ready** if Christ should come today."

ISSUE NINETEEN:
OFTEN MISUNDERSTOOD EGW STATEMENTS

Erroneous Presuppositions

1. Page 24.2: "To be pardoned in the way that Christ pardons, is not only to be *forgiven*, but to be *renewed* in the spirit and mind."
2. Page 24.10: "God's forgiveness is not like our forgiveness."
3. Page 24.8: " God's forgiveness is not *merely a judicial act* by which He *sets us free from condemnation.* It [God's forgiveness] *is not only forgiveness* for sin, but *reclaiming from* sin. It [God's forgiveness] is the *outflow* of redeeming love that *transforms* the heart." (TM 114).

Comments by The Author

Although faith, repentance, conversion, and the beginning of sanctification *occur together and at the same time*, they are *not the BASIS* on which God justifies us, but *the FRUIT* of Christ's atoning work and God's justification of believers.

God's *TOTAL* plan of salvation includes *ALL* aspects of salvation; it includes the atonement, justification, forgiveness, faith, repentance, conversion, sanctification, growth in grace, victory over our besetting sins, becoming more and more like Jesus in character, glorification, heaven and the new earth. See Volume One, Chapter 33 "The TOTAL Plan of Salvation".

But we must distinguish between *justification* and our being *forgiven* on the one hand, and our *conversion and sanctification* on the other hand, lest we **fuse and confuse** the two, thus making justification dependent upon conversion and sanctification as the Roman Catholics do.

I am surprised that our brother does not quote COL. 69: "When the character of Christ shall be *PERFECTLY REPRODUCED* in His people, then He will come to claim them as His own."

I have many SDA friends who interpret this EGW statement to mean that we can become as righteous (sinless) as Jesus was in the flesh when He was on earth. This used to be my favorite EGW quote.

Mrs. White calls this *"BLASPHEMY!"*   See page 125, number 9 of this book. We would do well to reread pages 122–127 and 149 again.

The Bible Teaches That:

Justification *(forgiveness) is the opposite of condemnation*, the remission of sin, freedom from guilt. Mrs. White does not always distinguish between the *basis*, *means*, *and fruit* of justification.

Strictly, technically, biblically speaking, justification (forgiveness) *is not conversion and sanctification*. In many other statements, Mrs. White clearly and correctly *restricted* justification (forgiveness) to *remission* and deliverance from *guilt and condemnation of sin*.

Ps. 51 includes *both* imputed and imparted righteousness. David wanted not only to be forgiven, but also to be reconverted and sanctified. He wanted a new heart and a renewed relationship with God.

Inner conversion, cleansing, sanctification, and transformation of character always *accompany* justification (forgiveness) but are *not* an "organic," "systemic" part of them!

Mrs. White was not a systematic theologian. The apostle Paul was the only systematic theologian Bible writer.

We must interpret Mrs. White to harmonize with the Bible and with her *balancing, complementary* statements on each subject.

God does not justify anyone whom He does not sanctify. Forgiveness and conversion and sanctification always occur together. But forgiveness (justification) is not based on our conversion and sanctification, but on Christ's doing and dying.

It was the Great Protestant Reformer, John Calvin, who said:
"We are justified MERITORIOUSLY by CHRIST'S ATONING WORK.
"We are justified INSTRUMENTALLY by FAITH.
" We are justified EFFICACIOUSLY by GRACE.
And, "We are justified EVIDENTALLY by WORKS."

REPLY TO PAXTON

In 1977, Geoffrey Paxton, an Anglican Bishop of Australia wrote a scholarly, well-documented book on the Seventh-day Adventist Church's understanding of **Justification by Faith**.

In his 172-page book, Bishop Paxton states that, "although Seventh-day Adventists claim to be **heirs of the Protestant Reformers**, they are guilty of teaching the Roman-Catholic doctrine of Justification which holds that **Justification includes both justification and sanctification**."

Bishop Paxton's book did shake up Seventh-day Adventists as he preached his gospel in many of our leading churches and universities in the U.S.A. But, tragically, in the end, his message was largely rejected by the Church. **What a great CATASTROPHY this was!**

Elder H. M. S. Richards, Sr. said, "**Geoffrey Paxton is a friendly critic, and we should listen to him**." **I fully agree with him and with Paxton.**

THE WEDDING GARMENT
THE ROBE OF CHRIST'S RIGHTEOUSNESS

Mrs. White teaches that:
THE WEDDING GARMENT REPRESENTS CHRIST'S IMPUTED RIGHTEOUSNESS
OF JUSTIFICATION, NOT THE IMPARTED RIGHTEOUSNESS OF SANCTIFICATION!

●

This chapter is based on Christ's parable of **THE WEDDING GARMENT** in Matthew, Chapter 22.

1.	**FW 106, 107**: "He sees the **ROBE** of Christ's righteousness, **WOVEN IN THE LOOM OF HEAVEN**, wrought by **HIS** obedience, and **IMPUTED [CREDITED]** to the repenting soul [which we receive] through faith in His name."
2.	**This Day With God p. 226**: "Today human beings [including sincere Christians] stand before God with **defiled garments**. All their righteousness is '**as filthy rags**' (Isa. 64: 6). Satan uses against them his masterly accusing power, ...But they trust in Christ, and Christ will not forsake them. He came to this world to **take away their sins**, and to **IMPUTE** to them His righteousness. He declares that through faith in His name they may receive forgiveness."
3.	**2ST 497, Col. 2, July 4, 1892**: "It is the **[imputed]** righteousness of Christ that makes the penitent sinner acceptable to God and works his justification. However sinful has been his life, if he **BELIEVES** in Jesus as His personal Saviour, he **STANDS** before God in the spotless **ROBES** of Christ's **IMPUTED** righteousness...He sees **the ROBE of Christ's righteousness, woven in the loom of heaven, wrought by His [perfect] obedience**, and **IMPUTED** to the repenting soul through faith in His name."
4.	**PK 584**: "As the intercession of Joshua is accepted, the command is given, 'Take away the **FILTHY GARMENTS** from him:' and to Joshua the Angel says, 'Behold, I have caused thine iniquity to pass from thee, and I will **clothe** thee with **CHANGE OF RAIMENT**.'""So they set a fair miter upon his head, and clothed him with **GARMENTS**.' (Zech. 3:5). His own sins and those of his people were pardoned. Israel was **CLOTHED** with '**CHANGE OF RAIMENT**'—the righteousness of Christ **IMPUTED** to them."
5.	**Letter 17a, 1891: Quoted in N.F. Pease' book, *By Faith Alone*, p. 241** "Jesus is perfect, Christ's [perfect] righteousness is **IMPUTED** [credited] unto them, and He will say, take away **the filthy garments** from him and **clothe** him with **change of raiment**. Jesus' [perfect righteousness] makes up for our **UNAVOIDABLE** [!!!] deficiencies."

6. **SM 396**: "He presents me to God in **THE SPOTLESS GARMENT** of which **NO THREAD** [not even one **sanctified** thread] was woven by any **human** agent. **ALL** is of Christ, and **ALL** the glory, honor, and majesty are given to the Lamb of God, which taketh away the sin of the world."

7. **SD 368**: "Only those who are clothed in **the garments of His righteousness [the wedding garment–the imputed righteousness of Christ]** will be able to endure the glory of His presence when He shall appear with 'power and great glory.'...**a special garment** called **the wedding garment**, which is the white robe of **CHRIST'S** righteousness. "Everyone who has on **this robe** is **entitled** [title] to enter the City of God."

8. **EV 186**: "Faith in Christ means everything to the sincere believer. **The merits of JESUS** blot out our transgressions, and **CLOTHE** us with **the robe of righteousness woven in the loom OF HEAVEN**," **NOT** woven on earth or **IN US!**

9. **MYP 35**: "**The righteousness** by which we are **JUSTIFIED** is **IMPUTED**... is our **TITLE** to Heaven."

10. **6T 297**: **God provides the wedding garment without and apart from our help**. "They should put on the wedding garment that **CHRIST** has [already] provided [before we were **BORN**.]."

11. **6T 296**: "**The wedding garment**, [is] the robe of the righteousness of **CHRIST**."

12. **COL 316, 317**: "Those who reject the **GIFT** of Christ's [**imputed**] righteousness are rejecting the attributes of character which constitutes them the sons and daughters of God."

13. **1 SM 333: "Our sinfulness**, our weakness, our human **imperfections** make it impossible that we [Christians] should appear before God unless we are **CLOTHED in Christ's spotless righteousness**."

14. **SD 368**: "If you are to sit at Christ's table, and feast on the provisions He has furnished at **the marriage supper of the Lamb**, you must have a special garment, called **the wedding garment**, which is **the white robe of Christ's [imputed] righteousness**. Everyone who has on this robe is **entitled [title]** to enter the city of God.

15. **5 BC 1097**: "We must have on the **white robe of Christ's [imputed] righteousness**, which has been prepared for all the guests [by God Himself]."

16. **MB 8, 9**: Christ throws "His robe of righteousness" about those who are **NOT WORTHY**! "**We are not worthy** of God's love, but Christ, our surety, is worthy, and is abundantly able to save all who shall come to Him... "Our compassionate Saviour will meet you a great way off, and will **throw about you** His arm of love and **His robe of righteousness**.

    "He [Jesus] presents us to the Father **CLOTHED in the white raiment of His own character**, He pleads before God in our behalf, saying: I have taken the sinner's place. Look not upon this **WAYWARD** child, but look on **ME [!]**. Does Satan plead loudly against our souls, accusing us of sin, and claiming us as His prey? The blood of Christ pleads with greater power."

17. **FW 23**: "They need **THE WHITE RAIMENT** [the wedding garment] of Christ's pure character [which God **IMPUTES (CREDITS)**] to them in His gift of Justification."

18. **FW 108**: "Standing before the broken law of God, **THE SINNER** cannot **CLEANSE** himself; but, believing in Christ, he is the object of His infinite love and [**he is**] **CLOTHED in His spotless righteousness**."

19. **SD 240 teaches that the wedding garment represents Christ's IMPUTED righteousness!** "By faith he [**the sinner who is still a sinful sinning sinner!**] lays hold of the righteousness of Christ. Knowing himself to be a sinner, a transgressor of the holy law of God, he looks to the perfect obedience of Christ, to His death upon Calvary for the sins of the world; and he has the assurance that he is justified by faith in the merit and sacrifice of Christ...The active obedience of Christ [**the wedding garment**] **CLOTHES** the believing sinner with the righteousness that meets [fulfills, satisfies] the demands of the law."

20. **5 BC 480: "The wedding garment represents 'the righteousness of Christ' [that is imputed, credited, to us in justification]."**

21. **5T 509**: "**How plainly** the picture is drawn in the word of God, of His dealing with the men who accepted His invitation to **the wedding**, but who did not put on **the wedding garment** which had been purchased for him–**the robe of Christ's [imputed] righteousness!** He thought his own defiled garments good enough to come into the presence of Christ; but he was cast out as one who had **insulted** his Lord, and **abused** His gracious benevolence."

22. **FW 108, 109**: "Who can comprehend the nature of that righteousness which makes the believing sinner whole, presenting him to God **without spot or wrinkle [the wedding garment]** or any such thing? We have the pledged word of God that Christ is made unto us **righteousness**, sanctification, and redemption."

23. **COL 312**: "Then, as the Lord looks upon us [**Christians**], He sees not the fig-leaf garment, not **the nakedness and deformity of sin** [which all Christians continue to have until glorification], but **His own robe of righteousness, which is PERFECT OBEDIENCE to the law of Jehovah**, [which is IMPUTED to us in God's gift of Justification!]."

24. **SD 346; YI Feb. 8, 1894**: "The resolutions you may make in your own finite strength, will be only as ropes of sand; but if you pray in sincerity, surrendering yourself, soul, body, and spirit unto God, you put on the whole armor of God, and open the soul to the righteousness of Christ; and **this alone**–Christ's **IMPUTED** righteousness–makes you able to **STAND** against the wiles [accusations and temptations] of the devil."

25. **SD 240**: "He [the sinner] realizes that the law was obeyed in his behalf by the Son of God, and that the penalty of transgression cannot fall upon the believing sinner. The active obedience of Christ **CLOTHES [the wedding garment]** the believing sinner with the righteousness that meets the demands of the law."

26. **7BC 907**: "Through His sacrifice, human beings may reach the high ideal set before them and hear at last the words, '**Ye are complete IN HIM**,' not having your own righteousness, but the righteousness He wrought out for you. Your imperfection is no longer seen, for you are **CLOTHED [covered] with THE ROBE of Christ's perfection [which is imputed to you in God's gift of justification]**."

27. **OHC 52**: "They [believing, repenting sinners] are **JUSTIFIED**," [set right, given right standing] with God **ALONE** through the **IMPUTED** righteousness of Christ."

Conclusion

In this chapter, we have cited five EGW quotations teaching that **Christ's wedding garment, His robe of righteousness, represents** Christ's righteousness that is **IMPUTED** to us in His gift of **JUSTIFICATION**.

Strictly, technically, biblically speaking, Christ's wedding garment does **NOT** represent Christ's **imparted** righteousness of **sanctification**, but His **IMPUTED** righteousness of **justification**.

We are fully forgiven and accepted by God RIGHT NOW!

- **John 3:18**: "He that **BELIEVETH** [present tense] on Him **IS NOT CONDEMNED**."

- **John 5:24**: "Verily, verily, I say unto you, He that heareth My word, and **BELIEVETH** on Him that sent Me, **HATH** [present tense] everlasting life, and shall not come into **condemnation [Greek, Judgement]**; but **is passed** [present tense] from death unto life."

- **Romans 8:1**: "There is therefore **NOW NO CONDEMNATION** to them which are in [**BELIEVE IN**] Christ Jesus."

RIGHTEOUSNESS BY FAITH
What Is It?

Simply, Technically, Biblically Speaking,
What is "RIGHTEOUSNESS BY FAITH?"

Is Righteousness by Faith:
1. Our **conversion** and **sanctification**?
2. Our being **accepted** by God because He has converted and sanctified us?
3. Our being justified and forgiven by God because He has **MADE** us inwardly righteous, pleasing, and acceptable to Himself?
4. Our **obedience** by faith? Our rightdoing by faith?
5. Our **righteous living** by faith?
6. Our **becoming inwardly righteous by faith** and by God infusing His righteousness into us?
7. Our being **TREATED** by God **AS** righteous **because He has made us righteous.**

(The **JESUITS (Roman Catholics)** teach that Justification is **all of the above!** They teach that God accepts them **BECAUSE** they **ARE righteous. They believe that they are in a state of grace because God has MADE them inwardly righteous, through their faith and the seven sacraments of the Church!**)

OR is Righteousness by Faith:
1. God's **forgiveness** of all our sins?
2. Our being **credited** with Christ's righteousness?
3. Our being **treated** by God during this life on earth **AS IF** we were already perfectly righteous?
4. All of which we receive **solely by faith, apart from works?**

THE LATTER four are all true, according to the Bible. NONE of the first seven are true!

32 IMPORTANT TRUTHS
about Righteousness by Faith on the one hand, and Christian Perfection on the other

1. **The term, "RIGHTEOUSNESS BY/OF FAITH," occurs 8 times in the N.T. In every one of these 8 occurrences the CONTEXT is speaking of JUSTIFICATION BY FAITH, NOT Sanctification by faith and works.**

These Eight Texts are Quoted from the New King James Version.

1) **Romans 3:22**   "even **the righteousness** of God, **through faith** in Jesus Christ, to all and on all who believe. For there is no difference;"

2) **Romans 4:13**   ". . .the **righteousness of faith.**"

3) **Romans 4:13**   "For the promise that he would be the heir of the world *was* not to Abraham or to his seed through the law, but through the **righteousness of faith.**"

4) **Romans 9:30**   "What shall we say then? That Gentiles, who did not pursue righteousness, have attained to righteousness, even **the righteousness of faith**;"

5) **Romans 10:6**   "But **the righteousness of faith** speaks in this way," *'do not say in your heart, "Who will ascent into heaven?"'* (that is, to bring Christ down *from above*)

6) **Galatians 5:5**   "For we through the Spirit eagerly wait for the hope of **righteousness by faith**".

7) **Philippians 3:9**   "and be found in Him, not having my own righteousness, which is from the law, but that which is through faith in Christ, **the righteousness** which is from God **by faith**;"

8) **Hebrews 11:7**   "The **righteousness** which is according to **faith**."

The Bible never teaches that we are SANCTIFIED BY FAITH ALONE!
This proves that "Righteousness by Faith" is THE SAME as "Justification by Faith."

2.   Accordingly, Righteousness by Faith has to do with the **IMPUTED (credited)** righteousness of **JUSTIFICATION, NOT** with the **IMPARTED** righteousness of **SANCTIFICATION.** Sanctification by faith and works **is no part of** Justification by Faith (Righteousness by Faith).

3.   **There are TWO aspects of Sanctification. These two aspects of sanctification are: (a) the initial** setting apart for a holy use, consecration, dedication, surrender, and committment to God, and **(b) the continuing** obeying God, growing in grace, living a godly life, and developing Christian character.

4.   In number three just above, we said that there are **two** aspects of **Sanctification.**
   1) **The first aspect of Sanctification IS just like Justification—by faith alone, apart from our cooperation, obedience, and good works.**
   2) The **second** aspect of sanctification is **NOT** solely by faith apart from our obedience and good works. The **second** aspect of sanctification **is by faith PLUS our cooperation**—our personal devotional life, our obedience, and good works. **WE** have a part in our growing in grace.

5.   **Righteousness by Faith** is precisely the same thing as **Justification by Faith**—no more and no less. God does **not hold** our sins **against us** or punish us for our sins during this life on earth. During this life, all our sins are **"under the blood."**

6.   Justification is **three** things: (1) Justification is a legal, judicial, forensic **VERDICT OF PARDON**—of the forgiveness of all our sins. (2) Justifcation is God **CREDITING** Christ's righteousness (perfectly obedient life and His death on the cross) to us. And (3) justifcation is God **TREATING** us, during this life on earth, **AS IF** we were perfectly righteous. God's justification of unrepentant sinners **ENDS AT DEATH!** If sinners do not **respond** to God's love, truly **believe** in Jesus, and **repent** of their sins by the time they **die**, they will be **lost forever!**

7.   Justification is **NOT A MAKING** internally righteous **as the Jesuits and "Certain Independent SDA Ministries" teach!** Justification is God's gracious **ACT** of **IMPUTING**

(reckoning, crediting) Christ's infinitely righteous life and death to our account in heaven; **NOT His act of MAKING** us inwardly righteous, in a relative or absolute sense. Our growing in grace and becoming more and more righteous in a **relative** sense takes place in **sanctification**.

8. God's people will **NOT become perfectly** righteous within until **Glorification.** At that time, our sinful nature will be removed from us and we will be filled with the **FULLNESS** of the Holy Spirit.

9. **Justification by Faith** (Righteousness by Faith) does **NOT MAKE** us inwardly righteous; it **forgives** our sins; it **credits** Christ's righteousness to us, and it **reckons and accounts** us righteous. In justification, we are **accepted and treated** by God, during this life on earth, **AS IF** we had never sinned. Throughout our Christian lives, God helps us to become more and more Christlike.

10. **FAITH believes, trusts, and appropriates** God's gifts of Christ's righteousness and death to ourselves personally and **rests** securely in that perfect righteousness and eternal life. **This is Righteousness by Faith—Justification by Faith.**

11. We are justified **solely by faith**.

12. We are justified **apart from our obedience and good works**.

13. The **imparted** righteousness of the **second** aspect of **sanctification** does **NOT** make us perfectly righteous internally during this life on earth. **NOR** does it make us absolutely righteous in our outward lives. Therefore, **WHY** call Sanctification, **"Righteousness by Faith"**? To do so is to teach **contrary** to the Bible. Sanctification is **no part** of "Righteousness by Faith." Sanctification is the **FRUIT** of Righteousness by Faith.

14. Righteousness by Faith is **NOT OUR** becoming inwardly righteous by faith, **OUR** perfect obedience by faith, **OUR** righteous living by faith, or Christ or the Holy Spirit dwelling in us by faith.

15. We must repeat this important truth. Since **Sanctification** is by faith **and works and since**—our obedience and good works—do not **MAKE** us inwardly perfectly righteous during this life on earth, **WHY** call Sanctification by faith and works **"Righteousness by Faith"**? We should **NOT** call Sanctification by faith and works, **Righteousness by Faith** because sanctification is **BY** faith **AND** works. On the other hand, justification (Righteousness by Faith) **is solely by faith, apart from our obedience and good works**. To say that Righteousness by Faith includes sanctification is to teach Roman Catholic doctrine!

16. Righteousness by Faith is our being **ACCOUNTED** righteous. We receive this righteous **STANDING** before God in our sinful moral **STATE solely by faith, apart from works.**

    (See pages 62–69, 99–111). **Although sin REMAINS in Christians, it does not REIGN in them!**

17. Righteousness by Faith is God's sheer **GIFT to** unworthy sinners—**unearned, unmerited, undeserved!**

18. Christian perfection is **relative, NEVER ABSOLUTE. The best of Christians still come SHORT of perfectly obeying and fulfilling God's infinitely righteous law.** (See pages 119 to 127 on Perfection.)

19. It is impossible for anyone to be **lost** as long as he continues to **truly believe** in Jesus.

20. God's people will not become absolutely righteous within **until GLORIFICATION.** (See ISSUE 13, pages 119 to 127 for EGW statements to this effect. See especially page 126, numbers 1, 3 and 4).

21. Mrs. White says at least **27 times** that Christians become perfectly righteous **only by the IMPUTED** righteousness of Christ and of Justification—only by being **accounted** righteous— **NOT** by His **IMPARTED** righteousness of sanctification—**not** by being **made** righteous in nature, character, or life!

Mrs. White Says That:

22. **Although we are not perfect children of God, we are perfectly God's children the moment we truly BELIEVE in Jesus, repent of our sins, and accept Jesus as our personal Saviour!**

23. The moment we truly **BELIEVE** in Jesus (**repent** of our sins and are **converted**), we are **perfectly forgiven and accepted** by God unto eternal life.

24. We are to **COPY** the Pattern, but we **cannot EQUAL** it. 2T 549.

25. We are to be perfect in our **finite, human** sphere as God is perfect in His **infinite, divine** sphere. CT 365; 8T 64; PP 574.

26. There never was, and there never will be, another human being **as righteous as Christ.** 7BC 904.

27. The most righteous person in the history of the world is but a **DIM** reflection of the character of Christ. MB 49.

28. To teach that we can become as righteous as Christ is **BLASPHEMY**. RH March 15, 1887.

29. The prayers and praises of the most righteous Christian on earth **are not acceptable** to God unless **covered** with the blood of Christ and **perfumed** with the incense of His righteousness. 1SM 344; SC 62; 1 SM 367, 1 SM 389).

30. Our only **REFUGE** after the close of Probation is the **IMPUTED** righteousness of Christ, **NOT** His **imparted** righteousness—not our sanctification or character perfection.

31. Justification by Faith (Righteousness by Faith) gives us a righteous legal **STANDING** before God and His infinitely righteous law in our sinful moral **STATE** (condition).

32. We are to be diligent to obey God and to perform good works, but we are to be just as diligent not to trust in our obedience and good works for salvation.

It is very important for us to understand: (1) the one and only **meritorious BASIS** of our justification; (2) the one and only **instrumental MEANS** of our justification; and (3) the **inevitable FRUIT** of our justification.

John Bunyan, author of Pligrims Progress, said:
"It is the greatest mystery in the universe
that the righteousness that is in a Person in heaven
should justify me, a sinner on earth."
HOW TRUE!

RECAPITULATION

These are the 21 issues which the Challenger raises concerning the gospel in his 48-page CRITIQUE of the Campus Hill Church's Confession of the Gospel.

THE 21 BIBLICAL AND ELLEN G, WHITE TRUTHS WHICH WE ARE TEACHING IN THIS BOOK ARE THESE:

1. **SOLA SCRIPTURA**—The Christian's ultimate authority in religious matters does not include Mrs. White's writings, as she herself taught at least 16 times, but is restricted solely to the Bible. (See FUNDAMENTAL BELIEFS OF SEVENTH-DAY ADVENTISTS, "Preamble" and Belief Number 1, The Holy Scriptures). See also page 19 of this book for the 16 EGW statements.

2. **The NATURE of Justification:** Justification is not a converting, sanctifying, morally transforming act of God, but is instead a legal, judicial, forensic act of God in behalf of believers.

3. **The DEFINITION of Justification:** Justification is not God's act of converting, sanctifying and transforming us morally and making us inwardly righteous, pleasing and acceptable to Himself. Justification is God's acts of forgiving our sins, crediting Christ's righteousness to us, adopting us into His heavenly family, accepting us unto eternal life, and treating us, during this life on earth as if we had never sinned. Justification is three things. Justification is: (1) God's non-imputation of our sins to us, (2) the imputation of our sins to Christ, and (3) the imputation of Christ righteousness to us.

4. **The MEANING of the GREEK word,** *logizomai,* which appears eleven times in the fourth chapter of Romans, does not mean to impart, to infuse into, or to make righteous, but to impute, to reckon, to account, to credit, to consider (righteous) and to treat us as if we were actually righteous within.

5. **The RIGHTEOUSNESS which JUSTIFIES us** is never the righteousness of the Holy Spirit, but is solely the righteousness and atoning work of Christ! The Holy Spirit is not our justifier and Savior; Jesus is! The Holy Spirit is our sanctifier and perfector.

6. **Justification is OBJECTIVE**; it does not take place inside of us, down here on earth, but is always, in Christ in heaven.

7. **The meritorious BASIS** on which God justifies believers does not include his converting, sanctifying, morally transforming work in us, but is solely God's atoning work for us in Jesus outside of us, in Palestine, nearly 2000 years ago.

8. **The instrumental MEANS** by which God's gifts of justification are appropriated by us personally is not faith plus obedience. We are justified by God by faith plus nothing! Faith is belief plus trust, plus resting in Christ's completed work of salvation 2000 years ago!

9. **We must DISTINGUISH between THE ROOT AND THE FRUIT of justification**, between the basis and results, between justification and sanctification. Justification and sanctification are distinct, but never separate. God does not sanctify us in order to justify us; He justifies us in order to sanctify us.

10. **There are NOT MANY CONDITIONS**, which we must meet in order to be justified; there is only one; and that is faith.

11. **STANDING and STATE:** God's gift of justification gives a righteous legal **STANDING** before Him and His infinitely righteous law in the judgment in our sinful moral **STATE**. Although we sincere born–again Christians continue to be sinful beings with sinful moral natures, and although we continue to come short of perfectly obeying God's infinitely righteous law, because of and on the basis of Christ's atoning work for us, God justifies us and treats us **AS IF** we had never sinned.

12. **There are two aspects of SANCTIFICATION.** The first is a setting apart for a holy use, consecration, dedication, surrender, commitment to God, which is solely by faith apart from works. The second is our living the Christian life, overcoming our besetting sins, developing Christian character and becoming more and more like Jesus in character. In order to accomplish these in us, the Holy Spirit needs our knowledge, consent and cooperation. We are not to become spiritual zombies and remain inactive and wait for God to perfect our characters.

13. **Christian PERFECTION is never absolute during this life on earth.** Christian perfection is always relative during this life. The best Christians in the world still come short of perfectly obeying God's infinitely righteous law—of becoming perfectly sinless (righteous). The only way we meet God's requirements, the only way we become perfectly righteous during this life is through the imputed righteousness of Christ which God credits to us in His gift of justification, and which we receive solely through faith in Jesus. For entrance into heaven God requires of us perfect obedience, perfect righteousness from birth until death. But not one of us has that perfect righteousness to present to God. In love, mercy and compassion, God has come to our rescue. The perfect righteousness which He requires of us for entrance into heaven, He Himself has already provided for us in His Son Jesus Christ as a free gift, period.

14. **Jesus' SACRIFICIAL ATONEMENT** for sin was perfect, complete, and finished on the cross. Jesus is not now atoning for our sins in Heaven. Jesus is now dispensing to us the benefits of His atoning sacrifice nearly 2000 years ago. See page 130 for the two aspects of the great A-T-O-N-E-M-E-N-T.

15. **Getting through THE JUDGMENT**: "O, blessed Judgment Day! Hasten on, O blessed Judgment Day!" Why? Because Jesus stands-in for us in the judgment! It is **His** character that gets us through the judgment, not our own. The only righteousness that is good enough to get us through the judgment is Christ's, which God **imputes** to us in His free gift of justification, which we receive solely through faith apart from anything else we may do.

16. **PAUL and JAMES.** Paul says we are justified solely through faith apart from works; James says we are "justified by works." There is no contradiction here. Paul was combating legalism—salvation by works; and James was combating salvation apart from a changed life. True faith will always lead to repentance, conversion sanctification, obedience, good works, a godly life and to the perfecting of Christian character. If it doesn't, it is not true faith, but is presumption! We are justified meritoriously solely through faith apart form works; we are justified evidentially by works. Our works are the result and the evidence that our faith is genuine.

17. **Our ASSURANCE of salvation** does not rest on what God does in us now during this life on earth. All our assurance of salvation rests solely on what God did for us, outside of us in Jesus in Palestine 2000 years ago. There is absolutely no justifying merit whatsoever in what we do, in what God does in us, in what God does to us, in what God puts into us or in what God develops in us! The Holy Spirit gives Christians the assurance of salvation. "The Holy Spirit testifies with our spirit that we are the children of God."

18. **HERMANEUTICS**: Our interpretation of the Bible rests not on the proof text method. We must consider the meaning of the Hebrew and Greek words and culture as well as the tense of the original words.

19. **ELLEN G. WHITE** was/is not "an inspired commentary on the Bible." We must not interpret the Bible by her, but her by the Bible. That which is an inspired commentary on the Bible is superior in authority to the Bible. See 16 statements by Mrs. White in Issue **One**, page 19 of this book. Also, see The Preamble to the Statement of Fundamental Beliefs, page 14.4 says: "Seventh-day Adventists accept the Bible as their only creed." The Bible must be our supreme authority or we are a cult.

20. **THE WEDDING GARMENT** of Matthew 22 does not represent the imparted righteousness of sanctification, but the imputed righteousness of justification. See page 143.

21. **JUSTIFICATION BY FAITH and RIGHTEOUSNESS BY FAITH** are exactly the same thing. These two terms do not refer to our rightdoing by faith, but to **Christ's** which God credits (imputes) to us, and which we appropriate to ourselves personally solely through faith, apart from works.

CONCLUSION

These are the 21 truths concerning the gospel, which this writer is respectfully appealing to our administrators and theologians to make clear in our **Statement of Fundamental Beliefs** in the next General Conference Session (2010).

It is this writers humble opinion that until an all-out global effort is made to enlighten our people concerning the gospel, He will not bless us with the Latter Rain of the Holy Spirit! This is my most mature Judgment: that it is the lack of understanding the gospel that is delaying the Latter Rain and the Loud Cry, the repentance, revival and reformation of our beloved church, and the Second Coming of Christ! **This situation constitutes A GREAT CRISIS in the worldwide Seventh-day Adventist Church!**

He who has eyes, let him see, he who has ears, let him hear, and he who has a mind let him understand what the Holy Spirit is trying to say to Laodicea!

If our beloved Seventh-day Adventist Church leaders, theologians, and pastors all over the world do not teach our people the pure apostolic gospel soon, will we be in danger of God writing "**Ichabod**" concerning us?—"The glory of the Lord has departed!" **How very tragic that would be!**

Gordon Wm. Collier, Sr.

Thank God, Dear Reader,
"They [our sins] are nailed to the cross,
They are nailed to the cross,
O how much He was willing to bear!
With what anguish and loss
Jesus went to the cross
And He carried my sins with Him there."
Old SDA Church Hymnal, page 123.

An Open Letter To Our Leading Administrators, Theologians, Pastors and Laymembers of The Seventh-day Adventist Church

Dear Brothers and Sisters in Christ whom we love in the Church:

SINCE most SDAs in the world do not have the **steadfast ASSURANCE** of salvation,

SINCE a clear understanding of the biblical doctrine of the gospel—the plan of salvation—Righteousness by Faith—how sinners are justified and saved at last—**is of transcendent importance** to the spiritual health and well-being of our beloved church,

SINCE most Seventh-day Adventists in the world are somewhat **legalistic and perfectionistic** because they do **not clearly understand the gospel**—Justification by Faith—Righteousness by Faith,

SINCE most SDAs in the world believe that they are **justified by faith plus obedience**,

SINCE most SDAs in the world believe that, in order to receive the Seal of God, to pass the Judgment and to be saved at last, they must become **perfectly righteous (perfectly sinless)** in character and life,

SINCE most SDAs in the world would answer the 21 questions on pages 146 to 148 of Volume One **incorrectly**, and would answer most of the 10 statements on the previous page incorrectly,

SINCE a very large percentage of **Protestants** in the world understand the gospel and, therefore, those Protestants who study what the SDA denomination teaches respecting the gospel (Justification by Faith), with a view to **joining** our church, **will be turned off by our inadequate teaching on this crucial doctrine of salvation**,

AND SINCE God will certainly not pour out **the Latter Rain** upon a church which **does not believe and teach clearly the truth concerning the gospel (Justification by Faith—Righteousness by Faith.**

I earnestly appeal to you and to your love for **God**, to your love for **truth**, and to your love for our beloved **Church**, please rise up today and earnestly request **our leaders** to publish, as quickly as possible, and by every means available, the full truth about **the WHAT and the WHERE of the IMPUTED RIGHTEOUSNESS OF JUSTIFICATION BY FAITH (Righteousness by Faith)!**

Please teach our people all over the world that the IMPUTED righteousness of JUSTIFICATION BY FAITH (RIGHTEOUSNESS BY FAITH):

1. **IS NEVER the Holy Spirit's converting, sanctifying, transforming work** inside of believers!
2. **IS NEVER Christ's or the Holy Spirit's presence** inside of believers!
3. **IS NEVER** a righteousness that is **INSIDE** of believers down here on this earth!

4. **IS NEVER**: in anything that **WE DO**,
   in anything that **God does IN US**,
   in anything that **God does TO US**,
   in anything that **God puts INTO US, or**
   in anything that **God develops IN US!**
5. **IS NEVER** the righteousness that God **imparts to us in sanctification.**
6. **IS NEVER** a righteousness that **MAKES** believers perfectly righteous, pleasing, and acceptable to God in nature or character or life (action)!
7. **IS THE ONE AND ONLY MERITORIOUS BASIS** (see number nine below) on which God **justifies** believers—**forgives** their sins, **credits** Christ's righteousness to them, **accepts and adopts** them unto eternal life, and **treats** them, during this life on earth, **AS IF** they were actually righteous within!
8. **IS CHRIST'S ATONING WORK** for all sinners in the world, outside of sinners, 2000 years ago which consists of His **Incarnation, sinless life, substitutionary death and resurrection.**
9. **CREDITS** Christ's righteousness to believers in Christ, **accounts** them legally righteous before God's moral law of Ten Commandments in the judgment, **gives** them **a righteous legal standing** (relationship) with God in their **sinful moral state** (nature) and **legally enables God to justly treat them** during this life on earth **AS IF** they were perfectly righteous in character!
10. **IS BELIEVED, TRUSTED, AND RESTED IN** by believers **solely by FAITH in Jesus, apart from** our repentance, conversion, sanctification, obedience, and good works which are the **fruit** of justification and of faith!

By doing the above, you will be HASTENING the enlightenment, repentance, conversion and revival of the worldwide Seventh-day Adventist Church, the Later Rain, the Loud Cry and the Second Coming of Christ!

May I respectfully request that the delegates to the next General Conference Session prayerfully consider adding to Number 10 (The Experience of Salvation) of our *statement of Fundamental Beliefs,* **a detailed explanation of Justification by Faith (Righteousness by Faith), making clear this wonderfully encouraging doctrine, as I have done in this book and in Volume One of this series of books and Volume Two—TWENTY ONE BASIC ISSUES CONCERNING THE GOSPEL—in the church today?** (See pages 146 to 148 of VOLUME ONE of this series and this entire book).

"WHO IS ON THE LORD'S SIDE?" LET HIM STAND UP AND BE COUNTED, FOR JESUS' SAKE AND FOR THE SAKE OF OUR BELOVED CHURCH!

Thank you for your serious consideration of this respectful request.

Very sincerely, your brother in Christ,

Gordon Wm. Collier, Sr., (retired SDA Pastor).
24414 University Ave., No. 149
Loma Linda, CA 92354

ABBREVIATION TO ELLEN WHITE'S BOOKS AND PAMPHLETS

Abbreviation	Book or Periodical Title	Abbreviation	Book or Periodical Title	Abbreviation	Book or Periodical Title
1888	Ellen G. White 1888 Materials, The	DG	Daughters of God	Pr	Prayer
1BC	Bible Commentary, The SDA, Vol. 1	Ed	Education	PUR	Pacific Union Recorder
1Bio	Biography of E.G. White, Vol. 1 (2Bio for Vol. 2)	Ev	Evangelism	RC	Reflecting Christ
1MCP	Mind, Character and Personality, Vol. 1	EW	Early Writings	RH	Review and Herald
1MR	Manuscript Releases, Vol. 1 (2MR for Vol. 2)	FE	Fundamentals of Christian Education	RR	Radiant Religion
1NL	Notebook Leaflets, Vol. 1 (2NL for Vol. 2)	FLB	Faith I Live By, The	RY	Retirement Years, The
1SAT	Sermons and Talks, Vol.1 (2SAT for Vol	FW	Faith and Works	SA	Solemn Appeal, A
1SG	Spiritual Gifts, Vol. 1 (3SG for Vol. 3, etc.)	GC88	Great Controversy, The (1988 Edition)	SC	Steps to Christ
1SM	Selected Messages, Book One (2SM for Book 2)	GCB	General Conference Bulletin	SD	Sons and Daughters of God
1SP	Spirit of Prophecy, The, Vol. 1 (2SP for Vol. 2)	GCDB	General Conference Daily Bulletin	SF Echo	Sothern Field Echo
1T	Testimonies for the Church Vol. 1 (2T for Vol. 2)	GdH	Good Health	SJ	Steps to Jesus (adapted from SC) or Sto
AA	Acts of the Apostles, The	GH	Gospel Herald	SL	Sanctified Life, The
AG	God's Amazing Grace	GW	Gospel Workers	SOJ	Story of Jesus, The
AH	Adventist Home, The	GW92	Gospel Workers (1892 Edition)	SpT"A"	Special Testimonies, Series A (Nos. 1-1
ApM	An 'Appeal to Mothers	HL	Healthful Living	SpT"B"	Special Testimonies, Series B (Nos. 1-1
AUCR	Australian Union Conference Record	HP	In Heavenly Places	SpTBCC	Special Testimonies to the Battle Creek
AY	Appeal to Youth	HPMMW	Health, Philanthropic, and Medical Mission	SpTEd	Special Testimonies to Educattion
BE	Bible Echo	HR	Health Reformer	SpTMMW	Special Testimonies Relating to Medical
BTS	Bible Training School	HS	Historical Sketches of the Foreign Mission Adventist	SpTMWI	Special Testimonies to Managers and W
CC	Conflict and Courage	Hvn	Heaven	SpTPH	Special Testimonies to Physicians and H
CCh	Counsels for the Church	ITT	Testimony Treasures, Vol. 1 (2TT for Vol. 2)	SR	Story of Redemption, The
CD	Counsels on Diet and Foods	LDE	Last Day Events	ST	Signs of the Times
CE	Christian Education	LHU	Lift Him Up	SW	Southern Work, The
CET	Christian Experience and Teaching	LL	Lion on the Loose	SW	Southern Watchman (if with date)
CEv	Christan Evangelist	LP	Sketches From the Life of Paul	TA	Truth About Angels, The
CG	Child Guidance	LS88	Life Sketches of Ellen G. White	TDG	This Day With God
CH	Counsels on Health	Lt	Letter, E. G. White	Te	Temperance
ChL	Christian Leadership	LYL	Letters to Young Lovers	TM	Testimonies to Ministers and Gospel Workers
ChS	Christian Service	MAR	Maranatha, the Lord is Coming	TIMK, TMK	That I May Know Him
CL	Country Living	MB	Thoughts From the Mount of Blessing	TSA	Testimonies to Southern Africa
CM	Colporteur Ministry	MH	Ministry of Healing, The	TSB	Testimonies on Sexual Behaviour, Adult
COL	Christ's Object Lessons	ML	My Life Today	TSDF	Testimony Studies on Diet and Foods
Con	Confrontation	MM	Medical Ministry	TSS	Selections From the Testimonies Bearin(1900)
COS	Christ Our Saviour	Ms	Manuscript, E. G. White	UL	Upward Look, The
CS	Counsels on Stewardship	MYP	Messages to Young People	UndMs	Undated EGW Manuscript
CSW	Counsels on Sabbath School Work	OFC	Our Father Cares	VSS	Voice in Speech and Song, The
CT	Counsels to Parents, Teachers, and Students	OHC	Our High Calling	WLF	Word to the "Little Flock," A
CTBH	Chtistian Temperance (EGW) and Bible	PaM	Pastoral Ministry	WM	Welfare Ministry
CTr	Christ Triumphant	PHJ	Pacific Health Journal	YI	Youth's Instructor, The
CW	Counsels to Writers and Editors	PK	Prophets and Kings	YRP	Ye Shall Receive Power, A
DA	Desire of Ages, The	PM	Publishing Ministry, The		
DF	Document File	PP	Patriarchs and Prophets		

Dear Reader, We print here the Table of Contents for Christian Classics, Volumes One, Three and Four so you will see them as MUST READ books.

Christian Classics • Volume One
Blessed Assurance!
Your Salvation Is Guaranteed

TABLE OF CONTENTS

1. Romans 3:20-31; 5;1-Justification by Faith, Righteousness by faith...v
2. A Key Prophetic Statement by Mrs. Ellen G. White vi
3. Acknowledgments.. vii
4. Dedication viii
5. The Fountain of Living Waters ix
6. Countdown to Eternity x
7. Dr. Heppenstall Discussing Righteousness by Faith with the Author and Others and some of EGW best definitions of Righteousness by Faith (Justification by Faith)...xi
8. More Startling Ellen G. White Statements on Salvation.. xiii
9. The Christian's HIGHEST AUTHORITY xiv
10. The WHOLE TRUTH ABOUT JUSTIFICATION BY FAITH xvi
11. WHY THIS BOOK? xvi
12. JUSTIFICATION: Seven Important Truths About Righteousness by Faith xvii
13. The True, Doctrine of Justification xviii
14. The TRUE and FALSE Doctrines of: The BASIS, Means and FRUIT....................................xix
15. An Honest Confession by the Author xx
16. My "Magnificent **Obsession**" xxi
17. WARNING!...1
18. Seventh-day Adventism' RENDEZVOUS with DESTINY 2
19. Forward...4
20. COVER LETTER - CIRTIQUE of The Confession of the Gospel by the Loma Linda Campus Hill Church of Seventh-day Adventist 5
21. A Personal Letter to the Reader of this Book 6
22. The Four-Page Loma Linda Campus Hill Church Statement of the Gospel................................7
CHAPTER 1   Understanding the Gospel Will not Lead Anyone 11
CHAPTER 2   For Enterance into Heaven, What Does God REQUIRE of Us?................................12
CHAPTER 3   Do We Have to UNDERSTAND Righteousness by Faith to be Saved? 15
CHAPTER 4   Ten Powerful EGW Statements Which Decisively Refute the Harvest Principal 16
CHAPTER 5   Sever Marvelous Aspects OF Justification..17
CHAPTER 6   "How Then Can Man be Justified With God?" Job 25:4 18
CHAPTER 7   Reply to Paxton: "To Disregard Light is to Reject It!" 19

CHAPTER 8   So Near to God, but LOST 20

CHAPTER 9   Five Crucial bible Truths Concerning Justification by Faith Which Most SDAs DO NOT UNDERSTAND...21

CHAPTER 10   15 Statements by Mrs. White on the IMPORTANCE of the Doctrine of   Justification by Faith 22

CHAPTER 11   "Our FIRST Consideration" - The Righteousness of Christ...24

CHAPTER 12   The Eight New Testament Texts Which Contain the Expression "Righteousness   by Faith".......25

CHAPTER 13   This Book is A COLLECTION of Some of the Author's Writings and Sermons on the Gospel over the Past 29 years 26

CHAPTER 14   Are Justification and Sanctification THE SAME THING 28

CHAPTER 15   The 1976 Palmdale, California Consensus Statement on Righteousness by Faith.......................29

CHAPTER 16   What God Does OUTSIDE of us and what He Does INSIDE of us 30

CHAPTER 17   24 TRUTHS You Need to Know about Justification by Faith (Righteousness by Faith)...........31

CHAPTER 18   At Least 18 Bible Texts Which Declare that We Are Justified SOLELY THROUGH FAITH APART FROM OUR OBEDIENCE AND GOOD WORKS 36

CHAPTER 19   Mrs. White's 15 Best Definitions of Righteousness by Faith in the book, *Selected Messages*, Volume One 37

CHAPTER 20   "Though Your Sins Be As Scarlet..." HOW NOT TO BE AFRAID OF THE PRE-ADVENT JUDGMENT 41

CHAPTER 21   14 E.G.W. Statements Declare That Justification by Faith is the Same as Righteousness by Faith 44

CHAPTER 22   OUT TITLE TO HEAVEN! THE IMPUTED RIGHTEOUSNESS OF CHRIST 47

CHAPTER 23   The Two Different Aspects of Righteousness CONTRASTED 55

CHAPTER 24   MORE Important Distinctions..57

CHAPTER 25   God's TWO ASPECTS, TWO PLACES, TWO USES, TWO PURPOSES, AND TWO ACCOMPLISHMENTS of Christ's Righteousness...62

CHAPTER 26   CHECK YOURSELF. WHICH ARE YOU? In your Understanding of the Gospel, Are You Protestant of Roman-Catholic?...69

CHAPTER 27   "Being Now Justified by His BLOOD" Romans 5:9 72

CHAPTER 28   The ABC's of Salvation 73

CHAPTER 29   TEN OFFICIAL ROMAN CATHOLIC DEFINITIONS of Justification and An Unbelievably Great SDA Theological Catastrophe. Truly   Our Beloved Church IS IN CRISIS! 78

CHAPTER 30   "Look Unto ME, and Be Ye SAVED, All the Ends of the Earth." Isa. 45:22 88

CHAPTER 31   JESUITS IN THE SEVENTH-DAY ADVENTIST CHURCH? 89

CHAPTER 32   The OBJECTIVE, MERITORIOUS BASIS and the INSTRUMENTAL MEANS of Justification Through Faith in Christ 99

CHAPTER 33   MARTIN LUTHER Discovers the Pure Apostolic Gospel of Justification Solely Through Faith, Apart from Works 100

CHAPTER 34   The ONLY Righteousness that is GOOD ENOUGH to Justify Us! 106

CHAPTER 35   SEVEN E.G.W. STATEMENTS Which Declare that We are Justified "ONLY," "ALONE" (SOLELY) Through IMPUTED Righteousness of Christ 107

CHAPTER 36   THE TRUE CHRISTIAN GOSPEL IN A NUTSHELL 109

CHAPTER 37   STRANGE BEDFELLOWS! Believe it of NOT! 116

CHAPTER 38   Three Different Doctrines of Justification...117

CHAPTER 39   THE IMPORTANCE OF SANCTIFICATION 118

CHAPTER 40   32 DIFFERENCES Between the Righteousness of Justification and the   Righteousness of Sanctification..122

CHAPTER 41   Let Us Exalt "the Precious Blood of Jesus" More and More! 127

CHAPTER 42   The Importance of the 1888 Message of CHRIST OUR RIGHTEOUSNESS—Justification by Faith...128

CHAPTER 43   JUSTIFICATION, SANCTIFICATION, PERFECTION 130

CHAPTER 44 A Thumbnale Sketch of the History of how the Entire Christian Church Went Astray on the Doctrine of Justification Solely by Faith Apart from Obedience and Good Works A.D. 400 to 1518-1545-1563-2005 132

CHAPTER 45 LOOK and LIVE! 134

CHAPTER 46 SEVENTH-DAY ADVENTISM: A CHURCH DIVIDED! 135

CHAPTER 47 The ONLY Way We Become Perfectly Righteous During this life on Earth! 136

CHAPTER 48 "I determined not to know anything among you, save Jesus Christ and Him Crucified." 1Cor. 2:2 141

CHAPTER 49 An **OPEN LETTER** To **THE LEADERS** of the Seventh-day Adventist Church 142

CHAPTER 50 My Closing **Appeal** To **THE LAYMEMBERS** of the Seventh-day Adventist Church 143

CHAPTER 51 Title Page and **TABLE OF CONTENTS** for Volume **TWO** 144

CHAPTER 52 ABBREVIATIONS TO ELLEN WHITE'S BOOKS AND PAMPHLETS 149

Christian Classics • *Volume Three*
ANGLICAN THEOLOGIAN EVALUATES SEVENTH-DAY ADVENTIST THEOLOGY AND FINDS IT WANTING!

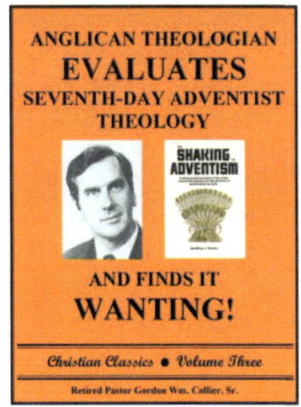

TABLE OF CONTENTS
PART ONE

- DEDICATION
- PREFACE BY Author
- FORWARD BY David McMahon
- INTRODUCTION BY Geoffrey Paxton
- THERE IS NO AGREEMENT in Adventism concerning the ESSENCE OF Christianity
- THREE DISTINCT Theological Schools in Adventism
- Dr Lindsell Believes that LIBERALISM Is Adventisms Biggest Threat
- THE CENTRAL ISSUE in Adventism Today is RIGHTEOUSNESS BY FAITH
- Righteousness by Faith is THE SAME AS JUSTIFICATION BY FAITH
- THE MAIN ISSUE of The Protestant Reformation ALL OVER AGAIN In the Seventh-day Adventist Church
- This CONTROVERSY In The Seventh-day Adventist Church IS A GOOD THING!
- Adventism Stands In A PIVILEGED POSITION
- Seventh-day Adventists and E. G. White's Emphasis on Sanctification IS VERY GOOD
- SPIRITUAL "ZOMBIEISM" The Dehumanization of Christians
- Adventisms' TWOFOLD CHALLENGE! Make Clear to The Christian World (1) SALVATION by GRACE Through Faith Alone and (2) JUDGMENT According to WORKS
- Adventism Is **FACE TO FACE** With The **GREATEST CRISIS** In Her History!
- FIVE ASPECTS OF THE CONFLICT Over Righteousness by Faith In The Seventh-day Adventist Church (1) Righteousness by Faith — JUSTIFICATION BY FAITHIs EQUATED WITH SANCTIFICATION

(2) Justification is **DOWNGRADED** by Subordinating It to SANCTIFICATION (3) Regeneration is Made **A CONDITION OR BASIS** of Justification (4) The Result is A **PNEUMATIC** LEGALISM (5) CHARACTER DEVELOPMENT IS Made THE CRITERIA In The JUDGMENT

- GOD'S WORK
- THE HOLY SPIRIT'S WORK
- THE MORAL NATURE OF CHRIST
- PAXTON'S FERVENT WISH
- The General Tendency of Adventism
- Adventisms BASIC P-R-O-B-L-E-M
- THE BIG ISSUE In Adventism today
- THE BASIS of Our-Acceptance with God?
- We Have An Apology to Make to the Christian World
- "THE GREATEST MISSION" of Seventh-day Adventists
- A Spectacle TO THE WORLD, To Angels And to The Universe!
- Echoes of Elder Herbert Douglas' Sinless FINAL Generation Demonstration - **"THE HARVEST THEORY"**
- The TOTALITY OF CHRISTIAN EXISTENCE
- Conclusion - **THANK YOU**, Dr. Paxton!

PART TWO

- IS CHRISTIANITY STILL RELEVANT TODAY?
- **Sound an Alarm! Part One**
- **Sound an Alarm! Part Two**
- A Christian MANIFESTO — 22 TRUE and 22 FALSE Doctrines of Righteousness by Faith (JUSTIFICATION BY FAITH) In the Seventh-day Adventist Church!
- President Neal C. Wilson's Letter to the North American Division Presidents About Geoffrey G. Paxton's Planned Visit to the Division Leaders, Pastors and Laymembers
- Dr. Heppenstall's ciassic Supplement to His Syllabus on Righteousness by Faith
- Pastor Larry Christoffel's 2008 Q. O. D. Message
- Quiz
- Advertisement for Volumes One, Two, Four and Five

The following are 20 E. G. W. Definitions of Justification by Faith—Righteousness by Faith—which teach that Justification/Righteousness by Faith is NOT A CREATIVE ACT of God in us, but that it is instead a legal, judicial, forensic verdict of God outside of us.

1. Justification is entirely **the GIFT of God** to unworthy sinners. Romans 5:15-18 -- six times.
2. Justification is by the **GRACE (goodness, mercy, kindness)** of God.
3. Justification is **SOLELY THROUGH FAITH in Jesus, apart from obedience and good works.**
4. Justification is **a LEGAL, JUDICIAL, FORENSIC law-court verdict of pardon (forgiveness, innocence, not guilty), of being in harmony with God.**
5. Justification is **OBJECTIVE – outside of us – in God alone. The fruit and results** of justification are inside of us.
6. Justification is **ESCHATOLOGICAL.** We have the final verdict of the final judgment **now**--the verdict of **not guilty, of pardon.**
7. Justification does **not change** our characters or natures. **Justification** changes **God's RELATIONSHIP to us**; and Justification **by faith** changes **our *relationship* to God.** (During this life on earth, God does not judge or condemn or forsake us!)
8. Because of and on the **BASIS** of (1) Christ's incarnation, (2) sinless life, (3) death on the cross, and (4) resurrection from the dead, in justification, God **CREDITS** Christ's righteousness (perfect obedience) and His death to us and He **reckons, accepts, and treats us as if we were righteous**.
9. Justification is **"the OPPOSITE of condemnation."**
10. Justification is **"a full, complete PARDON** of sin" by God.
11. Justification is our being **CREDITED** with Christ's righteousness by God.
12. Justification is our being **ACCOUNTED** righteous by God.
13. Justification is our being **DECLARED legally** righteous by God.
14. Justification is **NOT** God's creative act of **MAKING** us inwardly righteous in the flesh.
15. Justification enables us to **STAND** before God in our sinful **STATE AS IF we were as righteous as Christ**.
16. Justification is the **SUBSTITUTION** of Christ's righteousness for our **unrighteousness**.
17. Justification is our being **RESTORED TO FAVOR** with God in a legal sense.
18. Justification gives us a righteous legal **STANDING (relationship)** before God and His infinitely righteous law in our sinful moral **STATE (inner moral condition)**.
19. Justification is the **IMPUTATION (RECKONING, CREDITING, COUNTING, AND ACCOUNTING)** of Christ's righteousness to us by God.
20. This all amounts to one thing; **God does not hold our sins against us** during this life on earth. **He FORGIVES** all our sins and **CREDITS, IMPUTES** Christ's righteousness to us and treats us, **as if we were as righteous as Christ.** These are all truths taught by Mrs. White concerning Justification. Thank God for His wonderful **GIFT of Justification** which we receive **SOLELY BY FAITH, apart from our obedience and good works—PERIOD!**

Righteousness by Faith and Justification by Faith **ARE EXACTLY THE SAME THING.**

Christian Classics ● *Volume Five*
"THE INCREDIBLE CHRISTIAN GOSPEL"
COMING SOON

INDEX OF IMPORTANT GOSPEL SUBJECTS

A KEY STATEMENT by Mrs. White: 12.

ABBREVIATIONS to EGW Sources: 155.

ABOUT THE AUTHOR: Outside back cover.

AN OPEN LETTER TO OUR LEADERS (ADMINISTRATORS): 153.

AN OPEN LETTER TO OUR PASTORS and LAYMEMBERS: 154.

ASSURANCE of Salvation: 95, 135—137.

AUTHORITY, our ultimate: 16—20.

ATONEMENT: 128, 130.

BASIS of Justification by Faith, Righteousness by Faith: 70—74.

"CHRIST IN YOU": 121, 124.

DEFICIENCIES, UNAVOIDABLE: 142—144.

GOSPEL STATEMENT—Loma Linda Campus Hill Church: 6—11.

"HASTEN ON, O Blessed Judgment Day!: 132.

HEAVEN: God's Requirement for Entrance into: 12.

THE JUDGEMENT: 86, 131, 132.

JUSTIFICATION BY FAITH—RIGHTEOUSNESS BY FAITH: 146—149.

- BASIS, MEANS, FRUIT of: 38—40, 70—74, 88—92, 95—98,

- BASIS of: 38, 70—74,

- CONDITION OF—ONLY ONE CONDITION of: 75—86, 93—98,

- DEFINITIONS of: 25—51,

- FAITH—The only instrumental MEANS of: 75—87, 150,

- FITNESS FOR: 115—116,

- FRUIT of: 88—92,

- IMPORTANCE of: INSIDE FRONT COVER,

- THE LINGUSTIC (GREEK) BASIS FOR THE TEACHING THAT Justification by Faith and Righteousness by Faith ARE EXACTLY THE SAME THING: 57—58,

- JESUIT (Roman Catholic) DOCTRINE of: 32—35,

- Justification and Sanctification: DISTINCT, BUT NEVER SEPARATE: 45,

- Justification by Faith and Righteousness by Faith: The same thing: 57—58,

- MEANS of: 75, 87,

- NATURE of: 21—35,

- ROMAN CATHOLIC Doctrine of: 32—35,

- ROOT OF JUSTIFICATION: 88—90,

- STANDING AND STATE: 99—111,

- TEN TRUTHS ABOUT: 108–109,
- TWO BASIC VIEWS CONCERNING! 48–50,
- WHERE IS THE Righteousness that Justifies us?: 62–69,
- WHOSE Righteousness is it that Justifies Us? Christ's? or the Holy Spirit's?: 60–69, 115–116.

LOGIZOMAI: MEANING of: 54–58.

"NONE RIGHTEOUS, NO NOT ONE": 105, 109, 119, 125, 127.

PREFECTION: 109, 119, 123–127, 146–149.

"RECON YOURSELVES TO BE DEAD unto sin": 123.

RIGHTEOUS, RIGHTEOUSNESS, Righteousness by Faith (Justification by Faith):
- IMPUTED: 12, 52–59, 132,
- IMPARTED: 53,
- NONE RIGHTEOUS: 109, 122–127, 129, 146–149.
- OBJECTIVE righteousness: 62–69,
- Righteousness OF THE LAW: 37–39, 103, 106,
- SUBJECTIVE righteousness: 68–69.

SALVATION: 6–11, 14, 15, 40, 41, 125, 126, 134–138.
- Tenses of: 39,
- The TOTAL Plan of Salvation: 40–45.

SANCTIFICATION: 111–117.

SINLESS, SINLESSNESS: NOT UNTIL GLORIFICATION: 109, 122–127, 146–149.

"SINLESS Last Generation"–"NOT SINLESS UNTIL GLORIFICATION: 124–126.

WEDDING GARMENT: Christ's IMPUTED Righteousness: 143–145.

AMAZING!

2 Cor. 5:21 says: "For He hath made Him [Jesus] to be sin for us, who knew no sin; that we might be made the righteousness of God in Him."

This text does not mean that God made Jesus to be actually sinful. It means that:

> God took Jesus who was infinitely righteous
> and charged all our sins to Him,
> and reckoned Him to be sinful,
> and treated Him AS IF He were sinful,
> in order that He might take us
> who are exceedingly sinful
> and credit His righteousness to us
> and reckon us to be righteous
> and treat us AS IF we were righteous.

This means that God does not hold our sins against us. Instead, He freely forgives all our sins and treats us AS IF we had never sinned! Isn't that wonderful, Dear Reader?

"Look and Live!"

"And as Moses lifted up the serpent in the wilderness, even so must the Son of man be lifted up; that whosoever believeth in Him should not perish, but have eternal life.

"For God so loved the world, that He gave His only begotten Son, that whosoever **believeth** in Him should **not perish**, but have everlasting life."

"For God sent not His son into the world to condemn the world; but that the world through Him might be saved. He that **believeth** on Him is **not condemned**, but he that believeth not is condemned already because he hath not believed in the name of the only begotten Son of God." John 3:14-18.

On the cross, Satan hoped to destroy Jesus forever.

Instead, by that event, Satan sealed his own eternal destruction forever.

Design by Gordon Collier Art by O.G. Zell

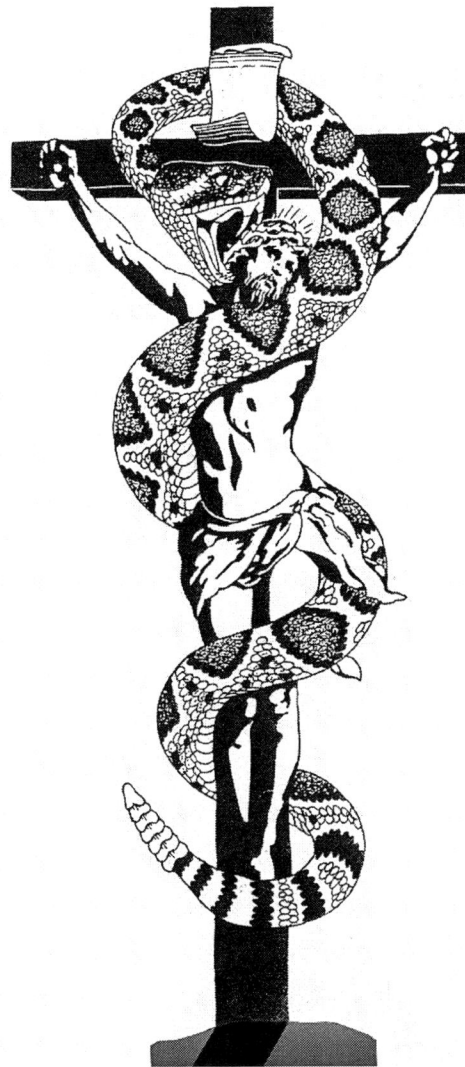

Our sins were reckoned, charged, <u>IMPUTED</u> to Christ in order that His righteousness might be reckoned, credited and ACCOUNTED to us!

Jesus was reckoned, counted, and treated AS IF He were sinful in order that we might be reckoned, counted, and treated AS IF we were righteous!

He was made [accounted] sinful for us in order that we might be made [accounted] righteous for Him. 2 Cor. 5:21.

**SATAN ATTEMPTED TO CRUSH CHRIST'S HEAD,
BUT HE SUCCEEDED ONLY IN CRUSHING HIS HEEL!
Genesis 3:15**

163

THE TWO DIFFERENT ASPECTS OF RIGHTEOUSNESS: WHAT They are, WHERE They are, and WHAT each ACCOMPLISHES for Us

It is extremely important for us to understand that there are TWO different aspects of Righteousness, What each is, WHERE each is, and WHAT each ACCOMPLISHES for us in the plan of Salvation

TWO DIFFERENT ASPECTS OF RIGHTEOUSNESS

	The FIRST Aspect of Righteousness	The SECOND Aspect of Righteousness
1	Is DIVINE RIGHTEOUSNESS	Is HUMAN righteousness
2	Is the righteousness of **JUSTIFICATION**	Is the righteousness of **SANCTIFICATION**
3	Is CHRIST'S RIGHTEOUSNESS	Is the CHRISTIAN'S righteousness
4	Is CHRIST'S DOING AND DYING	Is the CHRISTIAN'S doing and trying by faith
5	Is always only in CHRIST in heaven	Is in CHRISTIANS on earth
6	CHRIST'S righteousness is PERFECTLY, INFINITELY, ABSOLUTELY righteous—the only righteousness that is GOOD ENOUGH TO SAVE us	The CHRISTIAN'S righteousness is NEVER, perfectly, infinitely, absolutely righteous—is always only RELATIVELY righteous
7	Was wrought out FOR us, OUTSIDE of us, by the SECOND member of the Godhead 2000 years ago	Is developed IN US by the THIRD member of the Godhead and us working together now—during this life on earth
8	Is IMPUTED (RECKONED, CREDITED) TO us in God's GIFT OF JUSTIFICATION	Is IMPARTED TO and DEVELOPED IN Christians in SANCTIFICATION
9	JUSTIFIES AND SAVES US	Does NOT JUSTIFY and SAVE; SANCTIFIES AND PERFECTS
10	Is God's GIFT to us, but it always remains in Jesus in Heaven	Is IMPARTED TO and DEVELOPED IN Christians in SANCTIFICATION
11	Is the one and only MERITORIOUS BASIS on which God JUSTIFIES us	Is the INEVITABLE FRUIT—RESULT—of Christ's sacrifice and justification of us and our faith in Christ
12	PERFECTLY ATONES for all our sins	Does NOT atone for our sins
13	PERFECTLY RECONCILES God to us and us to God legally—judicially, forensically	Does NOT RECONCILE God to us or us to God. Helps us to develop Christian character
14	PERFECTLY FULFILLS AND SATISFIES God's infinitely righteous law for us	NEVER perfectly fulfills God's infinitely righteous law for us. Always comes SHORT of perfectly fulfilling God's law ...
15	PERFECTLY GETS US THROUGH THE INVERSTIGATIVE JUDGEMENT	Is NEVER good enough or efficacious enough to get us through the Judgement
16	IS THE RIGHTEOUSNESS OF "RIGHTEOUSNESS BY FAITH"	IS "THE RIGHTEOUSNESS OF THE LAW"
17	This righteousness of JUSTIFICATION is received by us, as a credit, SOLELY BY FAITH APART FROM WORKS	This righteousness of SANCTIFICATION is DEVELOPED in us by faith AND OUR COOPERATING WITH THE HOLY SPIRIT
18	There is INFINITE JUSTIFYING MERIT in this righteousness	There is absolutely No justifyijng merit whatsoever in this righteousness
19	WE ARE SAVED AT LAST BY THE PERFECT, INFINITE, ABSOLUTE, IMPUTED RIGHTEOUSNESS OF CHRIST	We are NOT saved BY this imparted righteousness, but NEITHER are we saved at last WITHOUT it.
20	All our hope of heaven IS IN THIS RIGHTEOUSNESS	NONE of our hope of heaven is in this righteousness
21	Is our KEY, TICKET, TITLE & PASSPORT to heaven	Is the VALIDATING EVIDENCE that our faith is GENUINE